More Praise for *Finding Fontainebleau*

"Charming and vivid and sweet, *Finding Fontainebleau* is full of the hopeful ambiance of Americans discovering France in the post-war era." —Alice Kaplan, author of *French Lessons*

"A delight, at all its levels. I've read it twice already. . . . It's a book to come back to again and again."
—Rosalind Brackenbury, author of *Becoming George Sand*

"A … war France."
… (Northampton)

"Lovely digressions, along with Carhart's own family's story, illuminate French culture in an appealing way." —*BookPage*

"American casualness and exuberance meet French formality and grandeur in this lively, perceptive memoir." —*Publishers Weekly*

"I don't think I can pay it a greater compliment than to report that reading it sent me to Paris's Gare de Lyon, there to board a train to Fontainebleau, which I saw with new eyes."
—Penelope Rowlands, author of *Paris Was Ours*

"… pations of the French, past … writes about with humor, …"
… thor of *Brunelleschi's Dome*

"Beautifully written, Thad Carhart's new book is a delight, happily meandering down memory lane through storybook 'Phone-Ten-Blow.' Simply marvelous!"

—David Downie, author of *Paris, Paris: Journey into the City of Light*

"I learned, I laughed, I marveled, I yearned to transport myself to Fontainebleau."

—David Laskin, author of *The Family: A Journey into the Heart of the Twentieth Century*

"Long before mass tourism and globalization, France was simple, soulful, and every inch stimulating. Carhart knew it all and shares this with us with the deftness and insight of a master storyteller."

—Leonard Pitt, author of *Walks Through Lost Paris*

"Anyone who has ever felt like a fish out of water will be diverted and informed by *Finding Fontainebleau*."

—John Baxter, author of *The Most Beautiful Walk in the World*

PENGUIN BOOKS

FINDING FONTAINEBLEAU

Thad Carhart is the author of *The Piano Shop on the Left Bank* and *Across the Endless River,* a historical novel. He lives in Paris.

www.thadcarhart.com

ALSO BY THAD CARHART

FICTION

Across the Endless River

MEMOIR

The Piano Shop on the Left Bank

FINDING FONTAINEBLEAU

AN AMERICAN BOY IN FRANCE

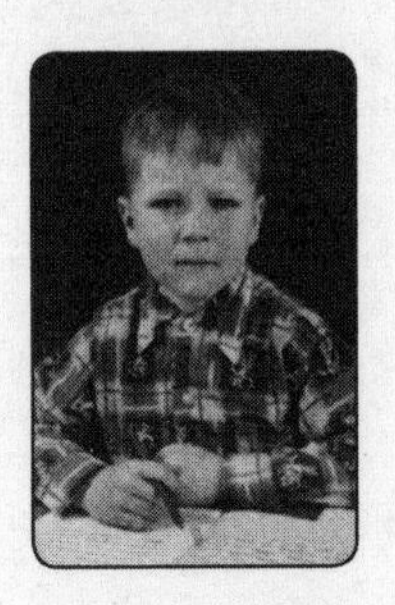

THAD CARHART

PENGUIN BOOKS

PENGUIN BOOKS
An imprint of Penguin Random House LLC
375 Hudson Street
New York, New York 10014
penguin.com

First published in the United States of America by Viking Penguin,
an imprint of Penguin Random House LLC, 2016
Published in Penguin Books 2017

Frontispiece: © François Brosse, 2015
ISBN 9780143109280 (pbk.)

THE LIBRARY OF CONGRESS HAS CATALOGED THE
HARDCOVER EDITION AS FOLLOWS:
Names: Carhart, Thaddeus.
Title: Finding Fontainebleau : an American boy in France / Thad Carhart.
Description: New York, New York : Viking, 2016.
Identifiers: LCCN 2016008395 (print) | LCCN 2016009173 (ebook) |
ISBN 9780525428800 (hardback) | ISBN 9780698191617 (ebook)
Subjects: LCSH: Carhart, Thaddeus—Childhood and youth. |
Americans—France—Fontainebleau—Biography. |
Boys—France—Fontainebleau—Biography. | Fontainebleau
(France) —Biography. | Fontainebleau (France) —Social life and
customs—20th century. | Château de Fontainebleau (Fontainebleau, France)
| Fontainebleau (France) —Buildings, structures, etc. | Carhart,
Thaddeus—Travel—France. | France—Description and travel. | BISAC:
BIOGRAPHY & AUTOBIOGRAPHY / Personal Memoirs. | TRAVEL / Europe / France.
| BIOGRAPHY & AUTOBIOGRAPHY / General.
Classification: LCC DC801.F67 C37 2016 (print) | LCC DC801.F67
(ebook) | DDC 944/.36082092—dc23
LC record available at http://lccn.loc.gov/2016008395

Printed in the United States of America
1 3 5 7 9 10 8 6 4 2

Set in Adobe Jenson
Designed by Nancy Resnick

Penguin is committed to publishing works of quality and integrity.
In that spirit, we are proud to offer this book to our readers;
however, the story, the experiences, and the words
are the author's alone.

To the memory of my parents,
May and Tom Carhart

CONTENTS

FINDING FONTAINEBLEAU

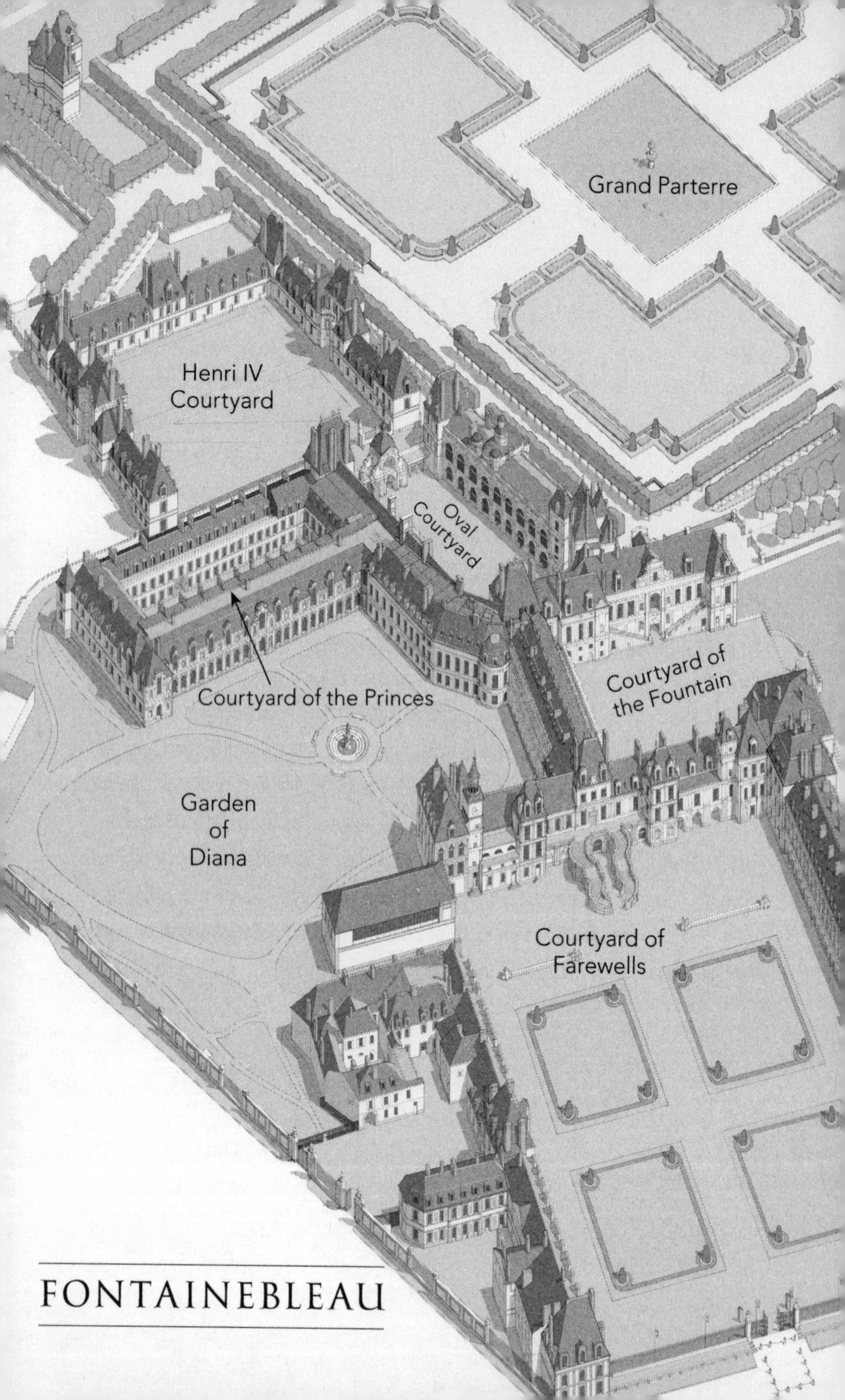
Grand Parterre
Henri IV Courtyard
Oval Courtyard
Courtyard of the Princes
Courtyard of the Fountain
Garden of Diana
Courtyard of Farewells
FONTAINEBLEAU

KINGS WHO BUILT FONTAINEBLEAU

1137–1180
Louis VII

1226–1270
Saint Louis

1515–1547
François I

1547–1559
Henri II

1589–1610
Henri IV

1610–1643
Louis XIII

1643–1715
Louis XIV

1715–1774
Louis XV

1774–1792
Louis XVI

1804–1815
Napoleon I

1830–1848
Louis-Philippe

1852–1870
Napoleon III

CHAPTER 1

FLIGHT

All these years later I can recall with keen precision the moment when the bottom dropped out, because that is exactly what it felt like: one moment we were flying, shaking a bit from turbulence, the next we were falling, in a calm, eerie quiet broken only by the sound of the four engines laboring uselessly. Then the air caught us again and it was bad: the plane pitched violently up and down, from side to side, every way imaginable. The passengers found their voice then, after the expectant dread of the free fall. This was active, maniacal horror, and people screamed. It was the first time I saw an adult—many of them, in fact—expressing fear without reserve. The woman across from us started to cry and yell, and there was nothing to be done but listen and watch with a kind of terrified fascination.

The other unforgettable occurrence was the almost simultaneous eruption of airsickness among the passengers. On a modern airliner, when you find one of those little "airsickness bags" in the seat pocket, you're looking at a quaint reminder of what was not so long ago a dire necessity. The bags used to be much bigger, there were several per seat, and people used them. When the serious shaking began, my mother managed to open a bag for my baby sister and give another to my brother Tom, known for his sensitive stomach. The rest of us were fine for a while, lurching against our seat belts as we heard the occasional crash of plates or glassware from what was then still called "the galley." Gradually, however, the smell overcame everything—not everyone had fished out a bag in time—and made me hopelessly, convulsively sick. This went on for what seemed like an eternity. The shrieks and yells of initial panic subsided into a generalized moaning punctuated by the occasional sob or an unproductive retching. Stomachs were by now empty and the plane's shaking went on: all you could do was wait.

My mother was a nurse who had dealt with her share of traumas and emergencies, and she had no particular fear of flying, but years later she admitted that the flight from Labrador to Ireland had been one of the most searing experiences she could recall. "Planes very rarely go down because of weather," my father had reassured her many times, and so she waited it out with the five children, aware—if not exactly accepting—that our lives lay in the hands of the pilots and in the airworthiness of what was reputed to be a very sturdy troop carrier.

We landed at Shannon at dawn, and the sense of salvation was absolute. One woman had become loudly agitated about an hour before we descended, as we plunged into yet another bout of turbulence. "Let me out of here! I have to get out of here now!" she wailed, but one of the crew members hastened to the back and somehow calmed her hysteria. For all I know she still lives in Ireland, though it seems more likely that she made her way back to America by ship, there to await the advent of jets to carry her above the weather.

When we staggered down the stairs and breathed the balm of fresh air, we were greeted by a team of workers who looked as if they had been assembled to deal with a chemical spill (which, in a way, they had): overalls, hoods, canvas masks, brushes, and pails.

They scoured the insides of the plane while we were being cleaned up in the terminal building as best my mother could manage, telling us repeatedly, as if to convince herself, "The worst is over." As she almost always did, my mother was telling us the truth, and I remember my next-oldest brother, Judd, saying that it sounded reasonable since we had indeed survived; short of a crash, he told me, nothing worse than the night we had just lived through could possibly be imagined.

Total uproar had reigned on moving day in the Virginia suburbs of Washington, D.C., when it came time to say good-bye to the family dog, our cocker spaniel Apple, banned from Europe by something called "quarantine" that my mother explained endlessly and that I never truly understood ("Why aren't *we* quarantined, too?"). In those days before FedEx, it was possible to send packages overnight by train all along the East Coast. The local hardware store fashioned a "traveling kennel," a big slatted box made of rough pine, and a Railway Express truck stopped by the near-empty house and picked up our childhood pet to transport her to her new home.

More than anything else—the chaos of bare walls and half-packed bags, of lawn furniture and plastic forks ("Pretend we're going on a picnic for a few days!" my mother told us, trying gamely to hold melt-down at bay), of teary-eyed friends and no car (our Chevy wagon had been shipped by boat two weeks previously)—the sight of our whimpering dog leaving for the comforting fields of Grandma's farm when we were going across the ocean to some strange country opened the floodgates. All five children sensed that this was some emotional point-of-no-return, and we cried and howled and fought like banshees as the Railway Express man tried to get the signature he needed for a quick getaway.

My mother must have anticipated some such disaster because she precipitated the perfect antidote: a family water fight. Northern Virginia was hot in June, and this day was no exception. With two outdoor hoses and plenty of plastic basins, we went at it for a full half hour, old and young alike, neighbors, too, in a simulacrum of war that I see now was some kind of ritual cleansing. Everyone was drenched, exhausted, and strangely happy—and everything I had known was about to change entirely.

Later I wondered at the ease with which my mother wrung out our shorts and t-shirts and threw everything in the dryer. Our clothes were soon wearable again and we shared the reassuring sense of calm that comes from braving a downpour together. I didn't suspect that the clothes dryer and the entire American suburban apparatus that went with it—streets of similar houses connected by open yards, rows of late-model cars at the curb, kitchens full of appliances, and living rooms with television sets—were soon to disappear from my horizon for years.

To be sure, the beginning of the trip was exciting. As many times as I had been near planes and airports, since my father was an Air Force pilot, I had never before flown. Like the children of most pilots, I was fascinated by airplanes, and I imagined a luxurious flight on a Lockheed Constellation, the glamorous triple-tailed flagship of Trans World Airlines. I saw the magic voyage the newsreels promised, with Ava Gardner or Gregory Peck being greeted in Europe at the foot of the staircase once the shiny plane rolled smartly into the perfect spot after a nonstop flight from New York. The Pentagon had other ideas. Since my father had left for Europe three months earlier, it fell to my mother to pack up the house, put most of our things in storage, and organize all five children for our transatlantic trip. I still wonder how my mother managed us all. Sally, the eldest, was twelve, and she helped with Brita, the two-year-old. Bracketed between them were the three boys: Tom, ten; Judd, seven; and me, four.

We left from a military base near Washington on a DC-4, a four-engine propeller plane that was solid but slow; this was before the era of jet airliners. Its military counterpart, the C-54, was used as a transport for troops and cargo. The DC-4's range, however, was limited, so rather than head directly across the Atlantic for France, we headed north, with the prospect of several refueling stops along the arc of the northern Atlantic. The first of these was in Labrador, a place I remember only as cold, dark, and windy; it had taken us eight hours. "Are we there yet?" The refrain had begun long before the plane landed in the Canadian mist, and our discovery that this was not France was a cruel disappointment. Fatigue and frustration, though, were nothing when compared to the trials of the next leg.

Labrador to Shannon was "only" six hours, but this was the North Atlantic and there was what was euphemistically referred to at the time as "weather." That is to say, major storms over the open ocean with no chance of flying around or over the clouds: straight through was the only possibility in those days. The consequences were worthy of an ocean crossing by boat in a full gale. Our seat-lined winged cylinder, though it vibrated and hummed loudly, was by now predictable, almost cozy. That all changed soon after we left the North American mainland and climbed into the storm that lay between us and safety.

When we were herded back onto the plane in Ireland for the last leg to Frankfurt, where my father would meet us, the interior was magically transformed. A strong smell of antiseptic filled the air, but this was more than welcome after the stench it replaced. The shambles of dirty blankets and fallen coats and sweaters had been replaced by a neatly ordered interior with fresh linen headrest pads adorning every seat. Several seats remained empty when we took off; whether they represented timorous passengers, or those whose destination was Ireland, I'll never know. The flight to Germany was in fact uneventful, though by now our excited anticipation was boundless. I am sure we looked forward to seeing our father, but mostly we just wanted to be out of the airplane once and for all.

At the airport in Frankfurt there occurred one near disaster, narrowly avoided, that ever since has become the stuff of family lore, when our destinies might all have veered into a chasm. After the plane taxied to a stop, a crew member pushed open the massive door, hinged on one side, directly in front of our seats. My mother had long since had us put on our jackets and sweaters, not because of a feared chill, but simply so that nothing extra needed to be carried. Standing, she held my baby sister in one arm and my hand with the other, telling the other three children to wait behind her until we could emerge into the afternoon air. As it happened, the stairs to the tarmac had not yet been rolled into place: a void loomed at the open door, fully fifteen feet down to the concrete. As an Air Force officer, my father had been allowed access to the flight line, and we now caught sight of him waving from below.

Suddenly my brother Judd shot from behind my mother's skirt and leaped into the opening: "Daddy! Daddy!" By some superhuman maternal instinct that bears no understanding, my mother wrenched her hand from mine, stepped forward to the edge still holding Brita in one arm, and caught Judd by the back collar of his shirt. For a long moment he swung over the abyss, cantilevered at the end of her arm. Had her strength failed her, had his shirt slipped over his head, he would have fallen straight to the concrete below, serious or even fatal injury the certain result. "Come back," my mother half grunted, and somehow she managed to pull him back into the plane. Quickly a crew member stepped forward and blocked the way until the steps were firmly in place. "You wait until I say so," my mom hissed at Judd, but each of us knew that her anger was a mask for her relief. We were all relieved in ways we couldn't find words for: Judd was okay! We were all alive! The plane was a thing of the past! And there was Dad, bounding up the stairs now, ready to take us to this new place called France.

CHAPTER 2

FRANCE

My father was a newly appointed staff officer at the NATO command, whose headquarters were in a wing of the *Château de Fontainebleau.* In that summer of 1954, he had rented an immense house near the center of the town of Fontainebleau, as different from our home in suburban northern Virginia as one could imagine. There still remained repairs to be done on the interior before we could move in, so the seven of us stayed in the officers' guest quarters, a cramped affair of two rooms, at the local allied military base. During that first week of what amounted to hotel living, we visited our new home several times while my father was at work, so that my mother could get a sense of the practical arrangements. Our guide for these outings was the ancient and doughty real estate agent Mademoiselle de Chêneville, a tiny woman wrapped in a well-worn fur coat even in the July heat. She had taken a liking to my mother, and shepherded us through the house and grounds with a protective air.

In Arlington, outside of Washington, we had lived in the classic American postwar suburb, a vast series of brick tract houses in a variety of Colonial styles covering the wooded hills of northern Virginia on half-acre lots. Most everyone's yard ran into the next in an unbroken swath of carefully maintained grass, a perfect playground for the swarms of neighborhood kids who gathered for games of "Capture the Flag" or "Kick the Can" every evening in the summer. Cars were parked in the attached garages or at the curb out front—this was the era of mammoth Detroit metal. On summer afternoons, the Good Humor man, a white-uniformed guy driving a small white refrigerator truck filled with ice cream treats, rang the four bells that sat on the roof of his open cab at every neighborhood corner.

On our first few walks around the center of Fontainebleau, we saw a town that looked like another planet to us, one where all the people had disappeared. The streets in our new neighborhood were narrow, paved with cobblestones, and lined with high walls. No yards were visible, no bushes or trees—just a continuous barrier on either side that incorporated stone walls, the sides of houses, garages, and the occasional wrought-iron gate. No one walked along the little sidewalks that widened or narrowed haphazardly and sometimes just ended altogether as the walls converged and the street became very narrow. No cars passed as we made our way to the new house, and only a few were parked along the street. I gaped at the tiny size and strange shapes of the French cars: a Citroën *Deux Chevaux* that looked like an immense vacuum cleaner on wheels, a Renault *Quatre Chevaux* with forward-opening doors and an engine in the rear, and a curious little rounded sedan called a Panhard with three headlights. Who drove these cars and how did they ever fit in them?

More than anything else in those first days, I think, the difference in cars impressed my four-year-old sensibility. Where I came from, cars were enormous affairs with huge chrome bumpers, shiny wheel covers, white sidewall tires, and huge hunks of sculpted metal worked as if it were cotton candy. Backseats were big enough to sleep on. Our car, a Chevrolet station wagon, even had a second backseat—the "way back," we called it—with a cargo area behind *that*. And I was used to colorful cars: blues and greens and reds, and even two-tone cars with great swaths of white or black down their sides and running up onto the trunk. Every French car I saw seemed to be gray or black, with a purposeful, utilitarian look.

Fontainebleau looked unbearably gray to us—not just the cars, but the walls, the cobblestones, the buildings: *everything*. Then, in the late morning on our third or fourth day, we got our first glimpse of what lay beyond the walls and the gates. Mademoiselle de Chêneville met us at the new house with the keys. She stood in the narrow street next to a tall wrought-iron gate whose lower five feet were covered from the inside with metal panels that blocked the view of the enclosure.

"Ees a verree beeg car," she announced, rolling the "r" in "car," once my mother had parked our Chevy at the curb. When my mother complimented her English, the response was quick and filled with laughter: "Madame, I 'ave spoke Ingleesh before you 'ave spoke Ingleesh!" She brandished a mass of long iron keys attached to a large metal ring. Finding the one she needed, she introduced it into the gate's lock with a great shimmer of noise, like bells, as the other keys struck the metal panel. There followed a minute or more of anxious coaxing—the key would turn only at the right point, far enough in but not *too* far—and I can recall my mother's doubtful look. Then suddenly Mademoiselle de Chêneville's face brightened as the key turned, and she lifted the gate's handle with some effort.

"Pleese 'elp me poosh," she said to us children, the five of us gathered on the sidewalk like spectators outside a fairy-tale castle. My eldest brother, Tom, was the first to apprehend what was being asked, and he sprang forward. The rest of us found room where we could, leaning into the right half of the heavy iron gate as it swung inward slowly on its hinges with a shriek. What lay revealed was a vision: all the gray was replaced by vivid green—trees, bushes, a wide lawn—and through some low-hanging branches we saw a massive house standing beyond the lawn, surrounded by a skirt of pale yellow gravel.

We hesitated for a moment, but Mademoiselle de Chêneville smiled at my mother and encouraged us in her thickly accented English: "Yes, shildren, enter. Eet ees your new 'ome!" We scurried through the gate with yips and shouts, running around the grounds to discover where we'd now be living.

The house stood at one side of an enclosed acre, at right angles to the gate, its front close to another wall. We approached it from the back where a spacious oblong of greenswards and gravel paths was bordered by trees and shrubs growing against the perimeter wall. The gravel ran right up to the house and surrounded it on all sides, as if it were an island rising three-and-a-half stories above a lake of light-colored pebbles. The first floor was elevated a half story above ground level; a broad stone staircase led sideways up to a sizeable landing at the back of the house. Red brick walls rose two more stories to a gray slate mansard roof; full-length windows nearly covered the façades, each surrounded by wide strips of white plaster worked in simple classical detailing.

At the top of the staircase, two tall wooden doors, each with a large brass boss for a handle set in its center, blocked our entry until my mother and Mademoiselle de Chêneville caught up with the overexcited group of kids. Again the ritual of the keys was played out, and one of the doors swung heavily inward.

This time none of us hesitated, racing through the door into the dark within. I was the last to enter and was still adjusting my eyes to the dark when Sally, Tom, and Judd all came rushing back down the three stairs that led up to the main hall, yelling in a mix of fear and excitement: "There's a monster!" "There are animals!" "They're alive!" I bolted out the door onto the landing with them, caught up in the agitation of the moment. Sally blurted out to my mother that there were "heads with teeth and fangs" in the hall. My mother had grown up on a farm and knew animals well enough to appreciate that, wild or domesticated, they were unlikely to be roaming in an empty house.

Mademoiselle de Chêneville gave my mother a quizzical look and said, "*Des animaux?*" A no-nonsense look on her face—this was a property she had found for the American family—she pushed past us all and entered the gloom. "*Ça, alors!*" she muttered as she walked up the three stairs just inside. After a moment we heard a long sigh of understanding, then she beckoned us to enter.

"Zey are trophees, shildren. Zey are dead since a veree long time."

Hesitantly we went back in and crept up the stairs, my mother leading the way. There in a darkened central hallway of grand proportions stood Mademoiselle de Chêneville, gesturing to the walls above her. On either side the mounted heads of animals protruded from the walls, horned deer and antelope hunting trophies from some distant past. At the hall's midpoint, over the entrance to an adjoining room, an immense boar's head stuck out from above, its mouth open in a menacing snarl of teeth and curved tusks.

Slowly we all took in the surroundings, and while the absence of monsters and wild animals was reassuring, the picture still didn't correspond to anything we had known before. "This is a *house?*" we were all thinking. "And we're going to *live* here?" The idea was both strange and thrilling, and we looked around us with new eyes.

CHAPTER 3

THE CHÂTEAU, THE TOWN, AND THE FOREST

First, the word: "PHONE-TEN-BLOW." Never mind the landmark hotel in Miami Beach and its pervasive (and perverse) effect on how the same word is pronounced: "FOUNTAIN-BLUE." No! There is, indeed, a fountain in the origin of the word, but not a blue one. Rather, it's a compression of *Fontaine des Belles Eaux,* or "Fountain of the Lovely Waters." The fountain here—actually, a spring—still bubbles forth on the grounds of the Château, and its stream meanders through the English Garden. Just shorten up the vowels, give it your best nasal concentration, and don't say it too quickly: PHONE-TEN-BLOW. Fontainebleau.

When my family arrived in 1954 the town numbered just under 20,000 inhabitants (that number is closer to 17,000 today). It had the aspect of a sleepy provincial town, even though it was only an hour from Paris. One thing set it apart from all of the other towns in France; indeed, it was why we moved from Washington, D.C., to Fontainebleau in the first place: the Château. A royal residence since the twelfth century, the *Château de Fontainebleau* is unlike any other site in France. By turns a hunting lodge, château, palace, seat of government, and museum, it is the single greatest assemblage of successive architectural styles and decorative arts in all of France.

It lies at the heart of the town, though it is more useful to consider that the town itself grew up to serve the king and his court when he took up residence for the hunting season from September through November. For hundreds of years, the Château was a fortified castle used by the monarch as a hunting lodge. In 1528 François I decided to bring the arts of the Renaissance to France and to lavish them on Fontainebleau in order to transform it into a royal residence worthy of him and his court. From his reign forward virtually every sovereign added to what soon attained the scale of a palace: entire wings of rooms, courtyards, gardens, fountains, works of art, chapels, theaters, even one of the first covered tennis courts.

During the convulsions of the French Revolution, the contents of the Château disappeared, though the buildings were largely undamaged. Fontainebleau is unique, though, in that its furnishings were reassembled and carefully restored by Napoleon I when he chose it as his preferred residence in 1804. After the last monarch left—Napoleon III, following his defeat in 1870 at the hands of the Prussians—the Château became the site of the French Army's artillery school. Not until 1927 was it declared a national museum, and the French Republic has conserved its intact treasures.

Also in the twenties, the American School of Music and Fine Arts was organized within its walls, offering generations of musicians, artists, and architects a three-month residency in town during which the Château served as their conservatory. Nadia Boulanger was its most famous teacher, and the list of those associated with her work reads like a who's who of American musical achievement in the twentieth century: Aaron Copland, Arthur Rubinstein, Yehudi Menuhin, Leonard Bernstein, Philip Glass, Virgil Thomson.

Occupied by the Germans for part of World War II, the Château escaped major damage. In 1949, the Henri IV wing of the

Château was designated the headquarters for NATO's Central Europe land forces, a command presided over by Alphonse Juin, a French marshal and hero of the Italian campaign of 1943–44. My father was named to his staff as the American liaison officer, and that is how a U.S. Air Force lieutenant colonel traded an office in the Pentagon for one in the seventeenth-century *Cour Henri IV* of the Château.

The Château didn't look like any of the government buildings in Washington; in fact, it didn't look like anything any of us had ever seen. The main entrance is a deep courtyard with two long parallel wings on either side reaching out to welcome you. Evenly proportioned, they are far from identical. The three buildings that make up this wide, U-shaped courtyard differ wildly in their details, and yet their roughly similar proportions maintain the illusion of balance.

Right at the center of the main façade extends one dramatically symmetrical element: the staircase. A long stone horseshoe-shaped ramp, its shallow steps lead on either side, along a sinuous curve, from the cobbled courtyard up to the massive oak door on the Château's second floor. As you pass from one courtyard to another, generally through dark sally ports into light-filled squares or ovals, a version of this same visual cleverness is played out: dissimilar elements are unified and balanced with a fountain, a portico, a statue.

The gardens have about them a rigid geometry typical of the French tradition, though the "English Garden" on another side of the Château is about studied abandon and the appearance of nature's randomness. In the outer park, the long oblong of the *plan d'eau,* a canal-shaped pool over a kilometer long, echoes a Washington landmark—the Reflecting Pool that lies between the Lincoln Memorial and the Washington Monument. But Henri IV's artificial lake was built over three hundred years before in 1609.

Gradually, in those long weeks of July and August when my mother was setting up house, we got to know our surroundings, so different from the Washington suburbs. The side street where we lived had virtually no traffic, and the quiet seemed eerie when we ventured out the big metal gate. Only when we reached the main street, a hundred meters or so away, was there activity, and we soon learned that even that depended on the time of day. In the morning, women did their marketing and men were at work. Some women had jobs, but it was the exception rather than the rule. Then, from 12 to 2 p.m., no one stirred; people went home for lunch and were all *à table* at the same time.

For a young child—an American child in particular—this strange place was a string of continuous discoveries. In our part of town, narrow streets, irregularly spaced and winding, led from one surprise to another. The town center spoke of the past, with a single large commercial avenue, lined with nineteenth-century shop façades, passing through the heart of town. The *Mairie*, or Town Hall, stood at the main crossroads, an undistinguished but respectable civic building with the pink brick walls, gray stone lintels, and blue slate mansard roof typical of the region. Diagonally across the intersection sat the Catholic Church, *l'église Saint-Louis*, a much more imposing structure than the Town Hall, all statues and stone garlands festooned as if for a perpetual *fête*. Down the street a short way, the Municipal Theater showed its own *fin-de-siècle* exuberance, always in the signature materials and colors of Fontainebleau: pink, gray, blue.

Away from the center of town, there were two main areas: a succession of small apartment buildings and little houses arrayed on a regular grid of streets; and an extensive area of very large homes along broad avenues, always behind walls, always approached by gravel-covered drives that led to forbidding wrought-iron gates, most of which had been built by rich courtiers in the nineteenth century. Our house was in this latter category, but it was unusual for being so close to the Château's outer grounds, with a large walled garden of its own. Rather than sharing leafy avenues with other mansions, our street was principally lined with small houses where shopkeepers and local tradesmen lived.

Abutting the town center lay the Château and its extensive grounds, the entire domain surrounded by gold-tipped iron pickets whose gates were locked in the evening. We first saw this when we drove by the Château's main entrance, the *Cour des Adieux* or "Courtyard of Farewells," where Napoleon said good-bye to his troops before his first exile in 1814. He returned to his favorite château in 1815, but only for a few hours; his "100 Days" of glory (that's how the French refer to it: *Les Cent Jours*) ended soon afterward at Waterloo. A large golden *N* on the main gates to the *Cour des Adieux*—in effect, the front door to the Château—marks his continuing presence.

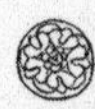

Fontainebleau lies at the heart of one of France's largest forests. Once you leave the close perimeter of the town, you run into the woods. They surround the Château and the town, except on one side where the road has been widened and leads to the nearby railroad line that was put through the forest in the mid-nineteenth century. To go anywhere by car, whether to Paris or the Mediterranean or to the open countryside where sugar beets were intensively cultivated, you had to cross the woods.

The woodland was always the draw for French kings. Hunting represented their chief activity when they left Paris, and Fontainebleau has long been known for its abundant game, principally deer and boar. The forest was the royal hunting preserve for over seven centuries, and the method used dated from the late Middle Ages: the *chasse à courre*, or pursuit of the animal on horseback with a pack of hounds. Over time the forest changed its aspect in response to this special and intensive use. Wide *allées*—broad avenues—were cut through the woods along unwavering axes, intersecting roads crossing each other at *ronds-points* dotted across huge expanses.

Armies of woodsmen cleared all underbrush and also culled any low branches on the trees so that horsemen could gallop without hindrance in pursuit of their quarry. Typically, the game wardens knew the exact number of animals on their terrain, and their sightings as the hunt began in the morning were relayed to the mounted hunters by a coded language of horn blasts. The king and his entourage then took up the chase, following the dogs' headlong dash after the prey. The pursuit could go on for hours, with new sightings signaled by those waiting along the *allées* when the hunted stag or mature boar crossed one of those meridians.

Eventually exhausted and brought to bay by a frenzied pack of hunting dogs, the animal was then dispatched with lances, pikes, and—if a *coup de grâce* were required—a long dagger thrust into the major arteries of the neck. No stalking, no wiles to speak of, just a wild pursuit stage-managed by underlings with a predictable result. In short, not very sporting. But one gets the feeling that the elaborate apparatus of *la chasse*—the horses, the hounds, the eating and drinking before and afterward, the echoes of horns and shouts in the wood—was far more important than bringing home the spoils of the kill for food. The entire complication of getting the king and his friends off into the woods and back again in one piece transformed the experience into an almost pure abstraction, repeated daily while the season was favorable. "*Tout prétexte est bon,*" the French say—any pretext will do—and surely "royal hunt" is one of those oxymoronic phrases that well illustrates this dictum.

This kind of hunting hasn't been conducted int
forest of Fontainebleau since the 1870s, but the w
the effects. Parts of the woodland closest to the Château are
cleared of their understory, and the effect of walking there is of a promenade in an endless glade, open and shadowy below the verdant canopy of mature oaks and sun-flecked Scots pine. It is beautiful in its way, but also decidedly unnatural in the strange openness, almost like a Disney forest that has been prettified for men prancing on horseback. Such is the legacy of centuries of royal hunts, though it must also be added that huge sections of the forest have been allowed to regain their wild undergrowth. The whole expanse has been open to the public since the late nineteenth century. Whether the abutting forest is cleared or grown over, the king's *allées* still make for wonderful walking in one of France's oldest domains.

The Château itself is full of the signs and regalia of the hunt, from antler-bedecked hallways to whole galleries given over to paintings of endlessly repetitive scenes: dogs, horses, snarling boar, uniformed equerries, concerned nobles. Leaving aside the question of the paintings' style and technique, which surely interests students of such things, the images in their profusion of sameness begin to take on the feel of photos from a too-long vacation that weren't erased from one's iPad.

Other, more evocative images of the hunt are to be found throughout the Château and its immediate grounds. Statues and paintings abound of Diana, the huntress, as do medallions and wood carvings of her symbols, worked into the furnishings: the crescent moon, the arrow, the oak leaf, the hunting dog. Henri II's mistress, Diane de Poitiers, infused the court with a power and a grace that eclipsed her rival, the queen Catherine de Medici, and she freely played upon these images to extend her influence.

Different than the numberless paintings and trophies cataloguing the kings' hunts, these elements are more carnal, more frankly erotic. They evoke a deep, even mystical connection to the hunt, the forest, the animal spirit that inhabits us all. Repeatedly the Château's decoration suggests a more poetic side to what *la chasse* meant to the king and his court.

A small garden, *le Jardin de Diane*, sheltered in the lee of one of the Château's wings, is given over to the cult of Diana. At its center, where the garden paths converge, lies a fountain that could only be French. You first notice the dogs: four of them, evenly spaced and facing outward, on the edge of a broad marble cylinder that rises at the center of a round basin. Identical bronze statues, they sit squarely on their haunches, looking just like hunting hounds anywhere: floppy ears, long snouts, and a taut musculature that makes it seem they might jump from their perch at the sound of a command.

On her own smaller column that rises above, a life-sized young woman strides forward in a short, loose dress that clearly shows the swell of her breasts. With her right hand she reaches over her shoulder to remove an arrow from the quiver on her back. Her left hand extends slightly and touches the head of a deer bounding at her side, as if to steady its leap. Below the dogs, on this wedding-cake arrangement at the center of the fountain, four full-sized heads of deer are arrayed symmetrically, alternating with the dogs in eight points of the compass. Only when you draw close do you see the source of the fountain's splash: each dog's penis sends a perfect arc of water to the pool below, as if he were only waiting to finish before running away.

The only way I can begin to comprehend the whole undertaking of the hunt is as a ritual that proclaimed the king's central role, his capacity to prevail again and again, and to underline his virility as the killer of animals supposed to be "wild." It's a ceremony that has ancient roots, certainly, but whose practical necessity for putting meat on the king's table was an empty conceit since before the Renaissance. Finally—and I don't think of this as a trivial consideration—it got everybody out of the house (or the château) quite regularly, which must have been welcome when "indoors" meant lots of people, lots of smells, and endless socializing, even for a king. *Tout prétexte est bon.*

CHAPTER 4

THE HOUSE

The house was big. In the United States it would have been called a mansion. To the French, it was a *maison de maître,* a "master's house," a manor: not a château, but more substantial than merely another big house. The walled garden and graveled walks, the wrought-iron gate and formal flower beds, the interplay of brick walls and white plaster cornices, the mansard roof covered with hand-cut gray slate shingles: all added to the importance of the dwelling in the French scheme of things. The front of the house faced a short dead-end street, not far from the town center, that ended in the entrance to the Château's outer gardens, a public park for more than a century.

The *rez-de-chaussée,* or ground floor, was actually raised up a half story, and so both the front and back doors stood at the top of broad stone staircases with a landing. There were three full floors and an elaborate basement: seventeen rooms in all, depending on how you counted dressing rooms, wine cellar, and the like. We used only the first and second floors, together with the basement, our parents declaring the top floor to be an off-limits attic for storage. Grand in scale and setting, this house left much to be desired for a family of seven at a time when modern appliances had already flooded postwar America.

The kitchen was actually two kitchens—adjoining rooms, spacious and drafty—that were floored with the ubiquitous blood-red hexagonal tiles known as *tomettes*. Each kitchen was dominated by a gargantuan wood-fired black cast-iron stove with brass handles and fittings, the brand name "*Rosières*" worked in brass tracery on the wall panel behind the burners. One of these had been retrofitted to use gas for two of its eight burners and a single oven, and my mother bent to the task of producing meals for our large family from this wounded behemoth.

The electricity system was both inadequate and fitful. My mother soon discovered that using the iron, say, required that you unplug the refrigerator; used together, they blew the main fuse. And since France—like the rest of Europe—is wired for 220 volts, use of any American appliance required plugging in a transformer, a murderously heavy column of metal coils with a wooden handle on top that you lugged from one outlet to another.

My parents assigned the various bedrooms on the second floor and gradually we settled in to the huge house. We had shipped over from Washington only minimal furniture, towels and bed linens, bicycles for each of us, and an already antiquated clothes washer. This last had an open, cylindrical washtub standing on three legs and a wringer device that was perched above the swirling stew of clothes. By the French standards of the day, though, it was modern. It was set up in the emptier of the two kitchens and, with seven people living under the same roof, was perpetually in use. The faucet in that room was commandeered for a feeder valve and a rubber tube was rigged so that wash water drained directly into the sink. Our second kitchen took on the air of a nineteenth-century laboratory, dominated by bizarre apparatus.

The wash cycle took over an hour, the soapy clothes swirling back and forth in the open tub, with an occasional "Splat!" of sudsy water flung onto the tiled floor. This washer had no spin cycle, though; you were left with soaked laundry sitting heavily in the tub. Dripping clothes and sheets then had to be lifted out, set in plastic bins, and the "wringer" mechanism engaged. This consisted of two rollers about two feet long and mounted horizontally one above the other about a half inch apart, turning against each other in opposite directions. Into their maw was then fed every article that had been laundered, individually threaded with a careful eye so that the rollers squeezed out the remaining water without becoming blocked. Pinched fingers were a real peril, too. Then the wrung laundry was put back in bins and carried to the adjacent sunporch, where the sizeable space was entirely given over to a network of lines and clothespins. A single wash involved a prodigious amount of labor and hours of watchful attention.

At some point in our first weeks there, the washer broke down, perhaps because of the voltage irregularity, despite the transformer. This was a disaster of major proportions, and a plumber was found to deal with the emergency. In the course of an afternoon he disassembled the heart of the washer, then put it all back together. He had changed the *roulement*, he explained to my mother—the main bushing, the dictionary told her—but it would, he said unapologetically, make a bit of noise. This was a small trade-off for a working washer, my mom reasoned, and she thanked him for his repair.

She immediately attacked the loads of dirty clothes and discovered that the washer now made a fairly loud, rhythmic, and distinctly repetitive series of squeaks and rubbery whines. The effect was strange, disturbingly like speech, and when my older brother Judd wandered into the kitchen, his response was immediate: "Hey, the washer is saying 'Mary Hotcakes'!" Once he put words to the noise, it wasn't hard to hear them, and they never varied. Ever practical, my mother's accommodation was to require that the door to the second kitchen be closed whenever the washer was going. Even so, it became a part of the soundscape of the house, a gentle and insistent whispering with an emphasis on the third syllable—"Mary HOTcakes, Mary HOTcakes . . ."—that meant that all was as it should be.

My father had already been in Fontainebleau for three months before our arrival, and he quickly disappeared back into his work schedule in that summer of 1954. It was left to my mother to organize the house and make it livable. The week after we moved in, Mademoiselle de Chêneville came by with a middle-aged woman who was dressed as if she were going to church—a hat, a fitted coat, gloves. She reeked of perfume. This was the house's owner, and she had come *pour faire l'inventaire,* to take inventory. We had rented the house *meublée,* furnished, and to our American eyes it seemed that the process would be straightforward and uncomplicated since only heavy pieces of furniture were left in the rooms: beds, armoires, the dining room table and chairs, and the like. My mother figured that this would be, essentially, a brief courtesy call so that introductions could be made and a perfunctory list of furnishings drawn up. In her ignorance of things French, however, she could not reckon the importance of this meeting and of its schematic code of behavior.

The two women were scarcely inside the door before Madame Duval, the owner, produced a thick, typed document which she cradled attentively. With the real estate agent as her hesitant translator, she proceeded to read from her list of everything that belonged in the house, starting in the entry hall. As she recited the description of each item—"an umbrella stand, brass, with a tin undertray and place for six umbrellas"; "a forged iron coat hook mounted on a walnut wall plaque, three hangers, each with a ceramic hook"—her eyes swiveled to its placement in the room and she nodded to herself. Before going on to the next item, she put out her arm and brushed her fingers across what she had just described, as if this ritual touching fixed the object in some special realm to which only she was privy.

My mom hadn't counted on a long visit, and this was glacially slow, taking in everything from door handles ("double-faced, bronze, with a sunburst pattern on each side") to doormats ("horsehair, oblong, 45 cm by 70 cm, slightly worn, in good condition"). What was really dragging things out, though, was Madame's comments, tinged with emotion, on every object she listed. "Madame says eet waz 'er fazer's clock," Mademoiselle de Chêneville pronounced impassively as Madame Duval withdrew her hand from the timepiece on the mantel, composing herself as her eyes returned to the list. "Two andirons, forged iron, in the form of pinecones; excellent condition."

Already half an hour had passed, and they had made it only to the *petit salon*, the first room off the hall that my dad used as an at-home office. Bemused at first by this visit, we children drifted off gradually to other parts of the house as the essential boredom of the adults' business became clear. In fact, it took the entire morning to walk slowly through every room, hallway, closet, and cranny under that extensive roof. During that time, my brother Judd and I, playing in a room that had already been "done," occasionally stopped and listened attentively to the strange sounds from across the hall. Madame Duval's voice would rise and fall dramatically, and at times there seemed to be real distress. "Is she crying?" I whispered to Judd, our faces attentive and quizzical. Together we listened for a minute or two more as a controlled keening emanated from the group of three women. Then he delivered his evaluation, the merciless wisdom of a big brother: "She's crazy!"

Nothing could be more French, nor more inscrutable to the outsider, than the reading of the inventory. And while much has changed in France since I was a boy, this has not: the reading of the inventory—before and after—is as much a set piece as ever, a neat two-act performance with an intermission that generally lasts for years. Because what Madame Duval was doing on that summer morning years ago was preparing the way for the second and final act. Her expressions of attachment and descriptions of provenance could be seen as irrelevant to a leaseholder; after all, the list existed and we could always have contested a description that didn't correspond to what was found on the premises. In truth, her incantation was a way of investing these things—her things—with emotion, and of preparing the way for bigger emotions when the final reckoning was made.

Later, my mom, in something like shock, told the story with relish, especially the part where Madame Duval caressed one of the looming hulks in the kitchen and called it her "heirloom stove." Mademoiselle de Chêneville made sympathetic noises, but she also insisted on entering the notation *"en panne,"* out of order, on the inventory list that described the broken stove. Like any good real estate agent, she was diplomatic, patient, and a shrewd judge of human nature.

Madame Duval was certainly an extreme version of a certain type of French landlord—*bourgeoise,* histrionic, and unimaginably petty—but the basic process of counting everything, down to carpet tacks, is profoundly French. In a country with a long history of war, privation, and loss, it's considered essential to know exactly what you own. In many ways, we were ideal tenants, a big

American family at a time less than ten years after World War II had ended when Americans were regarded as uniformly rich, vulgar, and "modern." Finding a French family to rent such an enormous place with considerable upkeep expenses wouldn't have been easy. But Madame Duval would have given the same performance for her countrymen; if anything, it would have been even more dramatic and fine tuned.

That hasn't changed. To this day, when you rent an apartment or house *meublée*, furnished, in France, there is a ritual counting of what is included, and a statement of its condition. The French know this—have known it for centuries—and are suitably prepared to defend their interests.

What most surprises Americans is the notion that an apartment or house that is *non meublée*, unfurnished, basically means the structure stripped to the bones. Bricks and mortar, floors and ceilings, plumbing and electricity—and that's about it. The French for "real estate" is *immobilier*, its root meaning "unmoveable," and that is the key point. Anything that can be moved (*le mobilier*) is considered a furnishing and is not included in a lease. What seems to foreigners an expression of miserliness—light fixtures, ventilation fans, door knobs are all *mobiliers*—is just the way this is done in France.

CHAPTER 5

FRANÇOIS I, HENRI II

Thirty years after I left France as a child, I returned with my wife and children when I took a job in Paris. We lived in the city, intending to stay for a few years before returning to America, but somehow we never managed to leave. We made our life in France then, raising our two kids there and sending them to French schools. I rediscovered France and, most pleasingly, I renewed my acquaintance with Fontainebleau. Inevitably I was drawn to the Château, full of curiosity about what it now looks like, and how it feels to visit its rooms.

As an adult I saw things differently. I realized what a remarkable stroke of luck it was to have lived in a place that was home to one of France's greatest structures, the Château of Fontainebleau. In my mind, the idea of France remained closely aligned with that great sprawling mass that embodied so much French history. It was both part of the local landscape in my boyhood and—something I understood only much later—a supreme repository of French style, taste, art, and architecture.

Unique in France, the Château was first built in 1137, fifty years before the Louvre was begun, and more than five hundred years before Versailles. In 1528, François I decided to rebuild and expand the Château, and the first of several transformations began.

He elaborated on what had originally been a fortified enclosure with a dungeon and transformed it into a Renaissance palace, starting a long tradition in which each monarch added to Fontainebleau.

To understand how the Château is configured, it's useful to know something about how the French monarchy evolved. Being king of France at the time of François I was no day at the beach or, as the French would put it, *un long fleuve tranquille,* a long tranquil river. The Valois dynasty was at least as violent and unpredictable as its contemporaries in England, the Tudors. Political intrigue and the threat of violent death were givens for the king. War, disease, and murder constantly loomed. So the pursuit of pleasure in the here and now was understood by all to be essential.

François had a kingly bearing: he stood six feet five inches tall and had a muscular physique, a giant for his day. He was known as *François au Grand Nez,* "The Big Nose"; his portraits show a long aquiline nose, expressive almond-shaped eyes, and a small mouth with the suggestion of a sly smile. He was what the French call a *coureur de jupons,* literally a skirt chaser, though the more refined version would be "a ladies' man."

François became king in 1515 at the age of twenty, and he soon took up France's continuing war in Italy against the Holy Roman Emperor, Charles V. No military genius, he was captured in 1525 by Charles's Spanish forces at the Battle of Pavia and was held prisoner in Madrid for a year against the payment of a ruinous ransom and the surrender of French territory in Italy. The final condition of his release was that his two sons, François and Henri, aged eight and seven, be held hostage in Spain until the ransom was paid. The young princes were not released for more than three years.

When François returned from the wars and captivity, he brought with him a passionate fascination with the accomplishments of the Italian Renaissance in the arts, sciences, and letters.

He invited numerous artists to his court—the most famous was Leonardo—and decorated his new châteaux with their works. His agents bought paintings from acknowledged masters throughout Italy; the masterpieces he acquired by Michelangelo, Titian, and Raphael were the foundation of the national collection now at the Louvre.

More than his rivals Henry VIII of England and Charles V of Spain, he saw himself as a Renaissance prince, encouraging the arts, befriending painters and poets, and experimenting with the new codes of architecture. He seems to have understood before his time the power of images to project an aura of grandeur and responsibility for his reign, and while his political and military record is mixed, he is still remembered in France for his support of artists, poets, and writers. Libraries flourished while he was king, and the French language was formally declared the official language of administration, supplanting Latin. French was codified, and its distinctive accent marks were made regular, as was a comprehensive grammar. In short, France began to cohere as a modern nation, no small achievement for a people who are notoriously independent.

Soon after he became king, François began work on the Château of Chambord, a Renaissance fantasy of white limestone in the Loire Valley. Before his defeat in Italy, he financed Verrazano's voyage of exploration to the east coast of North America, the first visit by a European to what is now New York Harbor. And then came the disgrace of captivity.

What might have broken a lesser man seems only to have made François stronger and even more determined to leave his mark on France. In 1528 he turned to Fontainebleau and commissioned his architects to make it into a royal residence worthy of his Renaissance court. The hunting lodge was eclipsed in a few short years.

François kept the *Mona Lisa* in his rooms at Fontainebleau, and he proudly showed the magnificent galleries and rooms decorated in the new style to royal visitors. His emblem was the salamander, still omnipresent in his elegant chambers, as is the associated enigmatic Latin motto *Nutrisco et extinguo,* "I feed upon the good fire, and I put out the evil one." This may be a reference to faith and the nascent religious conflict between Catholics and Protestants, but no one is entirely sure.

Once François transformed Fontainebleau into a veritable palace, its size and scope expanded with subsequent monarchs to meet the needs of a growing court. So began the practice that each successive king added to the Château, and this has created Fontainebleau's great charm and chief distinction. Rather than a single idea and unified whole, like Chambord or Versailles, Fontainebleau is an assemblage of many disparate parts constructed over a long stretch of time that magically coheres. François began his building projects there nearly five centuries ago, and every age since has left its traces. The result is a marvel of styles that are never quirky or dissonant, and yet never symmetrical or entirely regular, either.

Waging war, hunting, and making love were the three great preoccupations of French kings, and Fontainebleau was perfectly suited to the latter two. The king's principal duty once he inherited the throne was to consolidate his family's hold on power by producing a legitimate heir—a male heir, moreover, since the French monarchy always disallowed women as rulers. In order to be legitimate, the boy heir had to be born of the queen, herself necessarily of royal blood. So marriages were always arranged with calculations of power, treasure, and influence as precise as those used to assess the bloodlines of racehorses. Romantic love didn't enter into the equation; a solid hold on the throne was everything.

For the king's amorous pleasures, royal mistresses filled the bill. Not just an occasional courtesan, the king's favorite was a designated role at court in France, and often carried with it immense power. Generally of noble birth, and with a deep sense of political realities, a mistress who captured the king's fancy could exert influence unlike any other. At Fontainebleau, as in other royal residences, the Château was configured so that the bedchamber of the royal mistress was contiguous to that of the king, and splendidly appointed.

A singular example of this arrangement was that between Henri II, married to Catherine de Medici, and his mistress, Diane de Poitiers. Henri and his older brother François were the princes exchanged as hostages to the Spanish against their father's release. Twenty years Henri's senior, Diane was a lady-in-waiting to Henri's mother when he was imprisoned in Madrid, and she was entrusted with his education upon his return. Henri's path to the throne tells much about the convulsive politics of his day. As the second-born son, Henri was not expected to be king. The wife chosen for him was a Medici heiress, immensely rich but not a member of an ancient royal family. Intelligent but no great beauty, she was derided at court as "the banker's daughter." She and Henri were married in 1533 when they were both fourteen.

Three years later Henri's older brother François, the crown prince, died after drinking a glass of water offered by an Italian nobleman, and suddenly Henri was next in line to rule. The king's reaction was swift and pitiless. Suspecting Charles V of having his heir poisoned, he had the nobleman arrested, convicted, then drawn and quartered before the assembled court. However, persistent rumors pointed to the Medici family. By eliminating Henri's older brother, they ensured that Catherine would become queen consort of France. Poison was always suspected when a prince died in his youth. But it is equally plausible that the crown prince died of the pleurisy he had contracted while a prisoner in Charles V's insalubrious fortress in Madrid. We'll never know.

Henri became king when his father died in 1547, and Fontainebleau continued as a favorite royal residence. Ten years earlier Diane de Poitiers had become his mistress, and she wielded considerable power at his court. Henri didn't have his father's prepossessing stature, nor his extrovert's temperament; it is said he never fully forgave his father for the ordeal of his childhood imprisonment. But his less flamboyant style had its subtleties. He arranged for the marriage of his eldest son, François, to Mary Stuart, queen of Scotland, and placed his other children like so many pawns in royal marriages. The rising revolt of Protestants caused enormous upheavals, but the new king was inconsistent in his treatment of non-Catholics, tolerating them for a time, then repressing the free practice of religion as their numbers grew.

Under Henri's rule, the sublime *Salle de Bal*, the Ballroom, was added to the Château, and the court festivities in this imposing chamber were famously elaborate. On ceilings and walls can be seen his coat of arms, three interlaced crescent moons, alternating with those of his queen, Catherine de Medici. Their carved initials also appear around the room, a pair of back-to-back Cs superimposed on a single *H*. But the reversed C can also be read as a *D*—Diane. Goddess of the hunt, her regalia permeates the Château that started as a hunting lodge.

Diane and Catherine were in fact distant cousins, and each recognized the need to live without open conflict if not exactly in harmony. When no children had been born of the royal union after ten years, Diane even insisted Henri sleep with the queen more frequently in order to produce royal heirs. This turned out to be good advice for the Valois dynasty: within twelve years, ten children were born, of whom seven survived infancy, including four boys.

Intelligent, beautiful, rich, and discreet, Diane was ascendant in almost all matters at court throughout the king's reign. And then matters changed dramatically overnight. At a friendly joust among courtiers in Paris in 1559, Henri appeared three times in a single day. On the third occasion the lances of both riders broke and the match was called a draw. Ignoring the advice of his grooms and the entreaties of both his mistress and his queen, Henri insisted on a rematch. On the final charge, the lance of Henri's opponent shattered upon impact. A sliver of wood broke through the king's helmet, pierced his eye, and entered his brain. Henri languished for eleven days before dying in agony.

A macabre detail of his doctors' approach to the injury says much about the underlying barbarity of the age. Unsure of how deep the wood had penetrated and of how to treat the wound, they had four prisoners in Paris decapitated. They then tried to replicate the king's wound on each of the four heads, afterward sawing them open for guidance. Their efforts—and their cruelty—were in vain.

Diane was banished from court, though not entirely disgraced. Catherine forced her to exchange the *Château de Chenonceau* for the lesser fief of Chaumont. She died at her family's Château d'Anet seven years later at the age of sixty-six. In recent years her remains were reburied in the family crypt, and her bones were found to contain abnormally high concentrations of gold. In fact, in order to maintain the white pallor that was considered one of the glories of her beauty, Diane had drunk a daily potion of gold flakes. It almost certainly hastened her death.

One doesn't really feel sorry for these kings and their consorts. Materially they lived better than all of their subjects and exercised unquestioned power over their domain. But would you really trade places with them? If poison, war, or assassination didn't do you in, a simple infection could carry you off, royal or not. No wonder they sought delights in Fontainebleau, indulging in pleasures before the threat of an untoward end.

CHAPTER 6

THE EMPEROR'S OFFICE

When I moved to Paris with my own family in the 1980s, Fontainebleau—both the Château and the town, inseparable in my mind—exercised a kind of magnetic pull. Partly this was a matter of checking up on a place where I'd lived years before. I wasn't sure the house would still be intact (it is), but I knew for certain that the Château would be its age-old self, protected by the deep reverence of the French for sites that embody important parts of their history.

To my immense satisfaction, I learned that in recent years the Château had been undergoing restoration and rebuilding programs in several of its wings. This is not entirely new as an initiative—restoration has been an active concern of the responsible architects at least since Henri III was told that Primaticcio's and dell'Abbate's extraordinary frescoes, commissioned by his father, Henri II, were suffering from the extremes of humidity and temperature in the Ballroom and had to be shored up in the late sixteenth century. But the contemporary efforts are far more comprehensive than had been the case in the past, and are driven by a spirit to save and enhance the treasures of this unique palace for all French citizens, present and future. The impulse to preserve the *patrimoine,* the shared inheritance, is both strong and devoid of controversy. To the French, this is an obvious—and necessary—responsibility of the Republic.

What surprised me when I returned was discovering how deep my attachment was for the Château as a place that symbolized a certain idea of France itself, and of French attitudes. I found myself intrigued by the entire undertaking of preserving a series of buildings that had always assumed mythic proportions in my mind. Some of my strongest memories were associated with the Château from the boyhood years I spent in the town. Now, as an adult, I encountered its ongoing role as a museum, revered and respected by the French. When I inquired as to the possibility of learning more about the restoration programs, there were the usual hiccups with French bureaucracy, careful not to let itself be interrupted for no good reason. But once the architect in chief of the Château understood my deep attachment to the site from my childhood, and my honest interest in understanding what was included in his plans, he opened the door wide. I became an informal student of the work at hand, and was graciously tolerated in my desire to see how things were done, and why.

Architecturally, the Château is akin to an extensive labyrinth, a succession of five major courtyards arrayed haphazardly, each with a different sense of proportion. Its vast roof has a surface area of more than five acres and covers 1,500 rooms. On the day I met with him, Patrick Ponsot, Fontainebleau's chief architect, was worried about the roof.

"Any homeowner knows the perils of a leaky roof," he told me as we sat in his airy office in a quiet wing of the Château. "But when you're working on a scale like this, it opens up an entire universe of challenges." One of the windows in this pleasant attic room was open, and from its vantage point we could see a wide variety of roofs on adjacent wings. Each plane was different in both form and function: steep Renaissance peaks, squared-off mansard angles, pyramid-shaped masses atop pavilions, even a bell tower with a conical witch's cap, all of them interspersed with red brick chimneys, inset windows, stone detailing, and elaborate zinc rain gutters.

"Any leak compromises everything that lies below it," Monsieur Ponsot continued, his tone matter-of-fact. "So, assessing the state of the roof and then repairing it properly has had to be a priority."

A slender man with pink cheeks and bright hazel eyes, Patrick Ponsot could be a cousin of François Truffaut with lighter hair. The *Architecte en Chef des Monuments Historiques* for the Château of Fontainebleau, he is one of only forty-six such architects in all of France, each one appointed by the Ministry of Culture to undertake and oversee the maintenance, restoration, and appropriate development of France's preeminent cultural sites. Ponsot has had a lot of experience with troublesome roofs, having previously served as the head architect for the Château of Chambord, that sumptuous limestone pile in the Loire Valley whose roof resembles a baroque folly. Dressed casually in pressed jeans, loafers, striped cotton shirt, and a brown cotton bush jacket, he projects a French image of nattiness without pretention.

We are having a brief early morning talk in his suite of offices before heading to a *chantier*—a work site—in the Château. "Consider that a very great proportion of those five acres of roof is covered with hand-cut slate tiles, more than a million of them in all," he says, gesturing out the window to the broad expanses of blue-black stone rectangles laid upon one another in a symmetrical pattern. "Then consider that laying slate roof tiles properly is a fast-disappearing art. And, finally, factor in the challenge that the material itself is increasingly hard to come by." He told me that there remains only one quarry of sufficient size in France.

Ever since Napoleon III was driven from the throne by the Prussians in 1870, France has banished kings, sovereigns, and emperors from its political landscape. It now falls to the French Republic to care for the great châteaux of France. While some remain in private hands, sites like Fontainebleau and Versailles and Chambord are simply too big and too costly to maintain without government funds. Moreover, only the state can now bring to bear the kind of expertise that is required to maintain and restore such imposing buildings. Considering that these palaces were built by and for French monarchs, the undertaking is remarkably free of controversy. The Republic—that is to say, the people—now stand in for the aristocracy and subsidize the maintenance of such places in the name of French history. Very few French want to see a return to monarchy, but no one at all would argue for the destruction of the vestiges of their reign. That issue was settled long ago, and the secular Republic now cares for what is regarded as a common inheritance.

As we hurried across the main courtyard, past the double-horseshoe staircase where Napoleon I bade adieu to empire, Ponsot told me that work was well under way on the restoration of Napoleon III's office and the empress Eugénie's study, adjacent rooms on the ground floor of the Louis XV wing. Installed in this eighteenth-century part of the Château during the Second Empire (1852–1870), they were only now being brought back to a condition in which the public could view this private side of France's last sovereign.

We approached from the garden side, climbing over and around piles of pulled-up paving stones, stacked wood, sand, and various tools and building materials. Ponsot pushed open the floor-to-ceiling glass doors, and we entered upon a scene of frenetic activity. In a tall, amply proportioned room with a black marble hearth to one side, a dozen workers threaded their way around a floor littered with machinery and supplies: glaziers sealing windowpanes, painters climbing on several ladders, carpenters kneeling along pieces of ripped-up floorboards, masons fitting stone in the floor of the fireplace. One or two looked toward the door and then, gradually, work slowed as attention focused on the chief architect.

The next five minutes were given over to Ponsot's shaking hands with each and every worker there. This involved going into the two adjoining rooms and making the rounds, being certain that everyone got the extended hand and quick grip of the palm, whether leaning down from a ladder or shedding a paint-covered glove. This minor ritual draws no attention in France—a French friend assures me that pointing it out is like saying "Everyone was breathing"—but the more telling truth is that *not* shaking hands is unthinkable. That, surely, would be noticed and talked about. Foreigners, it should be noted, get a pass, but the price of avoiding the custom is that you are then not taken entirely seriously.

For as long as I've lived with this social form, and learned its rules, I still notice it in groups like this. And like any ritual, it has its subtleties. It's important, for instance, to know when *not* to shake. Ponsot, as the chief, took the initiative. He introduced me to three sub-heads—a curator, the chief carpenter, the head electrician—and I shook after him. But I did not then follow him as he walked around: these were his people; they were acknowledging his presence, not mine.

Groups of colleagues and friends always do this when they come together, most often as the first thing in the morning. It is still ubiquitous in French life: at a funeral, mourners shake hands in front of the church before going in for the service; at a murder scene, detectives, forensic medicine experts, and cops all shake hands before turning to the body. I once watched a group of young thugs emerge from a Metro stop onto the sidewalk, there to meet another group of rough-looking characters. They all shook hands before plotting the day's mayhem. If, as here, the boss arrives when work has already begun, there is a pause while his position at the top of the hierarchy is confirmed with the sequence of handshakes. A late-arriving mason, or carpenter, say, would not merit the same interruption; she or he would catch up on shaking individually during the course of the day.

Ponsot is an inclusive shaker, finding everyone on the crew for at least a quick "Bonjour." Among the three crowded rooms and the crew members outside working on paving stones and window sashes, that meant two dozen handshakes. Some supervisors just shake hands with their direct reports and leave it at that, the bare minimum required by convention and custom. A wide gulf—educational, financial, cultural—separates the journeymen workers from the likes of a Ponsot.

The position of Chief Architect of Historical Monuments is highly respected, even revered. Their ranks are extremely limited, and each one has prevailed in a rigorous competition that involves drawing, writing, supervising an actual restoration, and then comprehensive oral examinations. They are regarded as both guardians and proponents of a cultural continuity that is tangible, millennial, and unique. But the sense of respect extends in both directions. Only extremely competent artisans are called upon to work on a *monument historique*, and each is indispensable to the project. In twenty-first-century France, making a personal connection with each worker seems both shrewd and sincere; all the players need to cohere and cooperate in order to get the job done.

After the rapid ceremony of greeting, everyone returns immediately to work. The energy in the room is palpable, almost frantic. They are one month into this project, and the promised completion date is only two months away. Ponsot begins to discuss the paint color samples with one of the curators, but soon looks up to watch an operation under way across the room, both delicate and dramatic. A very large mirror, six feet tall by three feet wide, is being raised three inches within its molding above the chimney mantel. Four men, two of them braced on ladders, strain visibly to lift its weight, using large suction cups. Ponsot breaks away from his conversation and strides across the room. "*Doucement, doucement*"—"Easy, easy"—he says in a low, reassuring voice. This is an original Second Empire mirror, and it's important that it be repositioned intact. Up, down a bit, then up again. They look to him for the calibration, and when he nods, they secure it in place.

Ponsot continues around the crowded rooms, this time systematically spending time with the head of each group of craftsmen hard at work on the various tasks. The walls are being resurfaced and smoothed, then painted with primer before historically accurate wallpaper is affixed to their surface. Together Ponsot and the chief curator examine a tiny piece of the original paper that has been found beneath a window molding. Plenty of written evidence exists that describes for them the pattern and the colors that were used, but the actual palette of tones and materials has been a mystery.

The French tradition of comprehensive and repeated inventories was particularly strong with regard to the furnishings and appointments of all royal residences. For centuries, the royal architect and his staff kept elaborate lists and descriptions of what was to be found in each of the rooms at Fontainebleau. Now, with a tiny bit of physical evidence, the limitations of a written description no longer baffle them. The curator grasps a few square inches of frayed wall covering, hidden from the light for all these years, and this now sparks an animated discussion.

"You see, it's a much different brown from what we thought at first—*havane*."

The paint color, it happens, is called *havane*, "Havana"; they know this from the notes of their predecessors describing the furnishings and décor of Napoleon III's office when it was first installed in this wing in 1864, and now they have a scrap of the original wallpaper that reveals an important fact.

"Yes, yes. You're right: much different. It needs to bring out the warmth of that yellow stripe. This is Havana in the nineteenth century, not Miami in the twentieth!"

Their energy is that of two boys at a treasure hunt who have just figured out how to use a particularly telling clue. In this they could be like any pair of designers who are looking for appropriate solutions for an important room, except that the immutable standard for every choice they make, the perilous starting point for every option, is historical accuracy. More than any other, this consideration governs their decisions. The constraints are formidable. Ponsot sums it up nicely when we talk later in his office:

"Je suis comme un chef d'orchestre—je ne peux pas changer une seule note de la partition." "I'm like an orchestra conductor—I can't change a single note of the score."

"Well, yes," I respond, "but in a way it's trickier than that. You also have to fill in parts of the score as you go along."

He laughs and acknowledges that it sometimes feels that way, but that, like a conductor, he has a certain leeway to "interpret" matters. First they research the specifics rigorously. "This is, after all, a museum, and that consideration is paramount," Ponsot told me. "Once we do our work on the side of history, we must also determine how best to present the result while protecting it from a use for which it was not originally intended. It is a paradox."

Ponsot had addressed this paradox continually as he continued his rounds in Napoleon III's office earlier that morning. He verified with the glaziers, who were fitting panes into the window frames facing the garden, that the glass was double thickness. In this case, energy efficiency trumped authenticity. Running his finger along the wooden sash, he considered aloud that the window would almost never be opened, since the temperature and humidity must in all events be kept constant.

A curator produced a pair of bronze door handles, originals whose mechanism had been repaired and retooled. Ponsot took them in his hand and examined the stylized sunburst motif closely, then held them up to an unpainted door, imagining the effect. Delighted that original hardware had been found and could be used, he handed them back reluctantly, saying only, "That is a lovely handle."

Then it was time to go, and with a few hurried handshakes—the protocol of parting is nothing like the ritual inclusiveness of arrival—he was out the door, making his way carefully through the piles of supplies laid out on the cobblestones.

CHAPTER 7

MOVING IN

Once the inventory had been done, my parents, my siblings, and I got down to the work of settling in. The house was furnished—"*meublée*"—but this was a relative term. There was furniture in all the main rooms, but it was in keeping with the style of the house: heavy, dark, old-fashioned. The dining room table sat sixteen, with sixteen ponderous matched chairs, and it was solid but unwieldy. Sideboards and cupboards were also massive and immovable, though not attached to the wall. The bedrooms all contained wooden beds and no closets. This was standard in French houses and apartments until quite recently. Clothes were hung in individual freestanding wardrobe cupboards—*armoires*—both tall and wide, and invariably made of solid hardwood.

The *grand salon*, or formal living room, was initially filled with elaborate furniture in the style of Louis XV, featuring gilded frames and embroidered upholstery. My mother, Mademoiselle de Chêneville, and the landlady agreed that such heirloom pieces would not long survive the assaults of a family with five children—"*cinq enfants américains!*" "five American children!"—the landlady had noted. They were right: all those delicate chairs and tables and footstools were exiled to a locked room on the off-limits third floor, awaiting the departure of the wild foreign youngsters.

In the first week after we moved in, my mother discovered that the house came with a number of employees whose livelihood was closely associated with its maintenance. Certainly not servants in any conventional sense, they were more a group of retainers who knew the house and its grounds and were, for that reason, indispensable. We had a maid who drove her small motorbike from the outskirts of Fontainebleau three times a week, a gardener who came by every other day, a window cleaner who made infrequent appearances, and a man who cared for the hardwood floors and the big pieces of furniture every month. Painters and tradesmen also showed up irregularly, expecting to be paid for work my parents had not requested. After some initial resistance, my mom and dad acquiesced, adopting Mademoiselle de Chêneville's reasoning that the maintenance was usually essential, they did good work, and they were paid very little. But it meant that for those first weeks the house had the feel of a film set where a new character might walk in off the street and announce, in effect, "I'm in the movie."

Returning from an errand in those first days, my mother was startled by an older man in the *grand salon* doing a strange sort of gliding dance across the bare wood floor. Was he drunk? Some daytime prowler on a bender? Then she noticed the large brushes affixed to the soles of his shoes, his movements displaying a rhythmic pattern as he circled slowly, smiling all the while. "What are you doing dancing in my living room with brushes on your feet?" was far beyond her meager French, so she said the next best thing: "*Bonjour, Monsieur.*" "*Bonjour, Madame!*" This is how she met *Monsieur Jérôme, le frotteur*—literally, "the rubber," since rubbing and brushing is how parquet floors are maintained.

Later that same week she entered the second, darker kitchen

in the late morning to find a woman she had never before seen doing something she had never before imagined: sitting at the small table, prim and proper, eating a peeled banana with a knife and fork. She was, it developed, the maid's mother, who had thought that Madame—my mother—would not mind this "brief visit." She did mind—not the banana, of course, but the not being asked. And so she learned the age-old rule that if you don't set limits, chaos can ensue, far more quickly than one would like to imagine. As the mother of five, she knew this already, but now it fell to her to apply rules to the entire household, and that took some doing. No "guests," no "walk-ins," no unannounced visitors of any sort were to be admitted. The house sat on an acre of land, surrounded by a high wall and a wrought-iron gate; no one was to be let in from outside without the permission of Madame or Monsieur. There were exceptions—our friends from school, minor emergencies requiring quick repairs, the men who came by periodically to read the gas and electric meters—but the message was clear, and it was respected.

Gradually we got to know the town by foot; the center was only a five-minute walk from the house. We certainly weren't the first Americans the locals had seen—NATO had had a base in Fontainebleau since 1949. Still, we were something of a curiosity on the sidewalks: the tall mustached officer and his petite wife, with five children—two girls, three boys—from teenager to toddler. Two were dark-haired, three of us were towheaded and freckled. In other words, not the least bit French looking. The town center was full of the specialty shops for which France is known: the *crèmerie* for milk and cheese, the *boulangerie* for daily fresh bread, the *boucherie* for cuts of meat, the *poissonnerie* for fish, and so forth. On those initial outings, it was impossible to resist the delectable delights of the *pâtisserie*, and we each chose a different pastry confection, the likes of which we had never seen, much less tasted. The greatest discovery, though, was the outdoor market that was held at the center of town on the *Place du Marché*, just next to the Town Hall.

We walked through the market on one of those first mornings and the memory is still intense: boundless, frenetic activity on all sides, with screams arising from vendors and clients alike; piles of fruits and vegetables set up perfectly on the carts; big chalkboards announcing the prices, with selections weighed out on old-style balance scales with graduated counterweights; dead chickens and rabbits and ducks hanging upside down at the butcher's carts, their feathers and fur streaked with blood; smells that bombarded me, suddenly replaced by other, stronger smells in one long assault on the senses; flowers and herbs and cheeses, and people laughing and arguing and constantly moving. We emerged as from a downpour, blinking slightly. I still remember my surprise and disappointment when I discovered that, by the afternoon, the whole thing simply disappeared—gone, like a circus that had left town. But it returned in the mornings three times a week.

Over time my mom developed a pattern for her food shopping that combined weekly visits to the post commissary with occasional forays to the open-air market and the shops in town. We were relatively fortunate since we had unlimited access to the subsidized commissary with its array of American staples, and yet the favorable dollar/franc exchange rate also meant that we could shop locally for fresh fruits, vegetables, and French specialties like cheese and cold cuts. Like any others who have spent any time at all in France, we discovered early on that the bread is cheap, baked fresh daily, and sublimely flavorful. It was uncommon that a baguette, warm from the oven, made it home from the *boulanger* without one or both ends bitten off.

One of my dad's colleagues, a French officer, explained that wine could be delivered to the house and left on the back stoop, like milk in America. He suggested an acceptable *vin ordinaire* for daily consumption, with a visit to the *caviste*—the wine specialty store—when something better was called for. Soon after, a steel carrying rack of six bottles—two red, two white, two rosé—would appear on the gravel next to the basement door every couple of weeks. We emptied the rack, filled it with empties, and it disappeared as if by magic before morning. Every few months my dad received a bill for the equivalent of thirty-five cents a bottle.

Our house had one feature that made it resolutely modern in the eyes of the French, and extremely desirable: a working telephone. Phones were a government monopoly, one that didn't function very well. There was an entire ministry called PTT—for *Postes, Télégraphes et Téléphones,* or Mail, Telegraphs, and Telephones—but getting a new phone was nearly impossible without a contact inside the ministry who could pull the right strings. What seemed commonplace for us was a luxury to the ordinary French, and my father made sure we were aware of our good fortune.

My parents made an executive decision toward the end of that first summer that pleased all us kids: we would get a dog. Another of my dad's French colleagues had for sale a young *caniche royale,* a full-size male poodle. He was what the French call an *abricot,* an apricot-colored dog, but in truth that hue appeared only when his coat was long, and then only at the tips of his fur. His undercoat was a brownish gray.

He arrived with a pedigree that would have done justice to a prince of France: several pages of bloodlines bound in an old-fashioned French file folder. He came already named, too: *Capucine,* or nasturtium. It had something to do with his champion parents having borne names that both began with *Ca*, but it was ridiculous. We called him Kepi, the term used for the distinctive French military hat in the form of a low cylinder with a stiff brim.

Kepi arrived "looking like a million dollars," as my dad put it, with a formal cut that left no doubt he was a poodle. Not the ludicrous lion cut that is rarely seen in France, but a trim that left his torso close-cropped, his legs covered with fur (apricot!), and his feet and tail shaved. A pom-pom on his tail, a topknot on his head, and a kind of mustache on his trimmed snout completed the effect of courtly formality. That didn't last long, though. We kept him cleaned and brushed, but the fancy haircuts became a rarity, and he adapted to our more relaxed rhythm. To me he was like a French aristocrat who came to live with us, then quickly made the transition to an American dog. He fit right in, and the huge yard gave him plenty of space to run.

My mom grew up with animals on her parents' farm in upstate New York, and while she was in no sense sentimental about pets, she had a healthy regard for the bond between children and domestic animals. She used to say, "A good dog can keep two young children occupied for the better part of an afternoon." The operative term was "good," as in accommodating, and Kepi was in every sense a good dog. I used to wonder what my mom meant by that pronouncement until I had children of my own—only two—and the wisdom of her words became apparent. Kepi kept us occupied.

Before the end of the summer my mom began French lessons; twice a week she spent an hour with a French woman in town who taught foreigners. The Air Force had arranged for my dad to take a course in Washington, and he had a natural flair that lent itself to the somewhat theatrical adventure of learning a new language. Moreover, he had plenty of time to observe and absorb in his job at the Château since he was often in meetings with Maréchal Juin in which his duty was to listen to his French superiors rather than to speak. But my mom's responsibility for running the household required French. The retainers who came with the house, the various teachers at the schools we attended, the shopkeepers in town: none spoke English.

She resisted mightily the misguided inclination of many Americans who didn't speak French to make themselves understood without studying the language. There were two approaches, both of them fruitless and, in their way, offensive. One was to speak English loudly and clearly, as if the French were all hard of hearing and simply raising the volume would force comprehension. The other scheme was to speak English with an imagined French accent, which made everybody sound like walk-on characters in *Casablanca*. Some things never change; in Paris today, you can readily witness both of these hopeless notions in practice, and the reaction of the French ranges from frustration to utter contempt.

So my mom applied herself seriously and acquired a rough fluency before the year's end. But the accent eluded her, so that, while her French was basically correct, it was fundamentally lacking in the music that counts for so much. She was always aware of this limitation, and she herself made fun of some of its consequences.

One of her favorite stories concerned the time in early September of that first year when she met with the principal of the school that Sally would be attending. She sat in the woman's office and talked—in her rudimentary French—for a good five minutes about Sally's background and previous schooling. When she had finished, the woman leaned across the desk and said with an encouraging tone, *"Madame, s'il vous plait, parlez français."* "Madam, please speak French." My mother never tired of telling that anecdote, howling at the principal's look of concern and bewilderment after she had listened to my mom's flat American cadences. Things got better, but only gradually. Language is no light affair to the French, and meeting them more than halfway is expected. As my mom used to say, "Who can blame them?"

At the far end of the garden the ground rose almost to the top of the enclosing wall. On the other side it fell away in a sheer drop of twenty feet to a courtyard that lay at the edge of a French military barracks. The troops were mustered three times a day in close ranks, facing the wall while their drill sergeant—his back to our garden—harangued them with shouts and orders. Before long my brothers and I discovered that we could peer over the top of our wall and make faces at the soldiers, one of whom would generally break into a laugh, only to be set upon with fury by the sergeant while we hid below the wall's edge.

Our little game was brought abruptly to an end when my father discovered us at our mischief. Not only were we severely punished, we were also lectured and frequently reminded that we had no business bringing shame on our family or our country by making monkeys of ourselves in the eyes of the French. I began to see that we weren't exactly on display, but neither could we do what some French boys did all the time without consequences. I realize now, as I must have felt then, that we were in some kind of in-between category, American boys living like French boys but with different expectations some of the time. It took a while to understand the boundaries.

CHAPTER 8

SCHOOL

My parents chose to put us all in French schools, figuring that the opportunity to learn French was more important than going to the NATO-affiliated English-language school. At the beginning of September the four oldest children were enrolled in local schools; my two-year-old sister stayed at home. Both of my elder brothers, Tom and Judd, had already attended Catholic schools in Virginia, and they were entrusted to a boys' school run by priests. Their experience there was arduous, both because they had no French and also because the priests weren't known as indulgent, some pure French strain of a demanding religious order. I escaped this fate since I was just beginning school. My elder sister was sent to a Catholic girls' school, and for that first year I attended *maternelle*, kindergarten, at the same institution.

As with any preschool, the academic component was fairly informal. It was my first taste of school, though, and the formal introduction to language—the alphabet, the rudiments of reading and writing—all came at me in French. In that sense, I was the luckiest in our family since I was a newcomer, both to learning and to this other language. Among ourselves and at home we all spoke English, but I first learned to read and write in French.

Following the school's list, my mom assembled a puzzling collection of supplies from local shops: a satchel with straps that could be worn on the back (long before anyone had thought of backpacks and books in the same sentence); a small *ardoise* (a piece of black slate), framed in wood, together with three sticks of chalk; a tiny sponge in its own plastic container; a half dozen *cahiers* (notebooks) with graph-paper lines; an abacus; and a *tablier,* the pale blue coverall smock that schoolchildren all used to wear in the earliest grades to keep chalk, ink, and food from staining their clothes.

On my first day in a French classroom, all of the parents dropped off their children at the gates of the school. In France parents are not encouraged to enter the school grounds, and this is still the case. We were shown to the appropriate classroom and seated at ancient slanted desks with hinged wooden tops. Our teacher entered and, after quieting us down, greeted us formally: "*Bonjour, la classe!*" She then told us that we were to rise when she entered and greet her so that she could greet us, whereupon she walked out and, after a pregnant pause, reentered the classroom. We all shot from our seats and most knew the right greeting, which was screamed out gleefully: "*Bonjour, Madame!*" We practiced another half-dozen times until her appearance elicited a perfect singsong chant in unison. That same day we used the abacus for learning how to figure basic sums on the decimal system (a French invention, we were reminded), and the *ardoise* we used for spelling exercises, our efforts erased from the slate with the tiny moistened sponge before we began again.

One of the first problems I confronted as I embarked on learning a new language was the pronunciation of my own name. In every French institutional setting where there is a roll call, the code is invariable: you say your family name first, then your given name, military style. When she went down the rows and had each of us introduce ourselves by name, my teacher balked when I said it. "*Quoi?*" "What?" "CARHART" was already problematic, but my teacher managed an approximation: "CARARR" (the *H* and the *T* were unpronounced). Either "Thad" or "Thaddeus," however, was a logical impossibility.

In French, *Th* is always pronounced like a hard *T* ("Thomas"), never with the *H* sound. The *Th* that we regularly use in English, as in "thing" or "that," simply doesn't exist; it comes out as a *Z* or *S* sound: "ZING" or "ZAT." "THAD" became "SAD," and it was my turn to balk. "*Thaddé*" officially exists as the equivalent of "Thaddeus," but it is so uncommon as to be bizarre (even more so than "Thaddeus" in English). Finally, we settled on "TED," a pronounceable option that isn't French (the short version of Theodore in French is "Théo"), but it did the job. I became TED CARARR.

Even preschool followed the standard French academic calendar, which included classes on Thursday and Saturday mornings. Thursday afternoon was reserved for religious instruction and Mass in the Catholic schools. This made for a long week, with only Saturday afternoon and Sunday as a break. In that first fall we all discovered just how much farther north Paris lay than Washington, D.C., with a latitude equivalent to New Brunswick, Canada. Soon we were leaving home in pitch black—8:00 a.m. classes—and leaving school in pitch black, at 5:00 p.m. I had nothing to compare it to, so it seemed normal.

The kindergarten boys were the only male intruders in a building full of girls, its graveled courtyard spilling over with their uniformed bodies whenever the bells rang. We kindergarten kids were a frequent source of amusement to the "big" girls: not quite real, more like stuffed animals who decorated one part of the grounds. But my older sister Sally was among them, so there was a familiar face at the end of the day with whom I could head home. During that first school year, it wasn't a bad way to ease into the customs and rhythms of the school day in France.

Preschool introduced me to the social framework of French education; respect for authority was paramount. The subjects taught were the classic trio: reading, writing, and arithmetic. In addition to these substantive areas, we were graded on discipline, politeness and dress (*tenue*), and concentration, as well as religious instruction (this was a Catholic school). My mother saved the little squares of paper we were given every two weeks, each bearing the typewritten names of the various subjects. Beside each rubric was handwritten in black ink "*TB*" for *très bien*, "*B*" for *bien*, and so on. Then the overarching ethos of the entire French educational apparatus was distilled in *red* ink beside a final category—*MENTION: BIEN*. No initials here; the word *bien* is spelled out in full.

This system of notations amounts to a three-tiered honors scheme that applies at every level of schooling. When students are graduating from *lycée*, high school, they all take the national baccalaureate exam, *le bac*, and your *mention* on that test, should you manage to qualify for honors, follows you through life. All grades are numerically noted on a scale of 1 to 20. The overall average from the weeklong exam then determines whether you graduate or must repeat; an overall grade of 10 is required for advancement. The three *mentions* are: 12 to 14, *assez bien*, literally, "good enough"; 14 to 16, *bien*, "good"; 16 to 20, *très bien*, "very good." Any *mention* is respected, but the phrase *assez bien* exemplifies a certain grudging French attitude as concerns praise of any sort. "Let's not get carried away here" is an underlying message, never made explicit but clear to any French student with even a modicum of accomplishment. Success is both encouraged and highly suspect, a contradiction that underlies much of French life. It pivots on a fear of that most diabolical of sins in the Catholic order: pride. Damned if you do succeed, and most certainly damned if you don't.

The French take the long view. By the time the adolescent members of the nascent elite—make no mistake, there *is* an elite—complete the rigorous two years of preparatory classes that follow *lycée* and lead to the superselect *grandes écoles* (elite colleges), they have been told so often and by so many teachers that they know less than zero, that they are hopeless, that they are *nuls* ("nothing"), they are finally considered to be inured to the effects of disappointment and underachievement. It's as if they had been subjected to the academic equivalent of Marine basic training for two full years. Insult tempers the blade, it is felt, and when they do finally matriculate at their elite schools, the ego rarely rears its bothersome little head to raise an obstacle to serious learning. The individual's importance is vitiated, but the confidence of the group (many call this arrogance) emerges strengthened. And it all starts in kindergarten.

Every week one or another of my parents had to sign our homework notebook (*cahier de devoir*). My mom later admitted that she carefully reviewed the writing and reading exercises, not to catch any mistakes—the teacher had already corrected our scribblings—but to glean what she could, even at an elementary level, as she struggled to learn the language. One element caught her attention: in our rudimentary counting exercises, the example used was often bottles of wine, *bouteilles de vin*: "If my uncle brings two bottles of wine and puts them in the wine cellar with my father's five bottles, how many bottles of wine are there in the wine cellar?" How many American five-year-olds learned to count using wine bottles? she later joked, but already the units made sense to me. We had a weekly delivery of such bottles at the back door, after all.

Of the various subjects, I liked handwriting the most. There was a hypnotic quality to the alphabet, and I took to the French approach—endless repetition and replication by us students—like candy. The session began with the teacher's command to take out our notebooks and pencils. The top of the desk was hinged at its far edge as a single inclined plank of wood, so this involved clearing the desk with your seatmate before lifting it up to retrieve materials in the compartment underneath. Slamming of desktops was strictly sanctioned, so, depending on who you sat with, this could be a perilous maneuver. The first exercise was an introduction to vowels—*i* and *u* began the series—that the teacher had printed on the blackboard in large letters, whole lines of them. Underneath the block letters, perfect rows of script slanted across the board: *i,u,i,u*. Our task was then to fill our first page with as near a replication as possible of the perfect array of printing and script that we were looking at. Our notebooks were lined, both horizontally and vertically, like a special form of graph paper, but it required intense concentration to render our own fractured versions in pencil. Each of us also had a small book with a page devoted to the same two vowels that used images to show various ways of pronouncing the letter in a word. After filling two pages of our notebooks with *i*'s and *u*'s, we then opened our books and recited after the teacher the names of things that featured these vowels, each one illustrated: *hibou* (owl), *lune* (moon), *billes* (marbles), *bûchette* (stick).

It wasn't until many years later that I understood how much the intensity and newness of everything made me acutely observant. The utter necessity of learning French was akin to plunging into a fast-moving river and having to swim. I learned to watch and listen and name everything as if my life depended on it, which in a way it did—at least my social life. My memories from this time are correspondingly vivid. Both objects and experiences were imprinted on my brain a second time in a new language, and their staying power over time has often astounded me. There are many things I recall with greater precision from this tender age than, say, from the first year after our return to America. They sometimes feel like scenes from a movie, and the soundtrack is always in the French I first learned in Fontainebleau.

There remains from that year of kindergarten one singular memory that was rich with shame, though it has since mellowed to a kind of farce. In the fall of 1954, just as I started my schooling, Pierre Mendès-France, the progressive head of the government, decreed that all kindergarten and primary students in France would henceforth be given a glass of milk each morning; drinking the milk would be required of every student. Much discussion in the press ensued, about which I knew nothing.

The government reasoned that it would both set an example to counter the inclination of many families to give children wine or hard cider in the morning, and offset some of the poor nutrition throughout the country. Many families still struggled to put adequate food on the table, particularly at the end of each month before the next paycheck arrived.

So it was that, mere weeks after I had begun classes at the *maternelle,* still blinking my eyes at the newness of everything—the school, the language, my classmates—a glass of milk appeared on my desk one midmorning in October. Two glasses, actually, since my seatmate was served, too, by a pair of older women who walked up and down the aisles, one setting out glasses and the other filling them from a speckled blue enamel pitcher. Our teacher announced that this was now to be part of our morning *goûter,* or snack; we already received a slice of baguette and a thin bar of milk chocolate. She also told us that each of us was obliged to drink the milk unless we had a letter from our doctor.

We drank milk often at our house and poured it on breakfast cereal, and I liked it. My mother had been raised on a dairy farm, and though she didn't push dairy products on us, neither did she see danger in a small glass of milk. So I did the American thing: I drank the glass of milk, careful not to gulp, finishing it in one long swig. Before I had finished I heard some titters from around me, and some nervous laughter, too. When I set the glass down and looked around, I met the stares of my classmates, as if I were a circus clown. My desk partner looked on with saucer eyes, his features an amalgam of horror, fascination, and real concern. I might as well have just downed a cup of hemlock.

I now discovered that every other child had produced a letter from the family doctor, which they had unfolded and set on their desktops. These notes—many of them from the same practitioner and with identical wording—explained that little François or Claire or Michel or Madeleine was allergic to milk and was, under no circumstances, to be given any while at school. Unwittingly, I had kept the verdict against milk from being unanimous, had broken with my new schoolmates by the too-eager drinking of the milk I was served. Shock, derision, and a form of childish contempt were swiftly heaped upon me. As far as I was concerned, it was over even before it started, but there followed the tedious business of collecting the letters and taking note, aloud, that only "CARRAR, TED" was able to drink milk without peril to his life. In other words, the class freak.

This happened ages before anyone had heard of lactose intolerance, and there most assuredly was no constitutional predisposition to reject milk among the French. Not physically, that is: one has only to consider all the rich cheeses and cream-based sauces that are French staples to understand that much. But drinking milk was not part of the social landscape; it was something that only "Anglo-Saxons" (the catchall term for Americans and English speakers from the former British Empire) could dream up. Add to that Mendès-France's stated purpose of curbing alcoholism by steering children away from beer and wine, and you had a call to arms.

The French parents must have talked among themselves, and the loophole of the doctor's letter suited their purpose. My parents weren't in the know on that play, and now I had publicly displayed what a willing milk drinker I was. This complicated life for everyone. What followed was my first lesson in adapting to life in France.

Like most young children entering a group for the first time, I fervently hoped not to stand out, not to be different. Drinking that glass of milk certainly got me noticed, in a way I could have done without. "*Le petit 'ricain qui boit le lait de Mendès,*" "the little American who drinks Mendès's milk," was my new identity. How to turn this around?

At home I complained bitterly that I was the *only one* in my class who was even served a glass of milk, and—in the inscrutable logic of France—since it was served by government decree, it had to be drunk! This was played out as a surreal kind of pantomime for a few more days as the entire class watched me drinking my milk at 10:00 a.m. It was awkward for the teacher, and ridiculous for the poor woman who lugged her cumbersome pitcher to my desk to pour out a single glass.

My parents briefly considered asking for a letter from the American military doctor on the base, then dismissed the thought. My father was an officer, we had to play by the rules, and I was demonstrably not allergic to milk: not an option. The next day my dad made some inquiries among his French colleagues concerning "*l'affaire du lait.*" He came home at lunch with the name and phone number of the French doctor who had supplied the majority of my classmates' letters. That afternoon my mother and I entered the doctor's office, expecting him to examine me and question my mom. ("When did he first show symptoms of this allergy to milk?" "Three days ago. . . .")

The doctor's office was in his house—an arrangement still common in France—a single room off a narrow hallway. He wore a gray suit and a blue tie, and rose from behind his desk to shake my mother's hand. Settling herself in one of the two chairs, she began in her halting French: *"Mon fils n'aime pas le lait."* "My son does not like milk." A long pause, then she added, *"Il est à l'école maternelle."* "He is in nursery school." "Ah!" came the response, his face now bright with understanding. *"Je vois."* "I see."

And that was it! No exam, no questions, not even a mention of the word *allergie*. He reached for a blank sheet of paper bearing his letterhead, unscrewed the top of a fine fountain pen, and scribbled a note in less than a minute, asking only for my full name. He handed over the letter to my mom with a reassuring "This should be sufficient for this situation, Madam," and she paid him the equivalent of four dollars in old French francs.

I presented the letter the next morning and the milk lady never again appeared in our classroom. I could just about read "RELIEF"—okay, its French version, *"SOULAGEMENT"*—on my teacher's face. Without fully comprehending why, I had rightly understood that I needed a letter like everyone else's. It had long stopped being about milk: to drink or not to drink? Since the government's decree had the force of law, what I needed was *"une dérogation,"* an exemption to the rule, like all the other kids. A *dérogation*, I gradually learned, was an essential part of navigating the mysterious landscape of French administrative procedures. If you provide the document (it is *always* a document) that is defined as the permissible *dérogation*, everything is fine. Without that piece of paper, though, I could still be in nursery school, downing a daily glass of milk at 10:00 a.m. Or so it felt. Learning to play by the rules also meant learning to circumvent the rules, but always respecting the official form. My exemption didn't win me new friends, but it did help me to fit in when that was the essential dynamic.

As it happens, Mendès-France was forced to leave office six months later, not because of the milk, but because he had taken a principled stand against the conflict in Algeria, still a French colony. It's fair to say that he was ahead of his time. For decades afterward, the slang for a glass of milk was simply *"un Mendès."* He was reviled in many rural areas for ending the right of farmers to distill ten liters of *eau de vie* for their own use—the rough equivalent of making moonshine. A government advertisement in the Paris Metro stations at the time warned, *"L'alcool tue lentement!"* "Alcohol kills slowly!" Underneath, a wag scrawled, famously, *"Tant mieux! Nous ne sommes pas pressés."* "So much the better! We're in no hurry."

Gradually France has faced up to the problems caused by excessive alcohol consumption. "Designated drivers," "breathalyzer tests," "restraint" are all part of the landscape now in a way that would have been unimaginable in the fifties, and children rarely start the day with a glass of wine or hard cider to keep them warm. But among my French friends who are peers, many recall having produced the doctor's letter in that autumn of 1954 to save them from the strange notion of milk in a glass.

CHAPTER 9

HENRI IV

In the long line of kings who have ruled France and lived at Fontainebleau, one stands out as a favorite of the French, even today: *Le bon roi Henri IV*—the good king. This Henri has what we could call favorable press. His equestrian statue stands in Paris on the *Pont Neuf,* the bridge he had built, and it looks down on the tiny *Square du Vert Galant,* named for him. That phrase resists translation. *Galant* has a close parallel in the English "gallant"—amorous, flirtatious, chivalrous—but the *Vert* has a strong connotation of sexual prowess to it: lusty if not exactly lecherous. It is still said of an older man who remains sexually active, "*La touffe est grise mais la tige est verte.*" "His tuft [of hair] may be gray, but his stem is green."

Henri inherited the throne in 1589 when his cousin, Henri III, was stabbed to death by a Catholic fanatic. For more than thirty years under the reign of the weak Valois kings and the regency of their mother, Catherine de Medici, France had descended into a religious civil war caused by the rise of Protestantism throughout the land. Henri IV had himself been born to a Catholic father and a Protestant mother; he changed faith several times during his life merely in order to survive.

When Henri III, the last of the Valois dynasty, lay dying from his assassin's wound, Henri IV was a Protestant who had successfully led several campaigns against Catholic repression. Now he was faced with the political reality that he could not be crowned without professing the Catholic faith. His response to the facts has become emblematic: "*Paris vaut bien une messe.*" "Paris is well worth a Mass." A cynical pronouncement or a realist's assessment? Most opt for the latter, and this quality has ensured his popularity among the practical French.

He ruled from 1589 to 1610, one of the most tumultuous periods in France's long history. Managing to cool the fires of fanaticism on both sides of the religious conflict, he found common ground for Protestants and Catholics. Unlike his predecessors, he was known for his magnanimity in victory, and for his capacity to forgive and reconcile with his enemies. To a France exhausted by doctrinaire positions and merciless battles, this was a revelation. His success as both military leader and diplomat earned him respect, but it was his personal qualities that gripped the popular imagination.

He is the classic *bon vivant*, lover of life, famous for his amorous escapades and for his love of good food and wine. With the possible exception of Charles de Gaulle, no Frenchman has been credited with quite so many aphorisms, witticisms, and bits of wisdom. Some are no doubt apocryphal, others verified, but all combine to build the myth of Henri IV, a largely positive and appealing portrait that has persisted across the centuries. "*Jusqu'à quarante ans, je croyais que c'était un os*" "Until I was forty, I thought it was a bone"—this in reference to his state of virtually constant sexual arousal. Father of six children by his queen, he recognized a dozen illegitimate descendants by a series of mistresses. As for occasional liaisons, he was notorious for constant assignations in his numerous châteaux.

"A chicken in every pot," "*Une poule au pot,*" was associated with

Henri IV more than three centuries before Herbert Hoover's claim in the 1928 U.S. presidential election. This suggests how much the evolution of his image was based on his concern for common people. It also indicates what attributes continue to resonate with the French: a lesser prince from the provinces (Navarre, on the border with Spain) who managed to prove his mettle by force of arms and clever negotiation.

In 1600 Henri married Marie de Medici. Like his predecessor, Henri II, he turned to the vastly rich Medici clan to prop up his fortunes. Marie arrived with a dowry that covered France's debt. In the manner of her forebear, Catherine de Medici, Marie had to tolerate the king's succession of royal mistresses, though none was so constant a presence as had been Diane de Poitiers.

Henri favored Fontainebleau, and his additions are among the most impressive parts of the Château. He inherited a Château that was substantially the creation of François I, and he expanded it considerably to the scale it has largely kept to the present day. His Baptistery Gate, to commemorate the christening of his heir, the future Louis XIII, is a triumphal entryway to the Oval Court, an elegant courtyard toward the rear of the Château that served as the entrance for the royal family. The Gate's squared dome and neoclassical detailing are quintessentially French. Henri also added an entire new courtyard and surrounding buildings on a mammoth scale whose style is both rustic and grand. For this practical lover of the good life, the new buildings were given over to extensive kitchens and storage facilities for the growing court. To house his retainers, he commissioned two additional wings behind the *Cour d'Honneur* with its grand staircase. The canal was his creation, too, in 1609. Over a kilometer long and thirty meters wide, it extends the Château's gardens through the surrounding forest. When it had been dug, he made a bet with one of his advisers that it would take no more than two days to fill with Fontainebleau's extensive streams. Since it required more than a week, the king had to pay out a sack of gold pieces.

The target of numerous assassination attempts throughout his reign, Henri IV was stabbed to death in his carriage in the streets of Paris in 1610. His murderer, Ravaillac, a Catholic extremist who feared the king's tolerance of Protestants, maintained to the end that he acted alone. Doubts persist to this day, with many believing that a conspiracy was organized against the king.

Unlike his Valois cousins, Henri was no dandy; it is said that he smelled always of garlic (still a staple of the cuisine from his native Navarre), and that of all his obligations as a ruler, he most detested bathing. He is usually depicted with lively eyes, a slight smile on his lips beneath his full beard, with an enigmatic air of knowing what he wants. It may have been his next conquest, or a surcease from the brutal wars of religion—quite possibly both. His contradictions have come to embody an entire French approach to life's often daunting challenges: do your best to fashion workable compromises, and make sure to enjoy yourself along the way.

CHAPTER 10

DÉSTRUCTURÉ

As it happens, the part of the Château that NATO occupied in the fifties and sixties was also the creation of Henri IV, and it's where my father had his office. Known today as the *Cour Henri IV,* it is also known as the *Cour des Offices,* or kitchen wing. Built in 1609, it displays a monumental scale in all its aspects, and uses to great advantage the essential materials of Fontainebleau: gray stone, pink brick, stucco walls, and steeply raked slate roofs. Its massive doorway, as large as a medieval city gate, announces a royal residence in clear terms. Nearly three hundred and fifty years after *le Vert Galant* had it raised, my dad rolled his bicycle through its concave portal and went to work every morning.

Soon after making his acquaintance, I accompanied Ponsot on an inspection of this wing. As we walked toward this most distant of the five major courtyards, he told me that the buildings that flank three sides of the square had recently been entirely renovated. A tall iron picket fence closes the fourth side adjacent to the rest of the Château. We could see the spanking new slate of the roof and the perfectly restored stone detailing as we made our way across the courtyard. Ponsot had come to this far corner to hear the engineer's assessment of the underlying soil before this part of the structure was adapted for new uses. Centuries-old documents mention traces of groundwater in this sector, and unless it could be shown that the soil was dry and drained efficiently, major excavations and rebuilding might be necessary. "Water is always the enemy in such situations," Ponsot told me as we approached one of the doors. "An entire budget could disappear with an unfavorable finding."

Just before we entered, Ponsot turned to me and said, "The insides have been gutted"—he used the term *déstructuré*. "Don't expect to see your father's office." *Déstructuré* was putting it mildly. Inside we found a shell stripped to the structural basics. Only the load-bearing interior walls remained, bare to the plaster, where in the fifties this had been a warren of wood-paneled offices. I remembered them as dark, draped with flags, sabers, and military insignia. All of that was gone, utterly. Overhead, only a few floor planks remained of what had been the second floor with its steeply pitched ceilings directly under the roof. Below, the floor had been ripped up, right down to the soil.

Ponsot now scrambled over a small hill of dirt, and the rest of us followed. On the other side of this pile, we found ourselves on the edge of a deep trench, excavated in one of the corners and braced from within against collapse. He peered down anxiously to three workers fifteen feet below and asked what they had found. "*C'est sec!*" came the shouted reply, "It's dry!" His manner eased as he took this in, then he climbed down the ladder to see for himself and discuss the particulars with the on-site chief. In a few minutes he scrambled out of the depths, a smile on his face, and huddled briefly with his colleagues before bounding over the dirt to two other similar trenches in other parts of the wing. He must already have known that the other two were also free of moisture, and the sense of relief—excitement, really—was palpable.

In truth, I had visited my dad's office only a handful of times. I was a young child, he was a staff officer, and children were rarely seen in the workplace in the fifties. But I did retain enough from those few times to associate it with a certain kind of military decorum: the shiny black Citroën staff cars parked outside, the uniformed guards at attention before the massive entrance portal, the ceremonial display of guns and battle streamers decorating the interior hallways—in short, all the coded symbols that announced the headquarters of a French marshal—*un maréchal de France*—in this storied place most closely associated with Napoleon and his legendary marshals. To see the Henri IV wing gutted was now strangely thrilling, an inversion of a child's sense of solidity, authority, permanence. Not for the first time—and certainly not for the last—it would now be used for something else.

Back in his office, I asked Ponsot about the plans for the Henri IV wing now that the interior renovation could go forward. "For now, the space in one of the three sides of the U-shaped courtyard has been committed to use as a training center for the tourism industry," he said. Appropriate tenants will have to be found for the buildings on the other two sides, and much of that will depend upon fashioning long-term financing for their viability. "Everyone has great ideas, but paying for them is another matter," he told me. In any event, the decision had been made to use the structure in some practical manner rather than refit it as the seventeenth-century kitchen wing of a royal residence.

This illustrates the complex considerations that are brought to bear in any decision to restore a part of the Château. At its heart a historical monument, this elaborate assemblage of buildings must nevertheless continue to evolve with time and its users, whether they be visitors or tenants. Economic and political factors also come into play: the Château reflects the French Republic in many of its aspects, both logical and contradictory.

I inquired about the work site we had inspected on my last visit, the Napoleon III office. "There is a lot going on in such a small space," I ventured. "Are you pleased with the progress?"

"Yes, they're doing good work. These are professionals."

"And how do you keep track of it all?"

He pondered my question for several seconds, then said, "Well, when I return to my office I write a progress report, of course. But it's up to me, after all, to keep the essentials in my head, to recognize where problems may arise."

His job, he explained, was not to micromanage every last element, but to supervise the standards and the pace of work. He confessed, though, that it was impossible *not* to notice things once he was on the site. "My eye is trained to do that. So it remains a balancing act between descending into particulars and keeping the artisans moving along."

No matter what the issues on a particular day may be, Ponsot always has to consider the effects on the entire Château. "There are 1,985 windows in the Château," he declared. "The *Cour des Adieux* alone has 865, if you count both sides of the wings." I sensed that he had counted each one, just as he had calculated the five-acre surface area of the roof. "My initial assessment was that we need approximately forty million euros just to stabilize what is here and prevent further damage, working from the top down. That is why the roof is key. Of course," he added with a half smile, "we don't have that sum in hand, so we do what is most critical."

Keeping a site like Fontainebleau solvent as a museum takes some imagination. The great model is Versailles, with almost seven million visitors paying to inspect the creation of the Sun King, Louis XIV. But, like Notre-Dame or the Louvre or the Eiffel Tower, Versailles is one of the handful of indispensable stops on the Paris tourist circuit. As such, it has become a cash cow, one so overrun by the sheer number of people that a visit is often a caricature of tourist hell. On a given day, twenty or thirty thousand tourists shuffle through the king's bedroom, the chapel, the Hall of Mirrors, gazing upon acres of marble and frescoes and very few pieces of furniture, their numbers almost overwhelming even in this palace's grandiose spaces. Versailles has its subtleties, but they are difficult to appreciate in a crowd.

As for its more obvious attributes, they differ starkly from the spirit of Fontainebleau. Louis XIV imagined Versailles as a declaration of centralized royal power, and the great majority of it was built in a mere twenty years. Its architectural program hinges on a relentless symmetry, baroque detail, and elaborate displays of grandeur. The sovereign occupies the center of a created world: the central axis of the gardens leads directly to the person of Louis, the one and indispensable king of France. This kind of manufactured splendor is easily readable. Linked as it is in the minds of tourists to the unbridled excesses that led to the revolution, the site is a must-see for those who come to the world's most visited city.

In the world of tourism, one of the principal points of difference is the revenue each of these two palaces generates. Although both are storied royal residences in the near environs of Paris, Versailles attracts more than fifteen times the visitors of Fontainebleau. "We must find a way for Fontainebleau to pay more of its own way," Xavier Salmon, the chief curator, told me. "But we must do so without destroying the visitor's experience." He mentioned a number of possible schemes: selling advance tickets by reservation in order to limit the overall numbers at peak periods, working more closely with tour operators, trying themed visits for special groups. But the fact remains that, despite its overall size, Fontainebleau's rooms are primarily intimate in scale. Moreover, its rooms are almost entirely furnished with period pieces, which makes it at once both alluring for visitors and comparatively more fragile than other châteaux.

Related to the question of how to attract more visitors is an important curatorial issue: what do you "feature"? There exists no single formula, and no dearth of choices. Kings? Styles? Uses? Aspects of court life? France takes seriously the pedagogical role of its national museums, just as the French take their history seriously, so it is important to get right the mix of storytelling and historical accuracy. In a place that was continuously inhabited and added to by French kings for over four centuries, contradictions abound. Each monarch made his own changes. Louis XV's wing was partly gutted to accommodate Napoleon III's theater; Marie Antoinette had a new apartment built to suit her tastes; Napoleon I adapted Louis XIII's bedchamber for use as his throne room. Which style do you bring forward, the original or its usurper? The answer is complicated, but generally curators have chosen to point out the changes, flag the original elements (if any remain), and then let the amalgam stand. Most often, monarchs respected their predecessor's additions and changes. "There were numerous programs for comprehensive change and architectural unification," Ponsot told me. "None was ever carried out. For that, at least, we can be grateful."

One of the most distinctive features that strikes a visitor to Fontainebleau is the palpable sense that its rooms were lived in. Even though its furniture and appointments are rich and elaborate, the ethic and the esthetic are profoundly human: it exudes a kind of social warmth and cohesion, like a very big house. From François I to Napoleon I, monarchs referred affectionately to Fontainebleau as their home, a sentiment rarely if ever expressed when they spoke of the Louvre, Versailles, or any other royal residence.

Tourists, who commonly know less than the French about the

intrigues and court life of all those kings and queens, clamor for certain names. "Napoleon I and Marie Antoinette are hugely popular, especially among the Americans and the Russians," Ponsot said. For the French themselves, the classical style of the seventeenth and eighteenth centuries is preferred. "There has been an antipathy toward the whole nineteenth century," he said with a shrug, "but that is starting to change, as it is bound to do." Not surprisingly, many more furnishings survive from that period, since the revolution's looting had subsided. "We'll use them to help the public discover another part of its past, closer to hand but—paradoxically—less familiar." I asked if the restoration of Napoleon III's office was part of this undertaking, and he paused, choosing his words. "It's a start."

Later that day, Patrick Ponsot and I walked along the garden side of the Louis XV wing, toward the small lake that lies along one side of the Château's flanks. This long mass of brick, stone, and slate was commissioned by the king whose fifty-nine-year reign was sandwiched between the glories of Louis XIV, the Sun King, and the ultimate debacle of the sixteenth Louis, who ended on the scaffold. Louis XV had neither an interest in, nor an aptitude for, statecraft; by the end of his rule in 1774 he had managed to lose the French colonies in North America and in India to the British. But he had an architect of genius in Ange-Jacques Gabriel, who fashioned an entire side of the *Cour d'Honneur* at Fontainebleau in a style of French classicism that magically balances the facing wing, even though that side of the *Cour d'Honneur* is only two stories tall as opposed to the four of Gabriel's creation.

We passed through a sally port to the other side of the wing, into the Château's main courtyard. As we emerged into the light,

Ponsot told me that his secretary had called to say his mid-afternoon appointment was cancelled, so he had more time than expected.

"Perhaps you would like to see Napoleon III's theater?"

I could hardly believe my luck.

Between 1853 and 1856 the theater was carved out of another part of the four-story Louis XV wing, where court members had been housed before. One of the few remaining intact theaters from the mid-nineteenth century, it was a sleeping beauty that had never been opened to the public. I knew that there were plans for its restoration, but I also understood that it would be a matter of years before the work was finished. From his briefcase, Ponsot pulled out an enormous set of old iron keys strung loosely on a ring. He led me to a locked door on the courtyard side as he searched for the right key.

"Which one will open the door to unseen splendors?" he teased, a conspiratorial gleam in his eye. Then, as the door swung inward, he hastened to add, "Remember, what you are about to see is a work in progress, with a certain amount of disorder." We entered the ground-floor foyer and, as Ponsot locked the door behind us, I looked upon a scene of splendid dilapidation. The floor had been partly torn up, and piles of dusty *tomettes*—the red six-sided floor tiles so common in France—lay stacked at the far end of the space. Huge, irregular swatches of peeling paint hung outward from the high walls, like dust-covered blue and gray tongues whose crazy arcs revealed panels of bone-white plaster underneath. A thick mantle of fine dust lay on the floor, clung to the walls, seemed even to hang from the cracked ceiling. The very light that filtered through the powder-covered windowpanes was gray. Ponsot crossed the space and unlocked another door, motioning me to follow. "We have checked the underlying structure, and it is sound," he announced, as if to explain the shambles that first greeted us.

Now we penetrated to a much cleaner area, the bottom of a stairwell whose dove-gray walls were faded but unstained and intact. To the right I could see a series of curved doors that led to the theater's ground-floor seats. The stage would be farther to the right, I understood, since the theater had been fitted lengthwise into the central section of this extensive wing. We were in the vestibule, and the light here shone silvery, descending from unseen windows. Up one flight and through another door, and suddenly the proportions were grander, the sense of space more generous, with wider doors and higher ceilings, and a sudden air of opulence.

"The emperor never entered from the ground floor," Ponsot told me. "He and his entourage walked from their rooms in the Château along a hallway at this level of the wing and entered directly to the royal box." We now ventured into a large round room whose curved walls were covered in deeply tufted yellow silk with powder-blue accents; two dozen tufted chairs were arranged around the edges, each draped in a thin muslin cover. The effect was of walking in to a voluptuous mid-nineteenth-century jewelry box. We were standing in the salon of the emperor's private box, where Napoleon III received favored guests, sipped champagne, ducked out of the center of attention when the fancy struck him.

Ponsot led me down three shallow, carpeted stairs to the balcony of a small oval theater, the stage just twenty meters in front of us and slightly below. Looking out across a richly painted railing, I understood the theater's symmetrical layout, with the monarch's special seats at the focal point of the central axis. The décor is both elaborate and beautifully proportioned, its arches and ovals echoing the sumptuous curve of the dome, all worked in yellow, pale blue, and gold gilt. Even here, some peeling paint is apparent, but the essentials are intact, and the overall composition is an object lesson in Second Empire richness tempered by restraint.

Ponsot led me now around to the empty stage, almost as deep as the house is long. "This is a very special part of our *patrimoine*," he said, using the French word that means both inheritance and an entire shared cultural tradition. As we made our way to the fly space over the stage, up a series of narrow stairs, he explained that a controversy had gone on for years as to whether the theater could again be used for productions, or merely provide a showcase for what a period theater was like and how it functioned. The latter position has prevailed, Ponsot explained, since using the theater for plays or concerts would mean, in effect, replacing it.

"The room is both luxurious and fragile, never a good mix when public use is contemplated," he said. "Moreover, the stage mechanics all date from 1854, and are hand powered. That, together with severe restrictions imposed by the fire department on the number of spectators, decided the issue." The plan is to organize guided tours and seminars for those interested in the history of theater. And the room itself is an exquisite example of period architecture. "The sheikh of Abu Dhabi has agreed to sponsor its restoration," Ponsot told me. I recalled the plaque one sees in a Fontainebleau sally port—there is a similar one at Versailles—thanking John D. Rockefeller for his ongoing contributions to the restoration of the Château in the 1920s. Now that the kings and emperors are gone, Fontainebleau still seems to find patrons who appreciate its singular position in the history of the West.

Standing just under the roof in the fly space, one appreciates what an undertaking it must have been to shoehorn this entire theater into part of a wing that had previously housed courtiers. The apartments had to be ripped out, the walls and roof strengthened, and the theater built, all within four stories and a low attic. Here one sees the massive iron girders that reinforce the faceted curve of the mansard roof. The industrial age had begun to mature by the 1850s, and its new materials and engineering had been exploited to protect a wing built under Louis XV more than a century before. From outside, nothing betrays the presence of a theater; only the absence of chimneys on this part of the roof suggests a different use. The tradition of respecting the additions to the Château of one's predecessors—of previous kings and their architects—was better observed at Fontainebleau than other royal residences. Its long accretion of styles and masterworks seems to have had a sobering influence on monarchs who may have been inclined to impose their will. "Add, if you like, but do not destroy," was the unspoken rule, largely obeyed.

Through the slatted wooden floor upon which we stand, we can look down four stories to the main stage. All around lie wooden wheels and massive pulleys for raising and lowering scenery, and even a huge fretted spool for pulling up the central chandelier during performances. The oversized wooden dowels and levers bear sweat stains where hands worked them long ago. "Even if it were practicable to rip out all of this and make it modern," Ponsot says, "I have a hard time seeing what would be gained." His hand moves over one of the huge spools that reel in fly lines. "The fact is that nothing like this is being made anymore. It is functional and beautiful, and entirely outdated. But how can we know the past if we don't save some of it?"

CHAPTER 11

ANNICK

During that first fall after our arrival, my mom decided she needed some part-time help with the kids, particularly the two youngest: my sister, a two-year-old toddler, and me, who was in kindergarten. As with so many practical matters, Mademoiselle de Chêneville had a suggestion. A young woman by the name of Annick was looking for work. She was "from the north," "from a good family" (*de bonne famille*, the classic French formula to signal respectability), and she had experience caring for children. That was as much as my mom was told and, after a pleasant interview with a young woman of about nineteen or twenty, my mom hired her for two days each week. Part of the deal was that she would help my mom with conversational French.

Brita and I both loved Annick. She had a sweet manner with everyone, it seemed, and she had a sincere way of being attentive that spoke to children immediately. To adults, too, for that matter. Dark-haired and soft-spoken, she was happy to play with us, indoors or out, so that my mother could have a break. She had some English, which in those days was unusual for someone her age, and my mother and she got by with bits of French and English. But to us she spoke French, and it was our delight to learn and practice with her as we played. She described how she had lived by the sea as a girl and how much she missed it up north. It was never clear whether she was in fact French or, possibly, Belgian, but the northern beaches were what she sometimes described as familiar territory.

When we moved in, Mademoiselle de Chêneville had mentioned to my mother that between the two World Wars our house had been an *auberge*, an inn, but my mom hadn't really registered this in light of everything else she had had to contend with. In the first months, though, two letters arrived requesting reservations for rooms in the ensuing months. Not confident at all in her written French, my mom gave the letters to Annick with envelopes and a few pages of blank stationery and asked her to write short replies in proper French, explaining that the house was no longer a commercial establishment. On her next workday, Annick handed my mother the inquiries along with her handwritten replies. Thinking to see how it should be expressed in French, my mom unfolded one of Annick's letters and read what she had written. Rather, she looked at the page, dumbfounded, and slowly grasped the contours of what seemed impossible.

On each of the single-page letters and on each of the two envelopes, where there ought to have been handwriting, there was scrawl. Not bad handwriting, not messy script done with a hurried hand, but impenetrable scrawl, rendered as loops and squiggles with spaces, as if they formed words. Each line was properly spaced, as one would for a name and address, a date, a salutation, a short paragraph, and a signature. The same was true for the envelopes, where two blocks of scrawl were placed where the sender and the addressee would be noted.

Determining in an instant that Annick was entirely in earnest, my mom took in the implications and decided to duck the blow.

"Will that be satisfactory, Madame?" Annick asked brightly.

"Yes, these will be perfect," my mom assured her. "Thank you, Annick. I'll mail them tomorrow when I have stamps."

Annick couldn't read. She couldn't write, either—not in French nor English nor any other language. My mom was stunned, and she was also concerned, protective, determined to do something. How was this possible? Never had she suspected that the lively, well-spoken girl who helped with the children was illiterate. Years later she told me that she quickly put together some things that hadn't previously seemed to make sense. On the few occasions when my mom had given Annick a short list of items to pick up when she took us for a walk, Annick had made a point of having my mom say each word out loud, slowly and clearly, explaining that this was for her to learn the proper English pronunciation. She would then repeat the list back to my mom in French, as if she were giving my mom a few tips in proper intonation. She was memorizing, of course, in two languages to be doubly sure. My mom's note was of no more use than scribblings in Chinese. At their first meeting, Annick had stated that she was not willing to help with my *devoirs*, my homework, and though it had seemed a strange condition to lay down, it was in any event a moot point since I was in preschool. My mom also recalled how Annick never read to us, claiming that she preferred to tell us French fairy tales. Often she'd recite fables from La Fontaine; Brita and I were happy with this arrangement since my mom often read to us in English, and Annick's stories were full of dramatic pauses and personal asides.

The next day my mother invited over Mademoiselle de Chêneville for a cup of tea and confided in her. The old lady was surprised, too, but not as shocked as my mom. She explained that Annick had been a refugee immediately after the war—the American term was "D.P." for "displaced person"—and that the details of where she had lived and what she had been through were vague.

She had ended up in Fontainebleau by the good offices of the Red Cross, but the family she lived with knew very little. She was hard-working, unfailingly polite, but given to bouts of loneliness. In any other time, one could attribute all of that to the ordinary moods of late adolescence. However, Mademoiselle de Chêneville pointed out, the surrounding facts suggested something more somber.

Judging by her age when we first met her in 1954, she'd have been just five years old when the war began. If she and her family had lived anywhere along the French or Belgian coast in 1940 when the Germans invaded, they'd have been trapped in the nightmare battles that led to the Allied withdrawal from Dunkirk and the fall of France. Thousands of families were uprooted, entire towns and villages decimated. Had Annick been caught up in the horror of the war? Mademoiselle de Chêneville knew only that she had "lost her family," but when and how remained a mystery. Perhaps she was orphaned at the eruption of hostilities, and then poorly cared for as the residents of the most severely affected towns drew themselves inward and tried to survive the occupation. A child without a family would have been far more vulnerable to the blows of fate, and schooling could well have taken a backseat to mere survival. Or is it possible she had Jewish relatives, and so was hidden from the Germans on some remote farm where learning to read and write was not possible? Whatever the specifics may have been, it seems clear that Annick had missed some essential part of her schooling. It is easy to forget that there were many thousands like her throughout Europe. When the fighting stopped, unseen wounds remained. If indeed she had had the rug pulled out from under her and yet had still managed to survive, against the odds, she likely would have developed strategies for covering up the fact that she could neither read nor write.

In fact, war or no war, there was still a considerable amount of illiteracy in Europe—even in France—between the wars. It would have sufficed for Annick to be shunted to a peasant household, say—warm, quite possibly loving and safe, but with no experience of reading or books. At war's end she'd have missed the critical years of school where those her age picked up skills that we take for granted. Then, whatever the wounds caused by the war, another one would have been created in her mind: shame. When those who can neither read nor write are plunged into contact with those who can, the abiding emotion is generally shame, coupled with a panic not to be found out. The consequence is often an elaborate set of procedures, including memorization, avoidance, and ruses to get others to read something in your stead so that you are not discovered in your ignorance. Even years after the war, in late adolescence, Annick was engaged in just that daily battle, and my mother had stumbled upon it unawares. After all, she had kept the French letters overnight, and yet still had no one to whom she could turn for a simple version of a reply.

It seems shocking to us to consider that a large percentage of the population in modern industrialized democracies should be unable to read or write. But widespread literacy is a very recent phenomenon in the grand scheme. As a species, we have generated and used writing for no more than ten thousand years. For about 99 percent of that time, writing and reading were the preserve of a tiny educated elite. The generation, use, and transmission to others of texts had been the business of clergy, government officials, clerks, and teachers. They occupied themselves with documents while the vast majority of the population made do without any direct knowledge. As recently as the nineteenth century in Europe, a widespread definition of literacy was the ability to sign your name to a legal document. Not until comprehensive and obligatory schooling was legislated and enforced did the rate of illiteracy diminish appreciably. I think that this is what so surprised my mom: the realization that the fortunes of war, more than ten years after its end, could still disrupt a young person's life and cause suffering.

Only years later did I discover the truth underlying Annick's situation when she worked for us, and what my mom did about it. Annick's need for daily subterfuge in the face of shame powerfully affected my mother, and made her determined to help. She and Mademoiselle de Chêneville contrived to have Annick take a course designed to teach adults to read and write, but presenting it to her was tricky. They decided they could not tell her that they knew her secret, and so Mademoiselle de Chêneville confided in another young woman, who would suggest an "interesting" course she had herself taken to brush up one's command of grammar. "There are students of all levels," the young woman assured Annick, "and they begin at a basic level so that everyone is sure of progressing together." The woman explained how useful such a course would be if the world of business interested her in the future. With such slender pretexts Annick was gently prodded to enroll, hesitant but no doubt fascinated, too. What transpired behind the closed doors of the classroom remained her story, but, to my mother's enduring satisfaction, she did learn to read and write.

CHAPTER 12

DICTÉE

Things changed considerably the following year when I was enrolled in the local elementary school, which accepted the children of the NATO personnel who worked at the Château—Canadians, Belgians, Dutch, Americans, Germans, British, and French. I was part of the *section française* in which the national curriculum was taught in French. Gone were the grandmotherly tones and welcoming cocoon of preschool. This was a large elementary school with girls and boys in all classes and a rigid scheme of academic discipline.

The building was new, built for the influx of NATO officers and their families, its exterior covered in an aggregate of nubby pebbles that were fixed in a thin layer of concrete. While its shape and materials were modern, though, its rooms were configured in an age-old French manner.

A hallway ran the length of each floor along an exterior wall, classrooms arrayed one after the other longitudinally against the opposite exterior wall, their windows looking out on a large courtyard and playground. Forged iron hooks lined the hallway at an adult's waist level, covered with students' coats and sweaters. In each classroom, the teacher's desk was invariably set on a raised platform six inches above the floor. Our desks were modern: blond rectangles of wood on green tubular metal legs, their surfaces flat rather than inclined. Neither our desks nor our chairs were bolted to the floor. At the upper right-hand corner of each desk was inset a white ceramic cup with a small center hole in the top.

Each morning began with a strange ritual that I had never before imagined, much less seen. On the first day of school, a girl with long brown hair was given a huge wine bottle (in France, where every size of wine bottle has its own special name, this one was called a *jéroboam* and held three liters); a boy with thick, wire-rimmed glasses was given a folded hand towel. The teacher whispered her directions to them. Then the two students proceeded down the aisles of desks, pouring ink deliberately and cautiously from the wine bottle into each of our inkwells, any spills immediately wiped up with the towel. We were then told to prepare a *plume*, one of the old-style pens with removable nibs that had to be dipped continually in ink. So began my introduction to the French art of penmanship, still taken in France to be one of the key indicators of one's personality.

In our notebooks our teacher had written in her perfect hand a series of letters at the beginning of each line. Uppercase letters, then the same letters in lowercase, were finely inscribed below, all in maroon ink. Each notebook's pages were printed with horizontal lines minutely separated, every fourth one printed slightly darker. These separations were critical for the formation of one's letters: lowercase letters rose only to the first horizontal line, though the tops of *l*'s and *h*'s rose to the third. Similarly, the bottoms of *j*'s and *g*'s and *y*'s descended two lines, exactly. *J*'s and *i*'s were dotted on the second line. Spacing letters evenly was also important: bunching them up or stretching them out within a word was relentlessly sanctioned.

But the hardest thing to master for us beginners, since this was done with pen nibs dipped in the inkwell, was forming a coherent and continuous line with the pen. The teacher's example sat at the beginning of each line—a perfect *f* or *y*, say—and you were meant to replicate it eight or ten times, all the way to the right margin. But in forming an *h*, for instance, she subtly turned the nib of her pen during her stroke to adjust the amount of ink that reached the page. The top of the *h* would be the merest wisp of a line, rising in a regular curve, then descending with a bit more heft; the front of the *h* was thicker still, as if it were somehow more solid and closer to the ground. Every letter had its formula, its magic balance: the back of an *s* was thin, its bulbous front thick; the back of an *e*, on the other hand, was where you wanted more ink, while its front was diaphanous.

Since the whole exercise was conducted using indelible ink, no corrections were possible. This raised the stakes considerably, like a high-wire act without a net, and we did our best to render convincing letters, then words, then entire sentences. We were all armed with a supply of *buvards*, blotters, that came in graduated pastel colors, like huge Necco wafers. They were indispensable: too much ink was a constant threat, and a moment's inattention with the nib on the paper would quickly leave a blot on the page the size of a squashed grape. Our *cahiers* came back to us marked in the left margin in the teacher's precise hand: *sale* (messy); *vu* (okay); *bien* (good).

For a six-year-old, filling an entire page with all those perfectly formed letters and words seemed an impossible thing to aspire to. A meticulous beauty emanated from a page of French written in a practiced, confident hand: a quality close to calligraphy came forward in the subtle curves and bends, at times as alluring—and as mysterious—as a Möbius strip. We sharpened our skills rapidly—in handwriting, but also in spelling and grammar—by the supreme challenge of the daily *dictée,* dictation. The teacher read a text aloud in a declamatory tone, pronouncing each word with exaggerated precision, and you begged your ear, your hand, and your brain to concentrate in a way that allowed you to reproduce on the page what you had just heard. Sentence by sentence, you advanced inexorably, fearing disaster but refusing the distraction when certain words didn't make sense in your mind.

Every day for ten minutes or so the entire class held its breath as we traversed together this perilous ground, rendering in twenty slightly different ways the carefully chosen words that described a snowfall, or animals in the barn, or a train leaving the station. Along with everything else, it was a daily grounding in the codes, the images, and the metaphors that mattered in France.

I still use a fountain pen for handwritten letters, but there are far fewer of them these days than when I was young. When I look at my *cahiers* now, it seems as if another person altogether fashioned the elaborate sequence of lines and curves that counted as French script in those days. Pen and ink are still very much part of the landscape in France—my own children were equipped with blotters and pens with ink cartridges, but they also had correcting fluid—yet things are changing, as they must.

When the bell rang for recess, we headed down the hall, usually stopping at the large toilets on the ground floor in order to pee. The scene there was pandemonium. After waiting for one of the urinals to free up, you did your business and then headed for the door around the corner. Before you could leave, though, you were required to wash your hands. A hall monitor often stood at the door and watched the long bank of sinks to make sure that every boy complied. In those days, all French schools, and many cafés, had the same setup for washing up: a series of sinks along the wall and, above each one, a large yellow ball of soap shaped like a small football. Each soap was fixed above the sink to a chrome bar that was curved downward. You wet your hands, lathered up by rubbing the smooth soap, then rinsed. A long loop of white cotton toweling—gray by day's end—hung on a bar near the door.

Inevitably, the washing-up procedure got carried away some times as boys jockeyed for sink and soap. A favorite trick of the older boys was to fling soapy water on the younger students—it stung if it landed in your eyes—and to generally harass and jostle us before we made it to the door. Once an older boy at the next sink leaned over to two of us six-year-olds and whispered conspiratorially, "*Vous voulez me voir masturber un éléphant?*" "Want to see me masturbate an elephant?"

I knew what an elephant was—I had seen them many times at the National Zoo in Washington, and again in Paris—but I had no clue what "*masturber*" referred to. The two of us were wary, though, since it was clear that the older kid wanted an audience, and we might get ourselves doused if we moved away. As we looked on, he then wet his hands beneath the faucet and proceeded to pull rhythmically on the large mass of yellow soap, one hand after another sliding down its slick ovoid surface and working up a lather. This was accompanied by muffled grunts and snufflings in a way that had nothing to do with what I knew about elephants. Finally he stopped and turned to us, a knowing grin on his features. We played along as if we had found his display impressive, then quickly moved away. In the hall I asked my friend if he understood what we had just seen, and he responded with a withering pronouncement: "*Il est fou, Jean-Charles! Fou!*" "Jean-Charles is crazy! Crazy!"

It was only many years later that I understood that the older boy—he couldn't have been more than two years older than us—must have overheard this routine from a teenager or possibly an adult, and played out the scene without any more real comprehension than we showed. The yellow soap attached to the wall in cafés is far less common these days, but whenever I come across one, an elephant enters the room, and I have to shake my head to banish it from the premises.

During recess on the *cour de récréation,* the playground, the boys played marbles. We each had a small cloth bag with a drawstring top, a miniature version of a pirate's sack of gold, filled with fired clay marbles in solid, muted colors. As soon as the bell rang we scurried down the stairs and gathered at a much-trafficked end of the courtyard where the gravel had been trod thin and a broad, flat expanse of hardened earth was laid bare. This was our Coliseum, and our matches were comparably fierce. There were a variety of setups—one against one, teams, one against a whole team—but they all involved some variation on the ability to knock out of the field with great precision your opponent's marbles.

The tension was often high, the consequences immediate: if you won, you gathered the other guy's marbles and popped them in your bag, its bulging contents a sign of your prowess. An empty bag was cause for shame, and elaborate cycles of triumph, revenge, and defeat were played out regularly. I first learned what a bully was on that playground, and a sore loser.

During that first September at my new school, a couple of boys two years older than us—they must have been eight to our six—would periodically appear, flanking both sides of our game where it abutted a corner of the playground. On one side our marble pitch ended at the high stone wall that enclosed the entire area; the other side was bounded by an open arcade, one step up from ground level. Those of us crouched down, intent on the game, were oblivious to the danger, but, as with any predator, the behavior of others quickly told us to be wary. Things grew abnormally quiet on our little corner of earth. The boys watching the game drew back nervously, their eyes calibrating the distance needed for escape. Then came an explosion of movement, accompanied by shouts of menace and fright, as the two stalkers pounced. They grabbed any marbles that were exposed on the ground, and they also made a point of jostling anyone holding a bag of marbles so that their contents would spill. These, too, they scooped up.

This scene was played out all fall about once a week, but never on a predictable day or at the same moment during recess. What I gradually understood was that there was no practical alternative to—yes—losing some of your marbles regularly. They were bigger than us, the threat of physical violence was real, and no adult supervised our play. In any event, telling a teacher or parent was unimaginable; like everywhere else, a snitch—*un cafteur*—was universally loathed in France.

Soon, though, I learned what everyone else seemed to know already: you didn't have to give all of your marbles, just some of them. An agreement, no less precise for being unspoken, governed all. Once, by some miracle of good timing, everyone managed to grab the marbles and run; the bullies got nothing. Nothing, that is, but one of our unfortunate classmates, held tightly by one of the big guys from behind, his neck squeezed in one hand. *"Aye, oh!"* the victim yelped, his eyes wide with fear. We all stood nearby, warily assessing our predicament, our marbles safely pocketed. No marbles for the bullies was not a possibility, and not just because they could do our friend harm; it simply wasn't in the order of things. As if to give voice to this truth, the bully who wasn't occupied with the hostage stated the terms matter-of-factly, as if reason would now prevail. "*Tout le monde donne deux billes!*" he barked. "Everyone gives two marbles." A pause descended, but only a short one, before the first boys drew the required tribute from their pockets and dropped it to the tamped-down dirt.

For me it spelled a first lesson in a certain kind of power and intimidation, and in the coded language that passes for acquiescence. It certainly wasn't about the value of the marbles themselves; no matter how many of them that those two eight-year-olds accumulated, they were still just fired clay, painted in sober colors. I sometimes wondered what they did with their loot, imagining them sitting on their beds covered with hundreds and thousands of chipped, slightly imperfect marbles. But this was to miss the point entirely, and I gradually took that in, too. In the grand scheme, this felt like a workable accommodation. They could have taken all our marbles, but they didn't. They could have beaten the daylights out of us, but they didn't.

In fact, we had—all of us—already made sure to cut our losses by playing only with the lowly fired-clay *billes*. Every boy had a parallel collection of *billes transparentes*, "clearies"—the glass cat's-eye marbles with a swirl of color worked across the inside center. These were far more expensive, but their value to us wasn't simply a matter of price. Their perfectly regular dimension, the machined precision of their spherical shape, and—this, above all—the cold transparency of the glass set them apart. You could hold one up to the light, and sight along the stripy ribbon of color as if you were peering into a planet's heart. When rolled, the asymmetrical band made fantastic patterns as its axis turned slightly askew. Identically sized and perfectly formed, each was unique because of that swirl of color floating in a crystal world of its own.

By comparison, the clay marbles were sad, pocked cousins,

homely and common, like a handful of speckled pebbles. The clearies were lustrous gems, shooting off sparks. Their hold on us was intoxicating, and by common consent we didn't bring them to school. That truly would have been regarded as madness, to put a treasure at risk; we kept them for ourselves, safe in a parallel world where "play" didn't expose them—or us—to danger. So we played with second-best marbles, and paid tribute to the ever-present enforcers. But I learned something useful: when you don't control the terrain, don't tempt fate with nice things.

CHAPTER 13
FENCING

Once we had settled in to the house and our various schools, we established a family routine for weekends that allowed us to see some other parts of France. The nearest big attraction, of course, was Paris, only forty miles away on the two-lane Route Nationale 7 (simply the *Nationale 7* in French) that ran north, straight through the *Forêt de Fontainebleau* to the heart of the capital. On most Sundays we all piled into the Chevy and drove up to Paris, where my dad would compete in an afternoon match at one of the principal fencing clubs of the capital.

My father was a prodigious athlete, but not of any conventional sort. He was, I now realize, a "sportsman" from a previous era whose chosen fields of competition were aristocratic, largely solitary, and arcane. My brothers and I sometimes called them oddball; Dad was never available for a game of catch in the yard or shooting hoops in the driveway. Not for him any of the big three American sports—baseball, football, or basketball—or even one of the wide range of activities covered by track and field. Instead, he excelled at sports that were closely associated with the European tradition of the officer gentleman: fencing, riding, shooting, and rowing. The first three of these he practiced during our years in Fontainebleau.

Ordinary riflery had long since ceased to interest him—months of infantry training at the beginning of the war were doubtless the cause—but he was a crack shot with a birding shotgun and regularly won competitions on the trap and skeet ranges in Paris and its environs. As for riding, Fontainebleau was renowned throughout France for its tradition of horsemanship. Napoleon had famously established stables there that furnished him and his imperial guard with mounts trained for battle. Even in the 1950s, morning rides in the near forest with some of the other junior officers assigned to the Château headquarters command were part of the duty; my dad rode at least once a week. But the sport that consumed my father above all others during the three years we spent in Europe was fencing.

He learned to fence before the war in the played-out mill town in upstate New York where he had been raised, and it seems he was a natural. My father happened upon a remarkable coach at the local gym, and the young man who wanted to be a pilot but didn't have the means turned all his energies to fencing and became truly good at it. By the time we got to France he had competed regularly in Washington, D.C., after the war, and he was ranked nationally in saber, the slash-and-attack cousin to foil and epée.

His fencing bag, a long canvas contraption with zippers and buckles that held his swords and screen-covered face mask, was propped up carefully to one side of the wide entrance vestibule at the back of the house. The points of the blades were blunted, the edges unsharpened, but they were still redoubtable weapons in the heat of competition. Every bit of the equipment was pristine white: his knee-length trousers and padded tunic that covered the torso—the "plastron," like a supple turtle's shell—were carefully arrayed on the sunporch where laundry was hung to dry. Several pairs of special white shoes were regularly polished and grouped alongside padded gloves and kneesocks until the next match.

In the fifties, *salles d'escrime,* fencing halls, generally had the look of old-style gymnasiums, with wooden floorboards, high ceilings, and several *pistes,* or strips, laid out for individual matches. Each *piste* measures 46 by 6.5 feet, clearly demarcated on the floor with a special textured mat. The two white-suited opponents square off at the mat's midpoint, fourteen feet apart, with a presiding judge standing alongside. In fact, the fencers don't square off but, rather, each presents his slenderest profile to the other. The object is to touch your opponent with your sword while avoiding being touched, a point awarded for each touch. Then the bout recommences at the midpoint of the mat until one of the fencers amasses fifteen points.

At the judge's signal, the fencers approach one another warily, brandishing their swords with menacing reserve. Then comes the inevitable explosion, especially in saber, with slashing swords, the metallic clash of blades, and much foot stomping as each fencer lunges, ripostes, parries, and tries to gain an advantage while avoiding being forced off the end of the mat, which counts against you as a point. Often there are shouts as the two engage in combat, then a standoff, both fencers ripping off their helmets and assuming indignant poses as they await the judge's decision.

In addition to the touches with the point of the sword that are counted in foil and epée, saber also includes touches from slicing and slashing strokes. It emerged from the cavalry tradition, its technique highly physical. Originally, saber matches were not confined to a mat and could range throughout a room, which, in an oblique manner, accounts for all that jumping on tables and swinging from chandeliers that Hollywood relishes. Now saber is very much more contained in competition, but is still turbulent at times.

It's no coincidence that in the fifties the Hungarians—reputed to be daring, impetuous, and wily—ruled supreme in saber, while the Italians and the French excelled in epée and foil. Saber in particular has a strong psychological component as a prelude to the fireworks, an elaborate dance of intimidation, posturing, and quiet testing before an attack. Half poker game, half knife fight. Alongside this edgy contest a parallel world of chivalrous decorum surrounds the proceedings: the fencers salute one another with their swords before and after each bout, then also dip their swords to the judge. The loser always removes his helmet and offers his hand to the winner, who returns the gesture with a courtly shake. If, as frequently happened, the judge was not certain who had touched first in an exchange, the fencer who first felt the blade announced simply "*Touché*," "Touched," to acknowledge the point for his opponent. (Tunics are electrified these days, even for saber, and a light instantly shows a touch, whereas only epée was wired that way in the fifties.)

If it sounds complicated, it was. I can tell you that fencing was not my kind of spectator sport. Never could I see who had touched the other's torso first with his blade. It was my father up there often enough, and of course I wanted him to win (and in fact he often did), but it was all too fast and frantic for me to follow. Dad's skill no doubt had to do with his extraordinary visual acuity and hand-eye coordination—the same things that allowed him to excel with a shotgun or a fighter plane. But in a sport where neither the competitors nor the judge are always certain of what has happened, it's asking a lot of onlookers to follow attentively.

It was a relentlessly male environment, and my mother and two sisters left after dropping off my father and the boys. For a few weeks we stuck it out, watching countless matches as the competitors huddled with coaches, friends, and officials. An apocalypse of sorts occurred on our third visit when another young boy and I were invited to push the reset button on the epée lights each time a touch was scored. That was the high point, and I soon understood why both my older brothers had declined the honor before me. The *longueurs* were simply too long.

The next time none of us stayed, though we returned occasionally now that we knew the lay of the land. My mom was interested in other things and she drove the Chevy with confidence to other parts of Paris, a small figure behind the enormous steering wheel, determined to explore.

On Sunday evenings, we regularly ate at a restaurant in Paris and drove home late. The *forêt* had its own mysteries in the form of wild game, hunted there for hundreds of years by the kings of France. On our nighttime drives back to Fontainebleau through the impenetrable woods, we often saw animals along the road: deer, wild boar, and sometimes the tiny antelope-like deer called *chevreuil* so prized by *gourmands*.

Once in that first autumn my father slowed the car to let a family of boar cross the road, and we watched three immense adults and five little babies trot across the roadway in our headlights. Then, unexpectedly, as if to assert some territorial prerogative, one of the adults charged the car. Whump! Whump, WHUMP! The Chevy was a big car but the whole thing shook mightily on its suspension as the boar gave the front fender a few good whacks with his massive snout and fearsome tusks. We watched breathlessly, both delighted and terrified, until the big animal walked casually away and entered the forest's gloom. We walked under the mounted boar's head in our front hall ten times a day, and yet had never imagined that it had once been attached to a body of such power.

As soon as we arrived home, we tumbled from the car and ran our fingers in awe over the small dent that now creased the Chevy's right front fender, astounded that such a thing could be caused by an animal—a wild beast!—that issued from the forest only miles from the safety of our beds. When, as sometimes happens, some unknowing American soul says "pig" and likens it to the wild boar, I say "buffalo"—muscular, aggressive, and fearsome—and tell what I learned that night on the *Nationale 7*.

CHAPTER 14

CARS AND PLANES

Gradually we started to make outings to destinations other than Paris, and it's fair to say that all of us saw a side of France that wasn't readily apparent in the capital or in our town. While the area around Fontainebleau had not been a battleground when the Allies landed in 1944, on our weekend drives toward Normandy and Brittany you could still see the scars of that conflict less than ten years old. The invasion beaches lie on the northwest coast of France, about two hundred miles from Paris; we drove there in less than four hours. Occasional houses and barns lay in ruins, and the roads had been patched and rebuilt with new macadam, new bridges and culverts, new grading. Most of the military wreckage had been removed—burned-out tanks, artillery pieces, jeeps and trucks, downed planes—but there still remained evidence of the colossal armored battle that had been waged on that corner of French soil. Concrete bunkers and "pillboxes" studded the coastal landscape, the reinforced remains of Hitler's vaunted Atlantic Wall that to this day deface the length of the coast. No one knows how to get rid of them. Many of the large guns had not been removed; disarmed and crippled in their housings, their long barrels pointed at crazy angles from within their blockhouse revetments.

The landscape itself had a strange look to it, a peculiar amalgam of old and new that didn't quite cohere. Close to the Normandy coast, less than two hundred miles from Fontainebleau, entire towns had been flattened by the Allied bombardment of German occupiers, then rebuilt along the existing grid of streets and roads. The result was numerous new housing developments with quirky layouts: spanking new buildings, relentlessly modern in the fifties manner, following the curves and contours of ancient paths. The occasional surviving stone structure, repaired and painted, called attention to the magnitude of the loss. Even the fields betrayed the huge amounts of ordnance that had fallen from above, with softened craters and long trenches drawing the eye to an aspect of a landscape that simply didn't belong to the normal contours of a rural setting.

Ten years after the war's end, you didn't have to wander far from the road to find scraps of metal left by the two armies that overwhelmed the land here for those brief months. The shell casings and spent cartridges and crumpled canteens that still lay within plain view, however, were harmless compared to the live explosives that sat just below the surface. It's hard to appreciate the quantity of bombs dropped on the Normandy coast and its near hinterland during and immediately after the D-Day landings. In the three months before June 6, British and American planes dropped 66,000 tons of bombs on the region, isolating it by destroying road, rail, and communications links that were then only partially repaired by the Germans. On D-Day itself, over 5,000 tons more were dropped near the landing zones. Inevitably, many of those 100-, 250-, and 500-pound bombs did not explode; some experts put the rate of duds as high as 25 percent. Add to that the accumulated weight of artillery shells and hand grenades that failed to detonate and you have a sense of the hidden dangers around the invasion zone.

When we drove out to Normandy to see the landing beaches in that first year, my mother wouldn't let us play in the field by the road where we picnicked. Like so many young boys visiting European battlefields in the fifties, my brothers and I hoped to find some "real" military hardware. Something German with a swastika emblem was a dreamed-of prize, tangible proof of the evil enemy's presence in a country not his own. But farmers and fieldworkers—and schoolboys, too—still paid an awful price when one of the countless pieces of live ordnance was unearthed by mistake. Death, dismemberment, and maiming were all commonplace in those days. Bombs, after all, are meant to destroy, and it often took a mere nudge on a bit of metal lodged in the ground to trigger disaster. We found only a few spent cartridge casings and whined about it, but my mother was right to be cautious. As I write, almost seventy years after the war ended, parts of French towns are still regularly evacuated and the expert squad is called in when another bomb is unearthed in this densely populated region. France continues to pay for its occupation and subsequent liberation.

The three decades from 1945 to 1973 are known in France as *Les Trentes Glorieuses*, the Glorious Thirty Years, a period of runaway growth, technological development, and relatively cheap energy. Like the rest of Europe, France rebuilt its economy fairly rapidly after the war's devastation, and it was quickly becoming a modern consumer society. The mid-fifties were still at the early stage of the process, though, and the changes in infrastructure—highways, high-speed trains, supersonic airliners—weren't yet apparent.

Most things worked well but were old-fashioned when compared to what we had known in America.

All of that changed in a generation. By the time my wife and I moved to Paris with our own children in the late eighties, France was utterly transformed, a showcase of shockingly modern development. The highway system—*les autoroutes*—would be the envy of our Interstate system: an extensive network of brand-new roads, impressively engineered for speed and safety. The world's fastest trains connected major city centers, and the supersonic Concorde made the flight from Paris to New York in three hours. The telecom system was comprehensive, efficient, and relatively cheap. French-designed nuclear power plants generated more than enough electrical energy. Militarily, the country had become a nuclear power with a redoubtable delivery system and a much-respected army. It was as if a wizard had passed his magic wand over the entire land and awakened it from the doldrums. Since leaving Fontainebleau, I had spent the intervening years in America and could well appreciate the progress that was everywhere in evidence. While this would all become apparent to me as an adult, in the fifties I was a child, and the things I noticed were a boy's preoccupations.

My two passions were cars and planes. We often drove to Orly airport to meet my dad after he'd been flying, and there were a lot of different planes to see at a major international airport, both civilian and military. Jets were just being phased in as airliners, and I knew the models to look for, the "livery" of the national flag carriers, the major routes served. Once in a while we would visit a U.S. Air Force base, too, and the latest fighters and transports were usually easy to spot. In those days the modern security apparatus didn't exist; most of the precautions taken were to protect people from injuries that airplanes might cause as they taxied or parked. Don't approach a plane's propellers! Stay away from jet intakes and exhaust! Stand well back from taxiways! But you were allowed to stand outdoors at the edge of what was called "the flight line," and once the planes were parked with their engines off and wheels chocked, you could walk close to them.

I was familiar with the principles of flight—lift, yaw, pitch, climb, descent were commonplace terms in our house. But it was always thrilling to be able to examine these huge hunks of metal up close and have my dad point out the subtle curve of the wing's surface, or the play of ailerons with all their intricate machinery. I could run my hand over the broad panels of shiny steel joined in seamless curves with thousands of flush rivets, a tactile delight that confirmed how ponderous and even cumbersome these giant machines were when immobile. Then ten minutes later, I'd watch from in front of a hangar not more than a hundred yards distant as the engines suddenly fired up and the plane came to life, taxiing with a piercing whine to the end of the runway—a final blast of the screaming jet engines with the wheel brakes still on, followed by the hypnotic acceleration as it rolled down the long stretch of concrete on its tiny wheels before raising its nose, adding even more thrust, and rising into the air as if in a dream.

When you watched a plane's takeoff—and I watched as many as I could—the unspoken rule was to stay with it visually until the landing gear was retracted: "Wheels up!" Then the cool-to-the-touch mass of steel that only minutes before you'd been feeling, the way you might run your hand over a car's fenders, became something else altogether: a flying machine with a grace and a power that were closer to that of a comet. The deafening roar added to the excitement, as if the center of the sky were being ripped open by an unseen hand from above. The moment passed, the shining plane turned into an ascending point of flame at the engine's exhaust, and calm returned. And I wanted it to happen again.

Cars were easier to come by, of course, and Paris was a terrific crossroads. Europeans loved driving, too, and France was a favored destination for people from all over. Even small countries had their own makes of cars, and big countries like France and England had multiple car companies that produced distinctive, even improbable models.

The family of a British boy at my school owned an Armstrong Siddeley, staid and formal, with a sphinx for a hood ornament. Our Chevy had a stylized rocket ship on the hood, which was a different kind of cool from a sphinx. German DKWs had quirky three-cylinder engines; you could hear them coming on a quiet street, sounding a bit like a large vacuum cleaner. A fighter pilot friend of my dad drove a Lancia open sports car, and you could hear that coming, too, though the sound was always exciting. France was full of *Deux Chevaux*, utilitarian jumbles of gray sheet metal, with a canvas top that rolled back like a window shade.

Spotting cars while we were on the road was an iffy business. Since most of the highways were still two lanes, you had to approach a car from the rear, or see it when it passed you from behind. My mom got tired of my entreaties: "Catch up with that guy!" "Slow down! Let this car pass us!" My dad sometimes indulged me a maneuver, but only if it was within the bounds of what he felt was safe. Walking around Paris was a great way to see lots of different cars, but it depended on the neighborhood. The embassies and the fancy hotels always had luxury models out front—Jaguars, Buicks, Mercedes—and sometimes a rare sports car like a Maserati or a Jensen.

There were a fair number of American cars in the city, too, and they always stood out. The visual impact of an American car in 1950s Europe is hard to describe since there exist no latter-day parallels. First, they were immense in comparison to most European models, great hulks of sculptural metal that were far longer, wider, and heavier than their European counterparts. Second, they were impressively modern looking with curves, vents, and chrome that were directly inspired by the forms and materials of jet planes. These weren't just functional boxes on wheels; they were a confident declaration of modern intentions, modern methods, and modern leisure. Finally, they were almost never the drab grays and dark blues of European cars. Instead, color was used with the seasonal flourishes that the French reserved for fashionable accessories. Yellow, red, lime green, even combinations of two or three colors: anything seemed possible. The message must have seemed both sensational and strange to the French: Americans decorate their cars with wild abandon, and they replace them at will. In a country still on the road to recovery from the war's privations, nothing could have been more foreign.

The flagship of the American fleet was the Cadillac Fleetwood limousine, a twenty-foot-long behemoth that was more like a living room on wheels than a regular car. And unlike its plebeian kin, the Fleetwood was invariably a highly polished black with dove-gray mohair upholstery, even on the jump seats, and a uniformed chauffeur at the wheel. The appearance of one of these cars on the streets of Paris in the fifties was sure to cause a sensation. As the French would say, "*Ça ne passe pas inaperçu.*" "That doesn't go unnoticed." Top American diplomats and generals had them, as did some very rich international bankers, businessmen, and impresarios. If a Marilyn Monroe, say, or a Cary Grant were being met at Orly, you could be sure that the newsreel would show a shiny Cadillac pulling away from the gaggle of photographers like a rolling hotel suite with fins, its gold-plated "V" floating on the enormous trunk lid above the single word "FLEETWOOD." This was as clear an expression of national pride and prestige as an aircraft carrier or the latest fighter jet, and it was a lot more visible to the man in the street.

Beyond this pinnacle of luxury for the high rollers, though, the presence of other American cars in Europe in the fifties—lots of them—was almost more peculiar in its way. Even a garden-variety Ford or Pontiac was huge compared to the little Renaults, Fiats, and Volkswagens of the day, and the exuberance of both their colors and forms was striking. Perhaps the most astonishing thing is that Americans brought their cars with them at all when they crossed the Atlantic. For a continent that had been blasted apart in the most devastating war in human history, the mere presence of all those cars, as if they were just another piece of luggage brought along, must have underlined the differences in wealth between the preposterously affluent United States and the still struggling economies of western Europe.

Our family car, humble though it was by American standards, was no exception. A 1952 Chevrolet station wagon, it didn't have any of the flamboyant fins or streamlining of current, fancier models. It actually had a certain functional look to its passenger compartment, like a large windowed box, of which I was secretly proud. But it could never, ever pass for anything remotely European for two reasons. It was, no matter how practical, at least twice the size of anything a French family would drive around in. Even more striking, it was what used to be called a "woodie," a regular station wagon with a conventional metal body—in this case, forest green—to which were affixed large panels and sculptural support beams of false wood, to give the illusion that its four door sills, rear quarter panels, and tailgate were fashioned of wooden slabs framed by timber.

The local baker referred to it as *une énorme boîte d'allumettes*, a huge matchbox (matchboxes in those days were fashioned from thin strips of wood), and his description gives a flavor of just how exotic our family car must have appeared. It, too, was an outpost of the American imperium in ways we can only imagine.

In the mid-fifties, two French cars captured the world's imagination—or at least that part of the world that follows cars closely. The first was a new flagship model from Citroën; it was called the *DS-19* (the way the letters *D* and *S* are pronounced in French replicates the word *déesse*, "goddess"). It was the successor to the famous *Traction Avant* model—familiar from French movies—a long, low car with a gangsterish air about it, invariably black, that had been introduced in the thirties. While the *Traction* had numerous technical innovations for its day, its style was old-fashioned, with a vertical radiator grill, long, sweeping fenders, and individual headlights perched at the front. It was a prewar car, and it looked it.

Then Citroën jumped from the past to the future, offering the entirely original *DS-19* in late 1955. It resembled no other car. In fact, it didn't even look much like a car at all, so rounded and streamlined were its lines. A long, low snout made one wonder if there were even an engine under the swoop of sheet metal, and the details gave it the allure of a spaceship: rear turn signals that extended from the roof gutters, a steering wheel with a single spoke, a perfectly flat floor (front-wheel drive) with seats that looked more like modern molded armchairs than upholstered benches. In the fairly predictable world of consumer automobiles of that era, the *DS-19* was a master stroke of its kind: futuristic, eccentric, stylish in a highly original way, and resolutely French.

The other French car that caused a sensation while we lived in France was a Renault prototype called the *Etoile Filante*, "Shooting

Star," an electric-blue experimental model (only two were built) designed to break the land speed record. In the fifties the Bonneville Salt Flats in Utah were the site of numerous attempts to increase the maximum speed of cars. In 1956 Renault sent its streamlined model, a twin-finned creation powered by a jet turbine, to the American desert. It raced across the flats at 308 km/h (191 mph), an unheard-of velocity for its category of less than 1,000 kilograms (one ton).

For six months the French laid claim to the fastest car in the world, and the American press featured the exploit prominently. Best of all, the actual racer was soon displayed in the main Renault showroom on the Champs-Elysées. My dad took me to see it one weekend, and we entered in hushed awe. Less than a meter high, the *Etoile Filante* gleamed in the spotlight like a slinky blue ribbon built for speed. You wouldn't see it on the road, but in its own way it staked a French claim for distinction among the likes of the Cadillac Fleetwood.

CHAPTER 15

BEING CATHOLIC

As a family, we were about as un-French as could be. We certainly didn't blend in: half of us blond and freckled, all of us blue-eyed. Nothing about us when we first arrived, whether clothes, diet, or pastimes, was akin to French habits. There was, however, one essential point of convergence that cut through appearances and gave us a special credibility: we were Catholic. Not only were we Catholic, we were Irish Catholic, a kind of supercategory that conferred added respect.

The ties between France and Ireland go back for centuries: two Catholic countries—one large and independent, the other tiny and occupied—whose bonds were forged by a shared antipathy toward Protestant England. When the British broke the back of the Irish Rebellion at the Battle of the Boyne in 1690, many of the Irish earls and their men who fled English retribution—the so-called "Wild Geese"—found refuge in France. A central chapter in the story of the Irish diaspora was played out on French soil, with numerous clans establishing themselves in the Gironde region around Bordeaux and turning to wine making. Three centuries later, names such as Lynch, Phelan, and MacMahon are to be found among the great vineyards. These same families provided soldiers to French kings for their European wars in the seventeenth and eighteenth centuries.

When we arrived in 1954, the church and the state had gone their separate ways, but it had been a long and bitter separation. During the French Revolution, the monarchy and the Catholic Church were regarded as indivisible seats of arbitrary power, and a popular fury was unleashed on both institutions. By the time Napoleon asserted himself in 1800, however, he understood the need to use the church to strengthen his hold on the apparatus of power, and so an arrangement was fashioned that survived under successive regimes right through the nineteenth century. By then, reformers had identified the pervasive presence of Catholic doctrine in the curriculum of all public schools as a fundamental structural problem that had to be changed. It wasn't until the 1905 law formally separating public education from any church involvement that a central tenet of the revolution, the right to a lay public education, was finally achieved. Before then, crucifixes adorned every public classroom and Catholic orthodoxy permeated the teaching of French history.

But in the 1950s, France, while a lay republic, was still culturally a Catholic country. Many continued to go to Mass on Sunday, and confessed their sins the day before. Priests and nuns were much in evidence—on the street, in buses and trams—and clearly played an important role through private Catholic schools. The cardinal archbishop of Paris was an important figure, both politically and in the world of the Church. His frequent opinions carried real weight, as did those of the austere Pope Pius XII.

So we had another entry ticket to France, almost like another passport, and it helped us enter more readily into the rhythm of French life. My two elder brothers were sent to a private Catholic school in Fontainebleau, respected and academically rigorous.

But it was expecting a lot of a ten-year-old and a seven-year-old, who had already begun their schooling in the United States, to sink or swim when the only language was French. Mostly they swam. My twelve-year-old sister similarly attended a girls' Catholic school and hated it, until—early on—she cracked the code of friendship among French adolescent girls. Then she swam, too.

We went to Mass at the Catholic chapel on the American base, celebrated every Sunday by a white-haired, bespectacled Irish priest, Father Riley. Whether in a French or American church, the liturgy in those days was always said in Latin; only the Gospel, the Epistle, and the sermon were spoken in a modern language. One of the peculiarities of the Catholic members of the U.S. armed forces in Europe was that they were officially part of the Archdiocese of New York, presided over by the intimidating, and strange, Cardinal Spellman, another American of Irish descent. Whenever a message from Cardinal Spellman was to be read from the pulpit on Sunday, a glossy color photo of him in full episcopal regalia—red satin cassock, white silk capelet, massive jeweled cross, and a scarlet *biretta* perched on his head—appeared in the vestibule of the church. To me, he looked like he had walked out of one of the countless religious paintings that filled French museums and churches. My parents, both from upstate New York, had opinions about Cardinal Spellman more grounded in his taste for political power. "Tyrannical" and "old-fashioned" were two of the kinder things they had to say about him. But at the time, he and J. Edgar Hoover were the self-proclaimed bastions against the Communists.

My parents came from markedly different backgrounds, and so their relation to Catholicism also varied. My mom was the third of five children in an Irish Catholic family. Her father's ancestors had arrived in upstate New York in the famine years of the 1840s (the eight million inhabitants of Ireland were reduced to half that number in five years, with over one million dead; the rest emigrated). In America they prospered as dairy farmers. As a young man, my grandfather returned to Ireland, married my grandmother, and brought her to live in rural New York State. Her way of coping with the separation from her family was to turn to the Church, and she became something of a fanatic.

My mom wanted to be a graphic artist. She was accepted at Pratt Institute, one of the best art schools in New York City, but her parents refused to pay the tuition. It wasn't for lack of money: they felt that preparing for a career was wasted on a woman. She was given two choices: become a nun (the path her elder sister had already chosen), or enter nurse's training. She made the reasonable choice. Initially, her life was even more circumscribed than it would have been had she chosen the convent. She trained at a Catholic hospital that was run by nuns—"Mean nuns!" my mother never tired of pointing out—whose chief mission seemed to be working the nursing students as hard as possible, then keeping them from the temptations of the world by adding chores on evenings and weekends. The Great Depression made a job—any job—a prize to be treasured, so no objections were tolerated; the mother superior of the hospital ruled supreme. It was just one part of a system that was comprehensive and absolute, as well as deeply patriarchal in its form. The Pope was the Vicar of Christ, then came the Cardinal Archbishop of New York, a "prince of the church" (Cardinal Spellman himself beginning in 1939), then the local bishop and all the priests, followed by nuns, who in turn ruled the lowest of the low, the nursing students.

Alongside the use and abuse of their little bit of temporal power, some of the nuns added a condescension that sprang from their supposed holier state as members of a religious order. This kind of sanctimonious pride sparked a lifelong skepticism in my mom for the forms of Catholic orthodoxy. In her mind, the disconnect was often too great between Christian ethics and the attitudes taken by the clergy; the nurse in her responded more readily to purposeful actions than high-minded words.

My dad's experience of Catholicism was far different. An only child, he rode a roller coaster of big money and then very little money as my grandfather speculated on real estate. He was sent to the Christian Brothers military school, an order reputed for strict discipline enforced by what was called "corporal punishment." Read "beating." He made it through, but by the height of the Great Depression my grandfather's fortune was played out. When the war arrived, my dad was among the first to enlist. As for so many soldiers, the experience of combat intensified his faith. In fact, it led directly to the naming of me and my next older brother, Judd.

Late in the war my father flew from bases in southern Italy, piloting fighter planes that accompanied American bombers over Germany and Austria. The antiaircraft flak that he encountered when approaching and flying directly over the target cities was extremely thick and very accurate. On one mission a piece of flak took out one of my dad's engines (he flew a twin-engine P-38). While his aircraft could fly on a single engine, the situation was nevertheless dire: he was marked as a sitting duck, far slower and more vulnerable than any of the other American planes. In that instant, my father made an undertaking to Saint Jude Thaddeus—in the Catholic pantheon, the patron saint of impossible causes. "If I get out of this alive," he promised, "I'll name my next child after you." (Sally and Tom had been born earlier in the war.) The fates were with him that day—and perhaps St. Jude was there, too. That incident gave Judd his name, even though he was born two years after the war ended.

My name was decided under similarly dramatic circumstances.

In a particularly thick barrage of flak, my dad took a piece of shrapnel through his cockpit dome; it pierced the Plexiglas and lodged at the edge of the headrest pad just to the left of his ear. His aircraft was undamaged in its essential systems, but he had to descend to a much lower altitude after the loss of the cockpit's covering. Again the hurried undertaking to St. Jude Thaddeus to name a child in his honor, and again my dad was lucky and wasn't spotted by the enemy. When he landed at home base, his crew chief inspected the shattered cockpit cover and then pulled an ugly, twisted piece of metal from the upper seat back, with a grim pronouncement as he presented it to my dad: "Two inches more toward the center line, Lieutenant, and this aircraft would have been flying with a headless pilot." That piece of flak sat on my dad's desk for the rest of his long life, a *memento mori* with a distinctive resonance. And that is why I was named Thaddeus when I came along several years later.

So my parents were both born into a part of the Irish Catholic tradition, and each fashioned his or her own relationship to a church in transition. My dad's arrangement was more personal and more sentimental in its associations. Salvation under fire must have counted for a lot—it had worked two times!—but it also had to do with his finding strength on his own when his father lost everything in the Depression. My mother was more pragmatic, and far more skeptical of the Church's hierarchical structure and its categorical directives to what it always called "the faithful." My dad's romantic streak about the Church's ancient history and the splendor of its cathedrals were the very things that gave my mother pause.

We were raised as Catholics, but not because either of my parents feared outsiders or thought, as the Church instructed, that so-called "mixed marriages" were wrong. My own great-grandfather

Carhart had converted from Episcopalian to Catholic in order to marry my great-grandmother, but of course he was obliged to promise that all offspring would be raised "in the Church." Rome has always taken the long view on this, figuring—correctly, if perhaps too cynically—that the demography would always play to its advantage after a single generation. Christian ethics were important in our house, but always tempered by my mom's filter for what she saw as the unreasonable claims of the Church. No, no son of hers was going to a seminary at the age of twelve (my brother Tom). Yes, Mass on Sunday morning was a given, but once a week was enough, despite the constant encouragement by nuns and priests to attend daily. Never mind the endless novenas, prayer groups, and weekend "retreats"; family time was more important. Had it not been for my mom's having her feet planted firmly in the world, any one of us might have swallowed the entire Catholic elaboration hook, line, and sinker. But the farm girl in her, as well as the nurse, gave her a sense for what was reasonable and what was not when it came to forming beliefs about God in heaven.

Europe provided plenty of instances in which these matters could be confronted in a way that didn't seem to apply in America. On a family outing one weekend my dad got it in mind to visit the tomb of St. Thérèse of Lisieux in Normandy. "Tomb" isn't quite right, since her remains were exhumed in the twenties. (She died in 1897, and was declared a saint by the Vatican in 1925.) A small chapel contains her "relics," and this is what we visited, all seven of us. Rather than a traditional sealed tomb within a church, what you see is a life-sized representation of St. Thérèse as she was said to have appeared on her deathbed, dressed in the habit of a Carmelite nun and wearing a crown of roses. This facsimile of a human—strangely shiny, like a life-sized version of one of my sister's dolls—was displayed in an elaborate glass box, raised on a marble pedestal, and engulfed in bouquets of roses. She was *La Petite Fleur,* we were told—the Little Flower—and her corpse was said to have given forth their scent rather than putrefying.

It was unclear to us all, amidst the clouds of incense, the banks of candles, and the hundreds of roses, whether we were looking at the body itself, somehow preserved like a Catholic Lenin, or at a "pretend body." Since I'd never before laid eyes on a corpse, this suddenly seemed a critical piece of information. Is it *really* her? Yes or no? And what does "putrefying" mean? I think that little bit of pious embellishment did it for my mom, as if allowing children to drink such a potion in undiluted form was a dangerous business. Among ourselves, my sisters and brothers and I agreed that—body or no body—what we had just seen was *creepy.* No one had nightmares, but neither did we want to renew the experience.

When my dad emerged, he announced that she looked "at peace," and we left it at that. In truth, the reclining "body" we kneeled in front of briefly is entirely fabricated. But if you read the fine print, some bones from among those exhumed when she became a saint were enclosed in a reliquary and sit on top of her glass box in a closed jewel chest. This golden coffer periodically goes on tour to the far ends of the earth.

CHAPTER 16

"DAD GUM IT!"

My dad's job was that of a staff officer at a headquarters command. Since he was American, though, and directly assigned to the staff of the French commanding general, his situation was different from that of the officers who represented the other NATO countries. The United States was by far the strongest of the Allied countries militarily, and it was phenomenally rich compared to the European nations that were still recovering from the devastation of the war. So my dad was the first among equals in the group of midlevel officers at Fontainebleau. His job involved a fair amount of diplomacy, particularly making sure not to suggest American arrogance even though the United States paid for most of the NATO operations. He traveled a lot, often with Maréchal Juin, to visit the various commands and bases in Europe. At the Château the pace was far from frantic, with the day split into two parts by a long lunch. Sometimes my dad came home for lunch; often he stayed to eat with his colleagues at one of the officers' clubs. There were also frequent meetings in Paris at the Palais de Chaillot, directly across the Seine from the Eiffel Tower. My dad once described these gatherings as "about as lively as watching a glacier move."

His true love was flying, and whenever he could find the time, he'd steal away and "take up an airplane," as he put it. In those days, before Charles de Gaulle Airport was built, Orly was Paris's main field. On the south side of Paris, right on the *Nationale 7* that led to Fontainebleau, it had a military base attached to it. If he could get away for the afternoon—and often enough it was possible—he could easily be in the air within an hour of leaving his office. He claimed that it was important for him to collect his supplemental flight pay with such a big family (no doubt true). To maintain his "flight status" required some minimum number of hours per month. But he never disguised his sheer pleasure in being able to fly a plane—any plane, really—and to see things from the cockpit. I think in many ways he was most himself when at the controls of an aircraft, whether on a "long haul" to some distant destination or during the more frequent short flights from Orly around northern France to keep his flight skills current. His responsibilities as an Air Force lieutenant colonel overlapped with his passion for flying, of course, but it wasn't always so easy to square that need with the demands of a large family.

On one of those long winter evenings during our first year in Fontainebleau, my dad returned from a two- or three-day trip to Germany. He landed his plane at Orly and drove down to Fontainebleau, arriving just as we were finishing dinner. In those days before cell phones and international calling plans, long-distance phone calls were a rarity. He had told my mom he'd be back in a few days, and here he was. But "a few days" can be an eternity when you have five children and a huge, cold house on your hands. My mom was clearly delighted to see him, to have him back among us. We all were: Daddy's home!

Instead of joining us at the table, though, my dad begged off, explaining that he wasn't hungry, and besides, he had to wash up before going to his fencing match. My mom's voice was shrill with shock, disbelief, and a tinge of rage. But my dad was already on the stairs, headed up to their bedroom. She followed him, her voice rising as she bounded up the big staircase two steps at a time. There was an eerie quiet, and then there were shouts: "You are not going fencing! Not tonight!" answered by "See if I don't!" Then the door was closed and the argument was muffled.

My dad had an invariable ritual before he went out to fence: He'd spread his pure white gear neatly on top of their bed. The bag full of his helmet and swords, each blade cleaned and lightly oiled, lay by the back door. After he'd arrayed his clothes carefully, he'd take a quick shower, then suit up and dash out. He said that the shower helped him relax before the frenetic demands of fencing.

My parents argued, they bickered, but they rarely fought. And if it got to that stage, they made a point of continuing away from us children. This was one of those times, and a strange calm prevailed in the dining room as we waited for something, anything, to happen. Then my brother Judd, with a mix of curiosity and boldness, turned to me and said, "Let's go see." If my next older brother was saying this, it must be okay. I followed him warily up the stairs, down the hall, and peered into the big bedroom through a crack in the door, only slightly ajar. We heard the shower running in their bathroom and saw my mother leaning over the bed with something in her hands. Snip! Snip, snip! Scissors! At first I thought she was cutting up their bedspread, clearly the act of a crazy person. Then Judd turned and hissed, "She's cutting up his fencing pants!" We both stared, transfixed with horror, as my mom carefully, methodically cut the bottom eight inches off each leg, so that they would end at midthigh. It was the wildest, most desperate, and most transgressive thing I had seen my mother do. She who sewed her own clothes, who knew how specialized and expensive and hard-to-come-by such pants were, was now taking her shears to them with jerky hacking motions. Both of us were paralyzed with a child's clear awareness that this was taking things to an entirely different level. This was serious. Somehow we knew enough to tiptoe down the hall.

We heard the shower water stop and then, after a brief pause, there were more words between them, the volume rising. Then my dad exclaimed, "Dad gum it!" This was an expression of heated anger in our household, the circumlocution for "God damn it!" An ominous silence ensued; then my mother strode swiftly down the hall right past us, unseeing, her eyes glistening with triumphant fury. But she hadn't counted on my dad's sheer willfulness—this was fencing night and Dad gum it! he was going fencing—nor on the adhesive properties of duct tape.

My father may be solely responsible for the success of duct tape in situations where no ducts are involved. As far back as I can remember he had a ready supply of it on hand, and in several different shades, including . . . white! No handyman he, but my dad did wield a roll of duct tape with a profligate indulgence, fixing furniture, toys, even cracked plaster walls with a smartly applied width of the stuff. That night, not five minutes later, he hurried from the bedroom, clad immaculately in white, the lower part of each pant leg taped neatly in place so that you'd have to know to look for anything even slightly amiss. As I consider the stark facts these many years later, it seems a wonder that my dad walked out of that bedroom with only his trouser legs hacked off.

CHAPTER 17

MARIE ANTOINETTE

Of all Fontainebleau's royal residents over the centuries, the most star-crossed is surely Marie Antoinette. Fourteen years old when she was brought from Vienna to Paris in 1770 to marry the French *dauphin,* the crown prince, she arrived at a court in rapid decline. Louis XV's fifty-nine-year reign was nearing its end. The loss of French colonies in North America to the British in the Seven Years' War had decimated the country's finances, but the apparatus of monarchy kept spending as if France still dominated the world. Consider also that the court protocol at Versailles was more rigid and arcane than any on earth, and the Austrian princess was regarded as the ultimate outsider.

Fontainebleau was part of the court's annual circuit of visits, when the royal retinue would travel to different châteaux, generally for six weeks each fall in October and November when the hunting was best. Marie Antoinette first arrived there in the fall of 1770 and found the forest enchanting. The court ceremonial was such that the young couple were expected to conform to the ideal of *Louis le Grand,* Louis XIV, who had built Versailles more than a century earlier. She had to fight for the right to ride a horse, since it was thought both undignified and dangerous for a future queen of France to be seen on a saddle. A ride in the Fontainebleau forest, even accompanied by courtiers, must have felt like an escape into nature, where judgments were suspended.

When Marie Antoinette's husband became king in 1774, all eyes at court turned to him and his young queen. Eating, washing, conversations, choice of clothes, even bowel movements, illnesses, lovemaking, childbirth—all were closely observed and commented upon by a palace full of hangers-on. Marie Antoinette's mother, the empress Maria Theresa, received constant reports in Vienna from her ambassador at the French court.

One of the principal subjects of discussion was the sex life of the royal couple, or, rather, its apparent absence. Since producing a male heir was paramount, rumors and conjecture were rampant. It wasn't until 1778 that their first child, a daughter, was born, followed by three more children in years to come, including two sons.

There exists an elaborate literature on the reasons for the couple's failure to produce children, but no reliable evidence has been produced to explain it. None, that is, besides what is perhaps the most obvious cause: these were actually two children, their marriage arranged for political reasons. Both were raised in strict Catholic households where extreme importance was attached to the ideals of chastity and purity. Then, aged fourteen and fifteen, they were thrown together and expected to make babies. Marie Antoinette was certainly a virgin; Louis had no experience. The third of five sons, he was timid by nature and not expected to accede to the throne. His two older brothers died as children and then his father died unexpectedly at the age of thirty-six; suddenly he was next in line to succeed his grandfather, Louis XV. The rest can be imagined: constant pressure for them both for eight long years must have been its own kind of shared agony.

In keeping with the age-old tradition of the kings and queens who preceded her at Fontainebleau, Marie Antoinette left her mark by building on to the royal apartments. The young queen left two remarkable rooms, both of them boudoirs, built at an interval of ten years: the first in 1777, its cousin in 1787. *Boudoir,* an eighteenth-century French word that meant a place to be alone, apart from social life, away from noise. The related verb, *bouder,* has come to mean "to sulk," but the sense of boudoir in Marie Antoinette's day was of a place of one's own. This was a novel concept in those times, especially for a queen whose very identity was as the center of social life at court.

The state apartments at Fontainebleau are almost all *en enfilade*—in other words, one room opening to the next with no adjacent hallway. This meant that anyone of greater rank might at any time open the door to a room you were in; there existed no sense of privacy as we have come to know it. It's not really surprising, then, that someone who was constantly the center of attention should try to fashion a refuge of her own. What strikes us today is that both rooms are decorated around an exotic theme, a dream of escape from the here-and-now.

The *boudoir turc,* Turkish boudoir, was a gift from the king in 1777. Tucked away on its own on an upper floor above the formal rooms, it is an elaborate orientalist fantasy of white and gold with "Turkish" themes (motifs of turbans, pearls, crescent moons, scimitars) that were both stylish and informal compared to the French furniture and décor of the day. A decade later, another boudoir was built for the queen on the main floor. This time the conceit is a neo-Classic chamber with wall paintings in the style of Pompeii. The appointments are almost impossibly rich—white gold used on the walls, mother-of-pearl tables and desks, sculpted classical figures over each doorway. It is a voluptuary's vision of luxurious calm, but by the time it was completed, there was no way to enjoy it. The revolution was two years away. What in another age would have been a sovereign's indulgence for his queen now assumed the proportions of a scandalous expenditure with the royal fortunes in free fall.

It is, of course, impossible to dissociate Marie Antoinette from what we know was her fate in her adopted country. Within six years of this second boudoir, she and her husband would die on the scaffold in Paris; from among their four children, only one daughter would survive to adulthood. Even if we actively resist the creak of the tumbrel that we know will come, the slam of the guillotine's blade, the sense we have as we consider Fontainebleau as Marie Antoinette knew it is of a headlong flight toward rarefied pleasures and, above all, an ideal of escape from prying eyes. Unlike François I, say, or Henri IV, the prevailing spirit is not of a strong monarch in command of his court. You feel that, by this time, the court with its endless machinations has achieved a preponderant weight, an irresistible momentum that determines the kinds of choices the royal couple can only imagine. An urge to escape into a private world is perhaps understandable, but what stays with us is the pathos of the inclination as the Bourbon dynasty, shimmering and irrelevant, slid into the maw of change. When you marvel at the two elegant boudoirs that concentrate so much refinement, taste, and luxurious detail for a single person, you can't help but ask, "Didn't anyone at the time think this might have been a bad idea?"

CHAPTER 18

A ROOM OF HER OWN

Patrick Ponsot was full of enthusiasm when I next arranged to visit him. He told me that we'd inspect a major restoration site that is like no other. "*Maintenant on va voir de belles choses!*" "Now we're going to see some beautiful things!" With this tantalizing description, we walked to another wing of the Château where, he confided, the next project for the restoration of a single room had recently been launched. It was Marie Antoinette's "*boudoir turc*," her "Turkish boudoir," conceived for her in 1777 as a private place where she could be well away from the ever-prying eyes of the court.

We climbed three long stories to the top floor, then made our way along a warren of corridors that led past literally dozens of small doors, dusty rooms, and several tiny staircases that led up to the attic floor beneath the mansard roof. The walls were painted a uniform dark gray below waist level, a lighter gray above; the effect was cheerless. As he led us along this maze, Ponsot told me that this was where lesser courtiers stayed when the king visited. "Many hundreds of people figured in the monarch's retinue, and many of them had their own servants," he said. "They all had to be lodged close by, and this was the less elegant side of things."

As I looked down the rude little passages and into the close quarters, it wasn't hard to imagine the noises and smells of cramped rooms, even in a château. The peculiar institution of a court, traveling with a reigning monarch, struck me then with its practical requirements. In modern times a head of state typically travels with numerous officials and a considerable security apparatus, but imagine if such an entourage were far larger and consisted mainly of near and distant relatives of the leader. Their chief preoccupation was to make sure they were in or near the king's presence. When they weren't, he and his queen and his mistresses would be incessant subjects of conversation. And if he died in a hunting accident, say, or got himself stabbed or shot by one of his many malcontent subjects, a family member would always be readily available to put on the crown and act as the center of a very circumscribed universe.

The rules of protocol determined all, hinging uniquely on one's bloodlines and the relative degree of royalty to which one could lay claim. For instance, under the *Ancien Régime*, only direct members of the royal family could enter the lovely old *Cour Ovale*, the "Oval Courtyard" at the heart of the Château, on horseback. Anyone else—whether a marshal of France, a government minister, or a simple messenger—was obliged to dismount and make his way by foot across the cobblestones to the formal entrance. Family trumped all, and this was insisted upon at every turn, on every day. Versailles was said to be even more rigid and humorless in its codes. No wonder Marie Antoinette wanted a room of her own at Fontainebleau.

Finally we stepped through a large metal fire door, a modern accommodation to the risks of a spreading blaze, and the proportions of the hall changed to a more spacious dimension. We had come a roundabout way, Ponsot explained, which would be supplanted by a much closer staircase that was still under renovation once the *boudoir turc* was opened to the public. In this case the "Turkish" appellation referred to the decorative elements that were meant to capture a certain fascination for "the Orient," a style of exoticism that swept French interiors a dozen years before the revolution. What better style for a queen's private room than the orientalist fantasy that was both opulent and mildly daring?

It is sometimes difficult to recall amidst the splendor of a pleasure palace like Fontainebleau that a revolution shook France—all of Europe, really—to its core. There were kings on both sides of that divide, but matters were never again the same after Louis XVI was deposed and executed in 1793. It took the better part of the nineteenth century for the Republic to gain ascendancy—the Third Republic that followed Napoleon's fall marked the definitive end of monarchs and the start of a fully constitutional form of government that has persisted. At Fontainebleau, as at other royal sites, the transition was swift: with the Bourbons and the Bonapartes gone for good, the state stepped in and appropriated the Château in the name of the people of France. To the French, the Republic honors itself and its ideals by assuming the role previously played by the king.

Fontainebleau is thus a place imbued with the history of France—Renaissance art and architecture, the frivolities of Bourbon aristocrats, Napoleonic intrigues—but it is also an expression of the Republic's power to appropriate the apparatus of royal legitimacy and make it its own. Its role in teaching citizens about the past is ongoing, and taken very seriously; the restoration of this boudoir is part of that program.

Ponsot led us through an open doorway, down a narrow hallway that had been stripped to the bare wood, and made a ninety-degree turn into the boudoir, a small rectangular room of about fifteen by eighteen feet. The work crew was already there and several more of us gathered in the space cluttered with tools, materials, and—now—people. Besides Ponsot and me, I counted a job foreman, a head carpenter, two journeymen carpenters, an electrician, a mirror specialist and her assistant, and two Château curators.

The room contained no furniture; its structure had been torn apart, then partially refitted. Elaborate original white wall panels had been fastened in the four corners, each one embossed with "oriental" decorative details of gold gilt: strings of pearls, ears of wheat, inverted stars. On the interior wall opposite the single large window, an alcove had been stripped to bare oak, as had the two opposing interior walls as well as a sliding panel that was half opened in front of the window. Each one had originally held a large mirror, a great luxury when the room was first designed for Marie Antoinette in the 1770s. The effect the designers of that era had created was both airy and sumptuous, light and wholly original for its time. With the window panel closed, all four walls would have been covered with mirrors, reflecting endlessly the queen's hideaway graced with dabs of gold, sheer muslin draperies, and creamy silk swags hung along the cornice line.

Superficially, the scene as we stood huddled together had the look of one of those earnest and purposeful home improvement shows, with specialists gathered to "solve a problem" and "establish an ambiance." But that was an illusion, since the starting point for each of the undertakings was entirely different in kind. In my talks with Ponsot and various curators I had heard the refrain "We are not decorators!" often enough to detect an underlying note of annoyance, if not injury, around this common misapprehension. The point of their work at the Château is to reconstitute as faithfully as possible the creation of another—a room, a theater, a suite of offices—from a previous era. The challenge is not to suggest a style or a spirit; it's to reassemble every detail possible, relying on careful documentary research. They combine the attributes of historians, anthropologists, artists, conservators, and craftsmen. If evidence can't be found for a detail, then you have to make your best guess, but that is the exception. Each of these experts and tradesmen is like a detective in her or his domain, helping to put together a particularly challenging puzzle. They are of course paid for their expertise, but the real excitement comes with getting it right in the historical context—far different from, say, a successful remodeling.

The supplier of mirrors spoke authoritatively. She offered all of us in the room a miniseminar on why particular mirrors mattered, insisting that the tint of the glass was critical ("Not too blue!"). It happens that modern eyes are used to perfect mirrors, often back colored with a blue or green. The slightly imperfect mirrors of the eighteenth century would give a more silvery light, more consistent with the particular illusion of whiteness that was being sought.

Each person had her or his say, and for every player it was a bit like a high stakes *grand oral*, the pivotal oral exam before a committee that determines entry into France's greatest public universities. On every detail of the discussion, ten pairs of eyes swiveled to the object under consideration, ten pairs of ears were cocked to any nuance of uncertainty, doubt, duplicity. As I watched and listened, it occurred to me how well spoken they all were, and how confident, without pretention. No "um's" or "ah's" here: they knew their business and were sure enough of themselves to speak about it with conviction. And this group was charged only with refashioning and restoring the room's architectural details.

The furniture was yet another matter. Marie Antoinette's ensemble was lost in the revolution. Napoleon's empress, Josephine, ordered a new set of furniture in 1806. It was being restored and reupholstered after a successful fund-raising campaign yielded 500,000 euros. No one can accuse the French of cutting corners when they are after the truth of a thing.

Eleven of us were crowded into a room whose dimensions were half those of a standard American bedroom in a comfortable suburban house. And yet this was anything but another contractor's makeover. The amount of expertise, talent, and resources brought to bear on this single space, in solving the puzzle not just satisfactorily but correctly, spoke volumes about the underlying ethos.

I noticed that the *garde-fou*, the wrought-iron railing that serves as a barrier against falls when the tall hinged French windows are open, was personal. The letters *M* and *A* were delicately interwoven in iron and inscribed in a circle, flanked on either side by a *fleur-de-lys*. The queen would have laid eyes on much the same view outside the window: the *Jardin de Diane*, Garden of Diana, goddess of the hunt—the tutelary spirit of Fontainebleau.

Suddenly the meeting was breaking up, and I turned from the vista. Ponsot enumerated decisions, prescribed next steps, and we filed out. Several of us then visited a storage area in a long, blocked hallway. The mirror expert and her assistant made their way enthusiastically over and around dozens of mirrors, framed and unframed, stored vertically. After careful measurements and inspection of the glass, they emerged satisfied that they had found old mirrors that would be useable for two of the boudoir's large panels. It was a question of millimeters, the mirror expert avowed, but she would see to it that they were properly fitted in the original moldings.

As we emerged, Ponsot saw me looking down from a corridor into an otherwise hidden courtyard, *La Cour des Princes*, a fairly narrow oblong flanked on all four sides by various wings of the Château. Its unbroken surface of large, dark paving stones bore traces of bright yellow paint, worked diagonally. *"Le jaune, ça date de l'ère de votre papa,*" he told me. "The yellow dates from your dad's time." He explained that yellow stripes had been painted on the paving stones by the Americans to mark parking spaces for NATO officers. "It's a very American solution," he said with a deadpan expression. Then the architect in him added, "It was very good paint to have lasted this long."

I watched the small groups of experts making their way slowly down a beautifully proportioned hallway, talking already about other restorations and other historical materials that would need to be found. It occurred to me that this constant and easy attention to multiple projects lay at the heart of my fascination with the restorer's art. On a given day they could be dealing with issues that arose under several different kings, with hundreds of years separating them, and yet their charge was to fashion a convincing and appealing interpretation under Ponsot's supervision. When I considered the depth of talent brought to bear, and the institutional commitment to preserving the past, I realized there would exist a Château of Fontainebleau substantially the same as the one I had known since boyhood long after I had left this life. The idea was oddly comforting, to know that its vast array of rooms would continue to demonstrate a certain kind of French beauty and teach history's lessons with its distinctive bricks, mortar, and slate. It felt as if the memory of my childhood were connected to something I was seeing in a new way: a place and a building and an idea that had fashioned my idea of France; a place I knew and yet that was changing as I watched the restorers work their magic; and also a place that, in some fundamental way, stood outside of time.

CHAPTER 19

LE JARDIN DU LUXEMBOURG

None of us had ever seen a city like Paris. Washington, D.C., was what we knew, with its blinding white monuments and pewter-gray government buildings, its scorching summers and slow-paced rhythms, its ubiquitous museums and the wide-open expanse of the Mall. The whole thing had been laid out by a Frenchman, of course, but still Paris was different. It, too, had wide boulevards and striking monuments, and the line-of-sight axes so dear to the French, but everything was closer, busier, and—to my child's eye—more "filled up." Grayer, too, and clearly more worn down.

My mom's favorite destination was the Louvre, and its endless rooms and corridors became like a second home to us on those long weekend afternoons. The museum was rarely crowded in those days, and one could watch the special *copistes*, copiers, at their easels with virtually no interruption. They are still there at their task, each one granted special permission by the Louvre to copy a single painting, but it is hard to imagine how they manage to concentrate with the numbers of visitors who now flood the halls. The principal restrictions set on the copiers are that the dimensions must be at least 20 percent smaller or larger than the original, and the artist's signature can in no event be copied.

I got to know the different collections at the Louvre as if they were old friends, long before they had been modernized, reorganized, and divided among different museums such as the Musée d'Orsay. My favorite was the Egyptian collection, an inexhaustible source of mystery and fascination for a young boy who knew the pyramids and the Sphinx only from picture books. One room in particular captured my imagination, where mummies of every sort—humans, but also cats, fish, crocodiles, and snakes—were displayed in the swaths of linen strips that wrapped them completely without obscuring the contours of their features. Many are still to be seen there today—the sharp profile of a cat's ears and even the nubbiness of an alligator's skin, bound tightly in cloth, a strange comment on the transience of the wrapped-up afterlife.

The Louvre of today could hardly be more different from the place we went to on Sunday afternoons when I was a boy. In the fifties it was never truly empty, but actual crowds were unthinkable. There were always people looking at *Winged Victory* or the *Mona Lisa*, but nothing like the smartphone-wielding, photo-snapping hordes that mob them now. Whole galleries—entire wings, at times—would echo hollowly to the sounds of only a handful of visitors working their way across acres of polished parquet floors. This was true not just of the Louvre, but of other major museums, too. My mom had taken us fairly frequently to the National Gallery and the Phillips Collection in Washington, and the prevailing mood was one of hushed awe. You dressed up to go to a museum the way you dressed up to go to church.

If the weather was nice on those Sunday afternoons when my dad was fencing, we often went for a walk. Making our way along one of the grand boulevards—the wide, tree-lined avenues laid out in the nineteenth century to open up the medieval closeness of the city center—was in itself an adventure. I recall the wonder of seeing for the first time those massive Haussmannian doorways, flanked by carved, half-naked giants—both straining men and bare-breasted women—seemingly holding up the entire façade. I'd never seen buildings like this before. This at a time when the very word "breast" was hardly pronounced in polite company. The sight of half-nude women carved on the fronts of buildings, bigger than life, was a strange thrill.

Stores were closed on Sundays. By government decree they still are, except in a few places with high concentrations of tourists. This is a point that Americans, especially, have a hard time understanding: why close stores on one of two weekend days, when people have time away from work in which to do their shopping? The practice originated from a traditional respect of the Sabbath, and the Catholic Church vigorously argued against any profanation of the Lord's day. But the answer is in fact more complicated than a mere appeal to conventional religious values suggests. France has a lay tradition, firmly anchored in its form of republican government, and yet the Sunday ban still enjoys widespread approval, whether from citizens who are churchgoing (a distinct minority) or not.

The fundamental reason is that the French value their family time, and another day of merchandising is considered an incursion on private life, both for merchants and shoppers. There exists a deep distrust of the market mechanism, with its endless siren song to consume. Sunday shopping isn't conceived of as a convenience, but rather as an interruption. Saturdays are errand day and, yes, it's a bit more crowded than it might be if Sundays were also given over to commerce, but the French continue to favor that arrangement.

Often, after a snack in a café, we'd head to one of the big central parks, either the Tuileries or the Luxembourg Gardens. Both, appended to former royal palaces, were transformed into public parks by the Republic. As at Fontainebleau, the outdoor delights of the aristocracy are substantially intact, displaying the familiar elements of the French garden. *Allées* of chestnut and linden trees are aligned in neat rows around the garden's perimeter; other areas are planted in perfect grids so that tree trunks form lines of columns on the eight points of the compass—horizontals and diagonals extending with sharp-edged regularity. Fine white gravel, slightly yellow in the sun, covers paths and wide expanses where people are permitted to walk. Low boxwood hedges and elaborate flower beds called *broderie,* embroidery, set off emerald greenswards punctuated with classical statuary.

All of this proceeds from the long French tradition of treating a garden as an extension of architecture, with severely clipped trees and bushes, a rigorously geometrical layout, and plants used to suggest walls, corridors, and entire rooms. In springtime, then as now, immense boxed plants—full-size oleanders and palm trees—would be taken from the *orangerie,* an indoor winter garden, and arranged in symmetrical patterns around the fountain and statues. Metal armchairs are still arrayed around the gravel-covered clearings, and they are occupied on a first-come, first-served basis, often dragged by their users to where the sun falls directly on the park. In the fifties, you were required to pay an old woman retainer ten centimes for half an hour in a chair. The fee was derisory—less than a penny in old francs—but the principle of paying for the privilege of sitting was still a feature of Old France. We used benches, since the bother for my mother of finding six chairs, and then paying in correct change, wasn't worth the trouble.

An entire area of the Luxembourg Gardens is given over to a

French specialty: the planting of a grid of trees in precise lines, and then the periodic trimming of their crowns so that a uniform volume is created overhead. On the side of the garden facing the Boulevard Saint-Michel, numerous benches are interspersed among the regularly spaced trunks. As spring arrives and the trees come into leaf, it's as if a room with rows of supporting posts is slowly given a roof. For two weeks or so, the transformation is unearthly, the light filtered through the first-growth green of the leaves giving a magical underwater effect. It is phenomenally beautiful without being wild in the least. But the French have been at this for a very long time, and the effects are deeply satisfying to the casual visitor. The elements are simple—tree trunks in line, foliage above, benches below—but it makes for an exquisite outdoor room, patterned by man but furnished by nature. It's not the countryside, but it invites conviviality surrounded by the soft rustle of leaves and the lambent light of a half-shaded lower world.

People meet for lunch on particular benches, or sit singly and read their papers or their books, or consult their phones. Lovers know about this netherworld that seems invented for them, not hidden but still discreet, and they, too, have their chosen benches. The conceit is both formal and artificial, it is true, but the effect is of a delightful, huge hall that allows a public kind of privacy. Put that alongside the French respect for what Americans might call "personal space" and the effect is supremely civilized. When you leave the park, you walk back into the city's maelstrom, but while you are there—beneath the trees or sitting in the sun in a green metal armchair—the sense of remove from the urban bustle is absolute.

For years I wondered how the gardeners of French public parks achieved the effect of perfectly rectangular planes with the tops of trees planted in a line. There are *allées* of chestnuts at Luxembourg that continue for hundreds of yards, comprised of trees thirty and forty feet high. Occasionally I'd see a small crew up on ladders sawing off a dead branch, but never a clue as to how the crowns of mature trees were worked into a knife edge of branches to create the illusion of elevated oblong volumes receding into the middle distance. Then one day in February a few years back, before any of the branches had begun to leaf, I happened upon the answer.

The entrance by which I usually entered the garden was closed, so I walked to the next portal and made my way back along the gold-tipped picket fence. Soon I came across a large sign in red letters: *Ne pas entrer—Danger de MORT!* "Do not enter—danger of DEATH!" Red-and-white-striped tape stretched along a line of tree trunks to indicate a safety perimeter, and I could see a crew of gardeners and some large equipment fifty yards down the double line of chestnut trees. A high metallic buzzing emanated from that area, punctuated by the sound of wood splitting and cracking. I made my way down the line of tape until I was directly across from the work crew, where I joined a small group of mesmerized onlookers.

We watched a man sitting in the open cab of a small tractor from the front of which projected upward at a steep angle a contraption that resembled a firefighter's extension ladder. At the tip of this metal arm were fitted vertically several large radial saws, each disc fully three feet in diameter, powered from the tractor so that the teeth spun in a plane perpendicular to the ground. The tractor operator could manipulate the height at which the saw blades cut, and he gunned the engine repeatedly as he and a group of helpers on the ground slowly advanced. They were trimming the leafless branches of the trees so that not a single twig trespassed into a space defined by the outer edge of the saw blades.

Occasionally the saws encountered six-inch branches, which they bit through as if they were licorice, and the wood snapped and popped as it scattered widely below. Clearly there was an entire art to the operator's job, and at times he'd back up, eyeball the line he had cut, and then take another pass to fine-tune the geometry. The noise created was as hypnotic as the process itself, like an angry, wood-chewing monster whose growls lowered as it got some substance in its teeth, then soared back to the high registers with the crackle of twigs.

After ten minutes or so, I found myself focusing on those wildly spinning saw blades, and the flash of metal in the treetops grew gradually more menacing. Visions of a blade thrown free fill my head as it rockets from on high to the placid scene beyond the safety tape, splitting in two all it encounters: flower beds, fountains, statues, the *Palais du Luxembourg* itself, where the French Senate sits. The death disc saws through all—stone, glass, wood, leather, velvet—and chews into the august Senate chamber on a perfect central *axe*, scattering members in both directions as it furrows through the raked semicircle and lodges itself in the raised speaker's dais. It splits in two the highly polished wood platform, bedecked with gold symbols of the Republic, as neatly as a cake. The French state rent asunder by the insurmountable impulse to trim all trees like topiary in the *allées* of its parks! A compelling image, and one that I found made my legs move faster than I had expected until I was well away from the shrieking, chewing beast cantilevered above and demanding that it be fed.

A portion of Luxembourg Gardens is called the *jardin anglais*, the English garden, where the layout is entirely different from the French formality and balance. Paths meander, trees and flowers grow in apparent abandon, views are asymmetrical and seemingly natural. While the English championed this form, the French adopted the idea as a variant concept, grafting it onto their graveled walks and *parterres* rather than letting it supplant their own vision. (There is also a *jardin anglais* at Fontainebleau.) They'll tell you that the English garden is as much an invention—*un monde factice,* an artificial world—as their own notion of plants made to reflect balance and order, and in this they are not wrong. The time, money, and trouble required to make a garden look "natural" is significant, so the real question has to do with the visual enjoyment of two different conceits. The French remain attached to their geometry, their boxwood and gravel, but they also make room for a bit of the "wild" spirit of the English model.

It's also useful to consider that they make far less of a distinction between fiction and nonfiction than we do in what they call *le monde anglo-saxon,* the Anglo-Saxon world. Where we ask, about a book's story, "Is it made up or not?" they see all writing as "construct," whether it attends to imagined people or events (which the writer will necessarily infuse with his or her own experiences), or to "real" events. Even in a strict documentary mode, they insist, the writer chooses to include some details and dispense with others, and generally structures his or her narrative in a way that makes it entirely personal. The initial intention is not always what is significant in the enterprise, and so it becomes a matter of nuance. "*Roman*" means "novel," yes, but no single opposite for "nonfiction" exists.

Though they both featured several traditional French attractions designed for kids—model sailboats for rent, pony rides, a carousel—when I was a child, I preferred the Luxembourg

Gardens to the Tuileries for the unique configuration of its merry-go-round. It wasn't bright or big or at all fancy. When it stopped and the previous riders were made to clear off, we raced to mount one of the animals on the outer circumference of the menagerie. We strapped ourselves loosely to these special mounts with worn leather belts attached to the poles, shiny with the sweat of young hands. Each of us on the outer circle was then given a short wooden baton, one end pointed but not sharp, like a giant blunt pencil, which we brandished expectantly in our right hands.

Already leaning far out to the right as the carousel began to turn, we aimed to snag a shiny metal ring positioned just at the edge of our reach in an old mechanical dispenser. The belt stretched taut while we grasped the pole with our left hands, and if we snagged a ring we kept it on our batons and prepared for the next pass, collecting them like a swallow swooping for bugs, and keeping them piled up one upon the other as we sailed on in the headlong race to the next try. Before the carousel wound down, the operator pulled in the dispenser arm, and it was time to tally. Some kids never missed. I suspect there was a professional gang of ring snaggers who practiced at night when the rest of us were in bed. But winning was largely beside the point: the prize for snagging the most rings was not any plush animal or showy doll, but a free ride on the carousel. The real thrill was in the wild delight of thrusting your arm out with that stick of wood, as if you were trying to hook a fish and yank it in, and knowing that, ring or no ring, the frantic turning continued and you'd have another chance in a matter of seconds.

CHAPTER 20

PARIS

Paris in the fifties looked very different from the sparkling face it presents to the world today, but to us it was all new and engaging. The biggest transformation in modern times was simply the cleaning of the stone edifices of the center city, initiated in the 1960s by de Gaulle's minister of cultural affairs André Malraux. No change could have been more surprising, or more deeply satisfying. When we lived in Fontainebleau, I was convinced that all of the buildings in France—the châteaux, the cathedrals, the monuments—were made from the same special dark stone, quarried in some remote part of France, black as night and so softened by centuries of wood and coal dust that the surface was a felt-like matte whose edges looked as if they would soon crumble. This was the "atmospheric" Paris of all those voluptuous black-and-white photos, the ponderous Paris of Buffet prints and countless tourist posters.

Then the government started to clean the major monuments one by one—Notre-Dame, the *Arc de Triomphe*, the Louvre—and the transformation was shocking, almost troubling in its strange newness. The buildings of Paris weren't black after all, but very nearly . . . white! It took almost two decades of careful cleaning and restoration, but Paris emerged from the process the albino twin of its former self. To appreciate the contrast, buy a vintage postcard aerial view, dating from 1970 or earlier, at one of the *bouquiniste* stalls along the banks of the Seine, then compare it with the present-day aerial shot: the era of dirt and grime looks like a photographic negative of the light and airy Paris that current tourists will recognize as the "real" Paris.

Paris smelled different in those days, too. In the winter the odor of coal smoke permeated the air, and a fine layer of pure black dust settled everywhere; after a single day, a clean surface would show the swipe of a finger. Most buildings were heated by coal-fired furnaces that powered a system of water-filled radiators.

I had imagined that this system of heating had disappeared entirely since I had lived in Fontainebleau in the fifties, but I was astounded to discover that it persisted in certain parts of Paris as recently as twenty years ago. When we moved to Paris with our two infant children at the end of the eighties, we lived in an apartment in a Haussmannian building not far from the *Arc de Triomphe*. At the time I worked a corporate job that periodically involved both long trips and long hours. On one occasion during our first winter in the sixteenth *arrondissement*, I was returning home shortly before 2:00 a.m. after a long series of meetings. I let myself in to the entrance hall of our building and crossed to the elevator. As I pushed the button, the adjacent door to the basement opened and a tall man stepped into the hall. It's fair to say that each of us startled the other: we both let out cries of surprise and stepped back. Clearly he was not expecting to see one of the building's residents at that late hour, and I was equally startled by the vision that stood before me. His jeans and sweatshirt were filthy with black grime, as were his face and hands. The effect was amplified by a pair of goggles that had been pulled up onto his forehead, giving him the look of a huge reversed-out raccoon, with a band of white skin across his eyes and temples, surrounded by soot. A burglar, I wondered, who had somehow made his way into the cellar to filch the vintage bottles in my neighbors' wine cellars? I stuttered the age-old French challenge: "*Qui êtes-vous, Monsieur?*" "Who are you, sir?" As if it were obvious to all, he answered, "*Mais je suis le livreur de charbon!*" "Why, I'm the coal delivery man!"

He explained that our building's furnace was coal fired, a detail about which I was ignorant since we were renters. He was in fact a student at the Sorbonne whose after-hours job involved stoking coal furnaces in the basements of apartment buildings throughout the sixteenth *arrondissement*. "From 1:00 to 5:00 a.m., I manage to shovel coal in twenty different buildings," he told me. "My scooter makes for a short trip, and there's no traffic at this hour." He showed me the huge pile of coal that covered much of the cellar floor, delivered in September through a chute that descended from the sidewalk. "This has been a mild winter so far," he said, "so that should suffice." An extended cold snap, though, would make necessary an additional delivery. He excused himself—time was short, he explained, and he had fifteen buildings left on his round—and he was out the door in a flash.

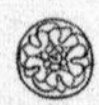

When spring arrived in the fifties, the lines of chestnut and plane trees along the major boulevards gave forth their varied perfumes, not quite sweet but strong enough to cover the fumes of traffic when the days turned warm. Another odor pervaded the air whenever we visited Paris, and on hot days it was inescapable: urine. Until recent times, a great number of standing toilets were to be found on public squares and sidewalks. Called *Vespasiennes* after the Roman emperor reputed to have cleaned the streets of Rome by providing free public toilets, these structures dotted the urban landscape throughout Paris. Always painted a forest green, they consisted of two wings of sheet metal that extended in a curve from a central core. These metal wings rose from knee level up to about six feet, supported by slender struts, allowing one to see whether either side of a *Vespasienne* was occupied. You entered at a central opening between the wings, walked part way around one side so that all but your lower legs were shielded from view, and peed onto the center core down which a constant stream of water dribbled to the floor drain.

Every Paris square or intersection had at least one of these *urinoirs* (more popularly, *pissotières*) and sometimes three or four, their surfaces covered with colorful ads for coffee, wine, and various throat lozenges offering relief to chronic smokers. Men would disappear for a minute, then emerge zipping up their pants, to resume their conversation at the bar, to continue to peruse the open-air bookstalls, to descend into the Métro or hop on a bus. No possibility existed of washing one's hands.

They were certainly convenient. Anything more than pee—and anything at all for girls or women—involved buying something at a bar for the privilege of using their toilets. My mother resisted the implicit contradiction in this arrangement, though, reasoning that to give a child a Coke or an Orangina as the price for access to a toilet would only make the child need to pee soon after, with no guarantee that a toilet would again be available.

For a five-year-old, figuring out how to negotiate successfully one of these *Vespasiennes* was not obvious; I felt both challenged and amazed by the whole setup. My father took me in once or twice, but, aside from the usual pee-shy concerns of that age, I had trouble gauging the distance. You had to stand close enough to the ammonia-encrusted wall at the center so that your pee joined the sheet of water that trickled down the surface, but not *too* close or your shoes inevitably ended up wet from the imperfect drainage system below. Moreover, the stink of accumulated urine was worthy of an unclean stable, even though chunks of naphthalene were periodically left in the drains to diminish the fumes. In general we avoided them unless it was an emergency, which occurred frequently enough with three young boys in tow.

Nor, for that matter, was a café's toilet a haven of peace and comfort. In the fifties, most cafés were presided over by a woman cashier, usually the bartender's wife, who dispensed slotted round tokens, *jetons*, for both the toilets and the public telephone from her perch behind the bar. After my parents made a cursory purchase, the gatekeeper would hand out a token, sometimes grudgingly, and we would make our way to the locked booths that were usually found in the basement. Inside the booth, the invariable configuration was the *toilette à la turque*, a "Turkish toilet": no commode or toilet seat, just a white ceramic panel laid flush into the tile floor with two ribbed footpads flanking a central hole. A water tank loomed overhead, from one side of which hung a long chain with a sweat-stained wooden handgrip fastened to its end. A thin pipe descended along the back wall from the tank and passed through the tile floor, ending in a fan-shaped fitting at the rear of the hole.

The technique needed for taking a shit was precise, athletic, and highly perilous. You first undid your pants and pushed them down to your knees, then turned around so that you were facing the door, and, with your feet planted squarely on the ribbed pads, executed a full squat. It was critical not to let your pants hang low so that they touched the usually wet—and filthy—ceramic plate. At this point, aim was everything: the trick was to position your rear end so that the excrement leaving your body fell neatly into the water-filled hole, then to make sure your pee was directed below, all the while relaxing enough to do your business while bent nearly double. Toilet paper was a scarce commodity in café toilets, so you were wise to have some Kleenex stuffed in a pocket for such situations.

Flushing was a directly mechanical operation—you yanked the chain, and gravity sped the contents of the water tank with terrifying force through the pipe's pressure fitting and into the hole. The explosion of pressure and whoosh of water were always dramatic, and the effects sometimes catastrophic. An improperly regulated feed pipe, or a partially blocked toilet, would send waves of filth rocketing across the floor, soaking shoes and socks. You learned to stand back as far as possible before pulling that wooden handle.

Though they were cleaned periodically, the *Vespasiennes* at street corners inevitably reeked, a heady ammoniac brew wafting around their environs. I tried to hold my breath, and would scurry out, gasping for cleaner air. If you landed sightless in Paris in those days, you could at least be sure of finding your way to the *pissotière*. But, while its stench could be overwhelming, the *Vespasienne* was not the only place that gave forth the pervasive smell, since Parisian men seemed to pee everywhere they could outdoors. Stone walls, exterior staircases, doorways: each bore the telltale smell of pee, streaks of discoloring a foot or two above the sidewalk, and sometimes the recent puddles dribbling toward the gutter. If it was a hot spell and hadn't rained for a while, you noticed it in the doorways and along walls, and hurried along.

This impressed me as a very different approach to urinating in public from that taken by Americans. Along French highways you'd regularly see cars pulled just off the road with several men and boys peeing on the far side of their vehicles. Women and girls went into the nearby woods—that was understood—but men just got out, stepped to the side, and let fly. What freedom it felt like at first! Soon our family adopted the same habit for longer trips—boys by the car, girls in the woods—and, aside from the voyeuristic peculiarity of performing for passing traffic, peeing in the open air of the countryside has ever since seemed to me one of life's minor pleasures.

The *Vespasiennes* are gone now, as are, for the most part, the *toilettes à la turque* in France's cafés. There remains a single *pissotière* in Paris, a piece of nostalgia saved by the municipal government as a reminder of the time when they were ubiquitous. By happenstance, it stands not far from where I now live, on a sidewalk in front of the notorious *Prison de la Santé*, a nineteenth-century pile of forbidding brown stone surrounded by high walls topped with gleaming, razor-sharp blades. It is a sorry affair for a *Vespasienne*, a two-person version painted the requisite dark green, tucked in among the line of chestnut trees on the usually deserted sidewalk. Taxi drivers know about it, detouring down to the prison if they are on the Left Bank, but I have never seen anyone else use it. That part of the Paris landscape belongs to the past, and its images are almost as old as the history of photography.

Squat toilets can still be found in villages and country cafés that haven't been gussied up, but they are rare in Paris. I can't truly say that I miss them, but—strange as it may sound—I do feel as if I learned something from having had to contend with their challenges. When one or another of us complained, my father would point out that, compared to the open-pit toilets he had known during the war as an infantry officer in the Pacific and a fighter pilot in Europe, *toilettes à la turque* were positively modern. Sometimes we'd remember those moments in France as if they were something out of the Dark Ages, and my mother's comment was typically succinct. "It didn't kill you," she'd say with a laugh.

Only much later did I understand that learning to squat in

order to defecate, like the rest of the world, was something that America had left behind in its surge of modernity. Now much of the world has decent plumbing, and "sit toilets" are increasingly the norm. Surely that's progress, and it's wrong to be sentimental about this. When my own children were infants in Paris, more than once I was faced with helping them negotiate the treacherous squat. It didn't kill us, indeed, but I'm glad those days are over.

In later years my family shared a memory of a café toilet that became a favored anecdote. It was on an outing we made to Normandy on one of our first camping adventures when, in the face of a driving rainstorm, my parents had taken us all to the village café, where we gathered over hot chocolate and croissants. The place was crowded with people from the town, filling the tables and standing at the bar in groups of twos and threes.

Suddenly the door at the far end of the bar burst open, and a very old woman, thin and dressed entirely in black, stood framed in the opening. The abrupt swing of the door quieted things, and the widow's appearance quickly reduced the room to a near hush. (Any woman of her age dressed entirely in black was understood, by the French conventions of the time, to have lost her husband.) The blood had drained entirely from her face, her legs were bent at the knee as if she were having trouble straightening fully, and one hand clutched the door handle for support. She confronted the room with a look of wild astonishment, then slowly composed herself before our searching eyes. Everyone in the place knew she had just come back from the *toilette à la turque* in the back, and her features were those of one who had just made a supreme physical effort.

She raised her free hand in a magisterial wave to the bartender and announced in a voice loud enough for all to hear, "*Alors, Monsieur, pour moi un coup de calva!*" "a shot of the local apple brandy." A murmur of approval passed through the room, and everyone returned to their talking. At the next table a woman whispered to her companion in a concerned tone that we could overhear, "*Ce n'est pas sa digestion qui lui fait mal, c'est les acrobaties aux chiottes.*" "It's not her digestion that's the problem, it's the acrobatics in the shitter." Ever since, the whisper of "*un coup de calva*" has elicited a smile of recognition in our family for the plight of that woman in the rain-swept village. Within five minutes, she was standing up straight at the bar, with color in her cheeks and an animated smile.

For a French friend with an intimate knowledge of his country's history, the matter and manner of disposing of waste is a better index of lasting social change than all of the ideological posturings that came in the wake of the revolution. "Running water, flush toilets, and a comprehensive system of sewers were, arguably, one of the greatest accomplishments of the nineteenth century. For the first time, the infrastructure in its modern expression served all the people, not just the aristocrats." He explained that Versailles, and Fontainebleau, too—all the great châteaux, really—had relied on a system of intensive human labor, not the least of whose expressions was the need to carry away daily mountains of human waste.

"Legions of servants, themselves producers of human waste, were made to remove the excrement of their betters in an arrangement that was only one step removed from indentured servitude," my friend declared. Unjust, demeaning, and brutally unhealthy, he reasoned, this sort of labor was taken for granted by those who benefited, but it was bound to lead to more and more resentment. "To understand the root causes of the French Revolution, you could do worse than to examine closely the means whereby the human waste of the ruling class was removed by an army of what amounted to slaves."

CHAPTER 21

WINTER

Men still wore navy blue berets when I was a child. Not everyone, of course, but enough so that they never looked out of place. And there was a great variety of ways to put a beret on your head: the classic pulled-to-one-side, cutting a rakish diagonal across the forehead; bunched up in front and then worked into a small peak over the brow; sitting flat as a pancake on the head, symmetrical and plain. You very rarely see a beret these days, and only on the old.

Cars had yellow headlights, a French particularity. The Chevy had to be fitted with yellow bulbs, which seemed like a disfigurement to me who cared so much about cars. Headlights were clearly a car's eyes, and to change from white to amber was as peculiar as could be. This standard was maintained until the early nineties. When we arrived with our own children in the late eighties, the Japanese van we bought in Paris had yellow lights. A few years later, I had to have them changed—expensively—to white, the new European standard imposed by Brussels. The tradition of yellow French headlights dates from just before World War II, when French military planners imposed yellow headlights so that French military columns could easily be distinguished from those of the enemy—at least at night. Whoever came up with that one didn't seem to have had *blitzkrieg* in mind.

In the fifties, we rapidly adjusted to a diet that included a daily baguette and lots of cheese. A fresh, warm baguette, straight from the *boulanger*'s oven, seemed like an entirely different kind of food. It had nothing to do with the spongy squares of sliced sandwich bread we had known. I can't remember a time when one of the two baguettes we picked up before dinner at the nearby *boulangerie* made it home intact; the temptation to take a bite from the warm, aromatic crust was simply too great. The French preoccupation with the perfect baguette hasn't changed; if anything, it has intensified with the modern foodie obsession with culinary excellence. The annual competition to designate the "Best Baguette in Paris" is taken quite seriously by *boulangers* and public alike. For the ensuing year, the winner becomes the official provider of baguettes to the Elysée Palace, the official residence of the President of France.

Once we all started at our new schools, we settled in to a routine of daily comings and goings. In those days we came home for lunch. Breakfast was fairly quiet, all about getting four children out the door in time for their first class at 8:00 a.m. (my infant sister stayed home). Lunch was boisterous, a real break in the long school day that ended at 5:00 p.m. We had no classes on Thursday afternoons, but Saturday mornings we were in school until noon. My mom devised a way of feeding all seven of us three times a day, using a combination of American staples from the post commissary (meat, canned goods, milk, cereals, peanut butter, and the like) as well as French fare from the open-air market and small specialty shops in town (fresh vegetables, cheese, cold cuts, baguettes, and an occasional patisserie). There was usually a maid around, and a young woman to help with my sister, but my mother always laughed when anyone referred to "the servants." "They were *help*!" she'd insist, before adding, "That's what I needed." We were very lucky to have the pressure valve of our huge yard as a play space, but there were times—rainy days in particular—when it felt as if the top might blow off with everyone cooped up inside. Then "the help" came into their own. The informal arrangement between them and my mother was "You watch those two, I'll watch the other three, and maybe—just maybe—we can keep things from boiling over."

In France we knew many members of *familles nombreuses*, big families. For many years the French have had an active policy of raising the birthrate by providing direct subsidies and tax incentives for large families. This was initially a response to the decimation of young French men during World War I: between the wars, an entire generation of women had a much reduced chance of finding a spouse, and France spent two generations recovering from this imbalance. Now its birthrate is one of the few in Europe that is positive, and cash payments as well as family services are still generously provided.

Beyond mere child care and housekeeping, my parents also did a lot of entertaining. In part this came with the territory because of my dad's job, with international contingents from the major NATO countries in residence. But it was also clear that they, and many others like them, thoroughly enjoyed a good party. It wasn't unusual for them to host a dinner party one night and a cocktail party on another evening in one week, and to attend a couple of other events as guests. And everyone, virtually without exception, smoked and drank. Liquor and tobacco were cheap through the commissary, and the quantities consumed were prodigious.

My parents had a practical approach: one drink each, and then sip from a highball glass with ice water. "Otherwise, we'd have been alcoholics in a matter of months," they explained. There were, of course, those who couldn't control their drinking, and it was sometimes a grim business. I once heard my father mutter "Demon drink!"—the Irish epithet of choice—when confronted with a garrulous guest who had drunk himself over the line of acceptable behavior. One of my mom's pet peeves was the habit of some guests of dropping cigarette butts into the remains of their drink. "An unnecessary mess," she complained, since every horizontal surface held one or more ashtrays. She wasn't against leaving dirty dishes overnight in the kitchen for the cleaning lady, but she systematically cleared the rooms of glasses, cigarettes, and plates herself. Besides, there were two kitchens, so it was no great problem to use one for party leavings.

By today's health standards, these people shouldn't have lasted more than five or ten years, but they persisted, even thrived. How did they do it? More than anything else, the pace of entertaining shows that other aspects of life were very different from what we know today. People worked fewer hours, and those hours were regular and predictable. Weekends and evenings were regarded as sacred, "family time." No one would have dreamed of calling a colleague at home for a routine business matter. "It can wait until the morning" was the widely repeated standard.

When we arrived in 1989 with our own children, this was still the rule among the French. Some of the indulgence has since gone by the wayside; two-hour lunches with wine, for example, have largely disappeared. But the attitude persists that time away from the office is both necessary and sacrosanct. It's as if the French have understood an essential element of social life: that what we call "down time" is the only way of having your own life.

There's another difference from those times, though, that

strikes me only from the distance of years. My parents seldom talked about it, and then only obliquely. Everyone was so happy to be alive! Even ten years after the war had ended, the general relief was almost palpable. They had all, in one way or another, looked into the abyss. Friends and relatives had been lost, whole cities and countries had been devastated, but they had somehow, miraculously, come through. Hitler did not prevail! And so parties seemed more than just appropriate. A facile generalization, perhaps, but how else to explain the almost juvenile glee that often fueled their get-togethers?

The war sometimes cast its long shadow in unexpected ways. Letters asking for reservations at the *auberge* continued to arrive infrequently, and my mother fashioned a standard response in French explaining that the inn no longer existed. One day two men appeared at the door, well-dressed in suits and ties. Thinking they were looking for the inn, my mother began to explain in her halting French that it was now a private house. One of them responded in passable English, with an accent that was not French, that he and his "brother officers" had lived here during the war, and they just wanted to see the house and garden where they had spent "so many pleasant hours."

Not entirely comprehending their interest, my mom took them around the side of the house and showed them the garden, its greenswards laced with gravel-covered walks and boxwood borders, with a ring of trees around the outer perimeter to mask the stone wall. This seemed to satisfy them and they nodded their approval. Finally the man who spoke English extended his hand and thanked my mother for showing them what had been for them a "special

The winter before we arrived had been the most severe since the war. From late January to mid-February a cold wave hit France with lethal effect. At the time, tens of thousands of poor lived in shantytowns on the outskirts of Paris. They were called *bidonvilles* since they were fashioned from the flattened-out *bidons,* or jerry cans, that were used to carry gas and kerosene. When the cold snap hit and then persisted, it meant an immediate catastrophe for the families trying to survive in the *bidonvilles,* especially for the very young and the very old.

When the first deaths were announced *en raison du très grand froid,* because of the intense cold, a young priest known simply as *Abbé Pierre* took to the radio and beseeched the French for help in the immediate crisis. The response was instantaneous, and the unprecedented gifts of blankets, clothing, and cash changed forever the way France looked at housing standards. Substandard housing was recognized as a blight, and Abbé Pierre's organization, Emmaüs, led the fight for assistance and solidarity among all French. Since that first consciousness-raising and outpouring of aid, he was regularly voted the most respected person in France. Considered against the dramatic events of the previous winter, our basement full of coal was in fact an extraordinary privilege.

The furnace, though, did not match the house's needs. Or, as my mother regularly put it with a sigh somewhere between frustration and fury, "This house can't be heated." Not only was the house huge and drafty, but the furnace had a range of caprices. A load of coal would burn in its maw for a day or two, but it had to be checked continually, and stoked if the temperature plummeted at night and more heat was needed. The man who polished the floors and cleaned the windows would ordinarily do this, but in the evening or on weekends the job fell to my dad. This involved putting on an old flying suit (in effect, a coverall against the clouds of coal dust when he dug into the pile), then going outside, whether or not it was raining or snowing, down the broad stone staircase, across the sodden gravel, and into the little green door that led to the basement.

Once inside, you heard a low rumble and saw a reddish-yellow glow from deep within, as if a dragon were asleep in the bowels of our house, breathing heavily. If you didn't hear the rumble and feel the deep vibration, things were truly serious as it meant that the fire had gone out and was no longer drawing air. In the evenings sometimes my dad would let one or another of us children watch his ministrations ("Stand well back!"), as he gingerly swung the heavy door wide on its hinges to reveal a cavern of red-hot coals. I loved this part. With the door open, the radiant heat was akin to a large oven: just on the edge of tolerable for any exposed skin, but deeply satisfying to some animal instinct as your clothes were heated and your bones slowly cooked.

I'd hand my dad the implements as he called for them in sequence, turning his face from the searing glow when it became too much: "Tongs!" "Shovel!" "Bellows!" At last he'd get it arranged to his satisfaction and swing the door shut with a muffled clang. The feeling of accomplishment was palpable at first, but was soon overtaken by the awareness that while the furnace had been given enough to keep it going, the heat it produced would always transform itself into little more than a feeble warmth in the house's radiators.

My dad purchased the French solution to cold rooms: several kerosene space heaters. My mother rightly regarded them as dangerous and forbade their use after bedtime. We used to huddle around them as we did our *devoirs*—homework—or listened to the radio. There was no television in our house (French TV of the day featured very few broadcasts), so reading and playing board games were the principal entertainment. Our beds were warm, at least, piled high with blankets. However, getting to the kitchen for breakfast—the enormous stove heated the room wonderfully—was a footrace each winter morning, like running through the frigid air of a mountaintop to make it to the climbers' refuge.

CHAPTER 22

"IN BETWEEN"

After dinner on those long winter evenings, my mother would often take over one end of the immense walnut dining-room table for her sewing. She was an accomplished seamstress, a skill she had learned thoroughly as a 4-H member on her family's farm. She loved fine clothes, and followed closely the changes in fashions. Moreover, she understood that the only way of having the latest styles was to make them herself. She bought the American *Vogue* and the respected French fashion magazine *L'Officiel,* as well as each edition of the *Vogue* pattern book. Since my father's travels took him throughout Europe and the Middle East, he was charged with bringing back materials that she wanted: brocades from Egypt, say, or tweeds from England and silks from Italy.

She had brought with her from America her trusty Singer, a utilitarian black machine that folded down neatly into its own small table when not in use. This served for a while, but then she made what for her was an extravagant purchase. She decided to buy a professional machine, since they were made in Europe. The choice was between an Italian Necchi and a German Pfaff; she bought the Pfaff.

Before the sewing itself, though, came the first step that always seemed wildly daring: cutting the material against the pattern.

She had a sure hand with her shears, and an unflinching eye as she cut a bolt of unblemished fabric into pieces of various size. The result looked like a pile of strange-shaped rags with pieces of paper—the pattern—pinned to each piece. Next came time at the machine, which she kept out of the way in a corner of the less frequently used of the two kitchens. Sometimes you wouldn't see what she'd been making again for days or even a week, but then she'd be sitting in a chair in one of the salons, doing finish work with needle, thread, and thimble on a dress or a suit that magically appeared as a recognizable piece of clothing. More than once she decided on the day of an event that she needed something new, and hours later she'd be going out the door with my dad in a green silk holiday dress, say, or a tailored suit for a ladies' tea.

It was one of those things I took for granted about my mom, that she could make clothes herself and that she was considered by many to be particularly well dressed. Several women asked her for the name of her seamstress, but she always demurred. It gave her considerable satisfaction, not principally that she had fooled people, but that she had mastered the techniques that amounted to a very personal art. To have your clothes admired in France—not just the style, but the actual craft of how they are fashioned—is no small feat. If there is a population that knows how a particular seam should be joined, how stitching needs to be worked unseen to give body to cloth, that senses all the solutions and tricks and invisible challenges that have been addressed in a particular piece of clothing, it is the French. They likely won't comment on it, but neither will it go unnoticed. *Couture* really just means "sewing," and *haute couture* is big-time sewing. It is taken seriously because it is a tradition that uses elaborate know-how to transform the practical into something akin to art. In France, the sophistication of specific knowledge deepens the appreciation of the result. My mom was not trying to "pass" as a well-dressed woman—she had better things to do—and "clotheshorse" was always for her a term of contempt. But she was in the right place at the right time to know the pleasures of creating her own clothes among people who understood and respected the process.

When the house became simply too cold in the evening, there was a place where we could be sure of being warm: the movies. The American post had a theater, and so did the British base. We went indiscriminately, the whole family piling in the car to go find real warmth for a couple of hours. The American movies we saw were the Hollywood standards of the day. Some were good, and some were plain awful. There were a lot of westerns and a fair number of conceptual cowboys (and Indians, for that matter), who were given to long, meaningful stares into the middle distance. My dad called these movies "gazers" because that's what the main characters were doing so much of the time. But we got to know Gregory Peck and Audrey Hepburn, Jean Simmons and Randolph Scott, as if they were distant relatives, familiar but not really approachable. I see now that it was one of the strongest connections we had to our own country, or at least to one idea it had of itself.

The British showed their own movies, and the standard was high. We saw the Ealing Studios comedies that made Alec Guinness famous; adults and children alike enjoyed the duplicity and madcap irony of a film like *The Ladykillers*. But even when the films were "gazers" or "dogs" (our two negative categories), we all left the theater warm.

In truth, there were limited possibilities for amusement on winter evenings. With no television, the options were reading, listening to the radio, and "spinning records" on the portable player the kids supposedly shared, but which was in fact monopolized by my elder sister, Sally, already a teenager. Reading in bed was the only possible place to be when the house was frigid. Experts were telling parents in those days (*American* experts, I hasten to add) that reading in bed was to be avoided, but my parents soon bent that rule. If only those same experts had had an inkling of what was on the not-too-distant horizon: the beneath-the-sheets freak show of computers, phones, video games, and chat that opens a world of violence, mayhem, and sex to toddlers if they can manage to push buttons (generally, they can).

At home we all spoke English exclusively, though our homework was always in French. We each developed fluency, outstripping our parents in a hurry, but the idea of carrying on our family life in French was simply never an option. We read American newspapers and magazines—the rudimentary *Stars & Stripes,* the paper published by and for the U.S. Armed Forces overseas; *Time*; and *Life*—as if they were dispatches from a strange frontier we had once known. But we also saw *Paris Match* every week, and its panoply of photos of French public figures. That, too, seemed a world that was removed from the one we lived in or, rather, that was a part of the amalgam that we fashioned without even knowing we were doing it. At times you ended up "in between" everything, it seemed: not really in an American setting like the ones we would see in the movies, and not really part of the French one that lay just beyond our front gate. In fact, we passed back and forth.

One day Sally brought back to the house a 45-rpm record by an American singer named Bill Haley, and that date marks the entry of rock and roll into my life—all of our lives, really, since none of us had heard anything like it before. His signature elements were a big spit curl on his forehead and the beat of his hit tune "Rock Around the Clock." The French loved him, too—Bill Haley was on French radio!—and it would be hard to exaggerate the impact his discovery had on their impression of Americans. Suddenly rock and roll was everywhere. Young French kids and young Americans, separated by language, instantly shared something on a visceral level. It was the beginning of a phase shift of major proportions. Soon after Bill Haley, Elvis Presley hit the airwaves—both American and French—and the effect was of a tidal wave. Quickly, the over-thirty Bill Haley and His Comets seemed almost quaint, safe, fun. Even at that young age, I knew there was nothing "safe" about Elvis Presley, and so did my sisters and brothers and many of our friends.

The rhythm of daily life was different in many respects, but the total absence of television, much less any interactive media, was perhaps the most obvious difference from today's habits. When we left Washington in 1954 we had a TV, but it was an entirely different animal from what became common within a few short years. The screen was tiny with curved sides, and it was housed in a large cabinet with hinged wooden doors covering the screen. These were opened ceremoniously by my father when a "telecast" was going to be viewed. The TV sat downstairs in a corner of what was called the "recreational room" or "rec room." (I always heard this as "wreck," associating the place with its condition after five kids had been playing there.) TV was not welcome in the main rooms upstairs; it was considered more of a newfangled appliance, and its masquerade as a piece of furniture did not convince my mom. The fact is, there wasn't all that much to watch in the early fifties, and it was generally understood that spending much time watching the programs that were available was a profligate waste of time.

I saw my first "modern," regular-screen TV in Paris, during our second year in France. My mom took us to one of the big department stores in Paris, *Printemps,* and as we walked around an upper floor we stumbled upon an extensive display of televisions, all showing the same thing. The effect was mesmerizing to me at six years old. All of the screens were tuned to an identical sequence from one of the Disney movies about Davy Crockett. We watched Davy and others have a fistfight as they stood in tippy canoes. But I was intoxicated with all the screens—a movie, like at the theater!—showing the action over and over again. I walked up and actually touched one of the screens, and Davy kept on trading swings with the bad guys. Such was my introduction to "real" television. Those demons were not again disturbed until we returned to America.

The Davy Crockett craze caught on in France as it did all over the world. Young boys clamored for coonskin caps—I was inseparable from mine for months—and they played in simulated versions of the frontier buckskin costume. We brandished Davy Crockett toy rifles and hunting knives when we weren't reading Davy Crockett comic books. Parents everywhere, including France, were pestered for the board game, the trading cards, even the bubble gum. Some of the French kids at school had bits of paraphernalia, and "The Ballad of Davy Crockett" ("Born on a mountaintop in Tennessee . . .") was a constant refrain. Never mind the Marshall Plan, never mind the Berlin Airlift, never mind NATO itself: at a kid level, this was the first palpable evidence I had that it was cool to be American in Europe.

Davy's movie incarnation, Fess Parker, had an initial hiccup in France that no one foresaw. As it happens, the word *fesse* (pronounced like the actor's given name, Fess) means "buttock" in French. "Fess Parker plays Davy Crockett" resonated for the French as "Butt Parker. . . ." Immediately his name in French was changed to *Fier* Parker, meaning "Proud" Parker. And so it remained through all the iterations and reruns dear to the French.

CHAPTER 23

CAMPING

After we had been in Fontainebleau for a year and had had our fill of day trips to Paris, my father decided that it was time we saw more of Europe. That year the world championships of fencing were being held in Rome, and my dad was invited to compete. Trying to stay on a budget with a family of seven was never easy, though, so he decided that this would be our first taste of that European approach to vacations, "camping." It happened that there were mountains of World War II–era surplus equipment at the military post in Fontainebleau, and the quartermaster let my dad take a massive brown tent along with sleeping bags, blankets, and lanterns. These we supplemented with a few pieces of modern, lightweight gear—a propane stove, flashlights, air mattresses—for our first foray into camping, a world the French embraced with the unalloyed enthusiasm of purists.

Setting off in the car on a long-distance trip of two weeks was a serious undertaking; we'd be going across the Alps. My father bought a massive roof rack, a commonplace feature on many French cars, and had it adapted to fit the Chevy. Since the equipment we were using was World War II vintage, suitable for an invading army supported by an elaborate logistical infrastructure, all of the components were both heavy and unwieldy. Somehow my dad and Tom, my eldest brother, wrestled the mountain of material to the top of the car, stuffed the various bags within the tubular metal framework of the oblong roof rack, and covered it all with a waterproof tarp. This last they secured with an octopus-like arrangement of eight heavy-duty elastic cords, bright yellow, each of which was attached on one end to a central ring and on the other by a metal hook to the far edges of the rack. This was my first sight of a bungee cord, common enough in Europe but virtually unknown in the United States. Our car looked as if a canary-colored starfish had fallen from the sky and adhered itself to our belongings.

Once the car had been fully loaded at the foot of the back stairs, we piled in: my father at the wheel and my mom on the passenger side, with my three-year-old sister perched between them on the massive front seat; the two oldest—Sally, thirteen, and Tom, eleven—in the far backseat; and my next oldest brother, Judd, eight, and me in the slightly narrower middle seat (the right-hand end of the seat was shortened to allow access to the side door from the rear). Judd always sat directly behind my father, a choice that left me in the middle. Unsuspecting, I soon learned that this spot was strategically vulnerable when the driver flailed out with back-handed swats. It was one more lesson in the anything-but-democratic rules that governed life in a big family. Our dog, Kepi, jumped in last to lie on the floor at our feet, though he often climbed up onto the seat with Judd and me, where he sat up straight, curious and attentive to all that passed outside the window. If he was not quite a sixth child, he was certainly a member of the family.

My father folded his road map a final time so that the first leg of our journey was displayed, the route outlined with a red pen, a pilot's habit that came from navigating and plotting his itinerary before each flight. Before we could drive away to begin a trip, we invariably observed a little ritual, solemn and quiet. My dad pulled down the sun visor over the steering wheel to reveal a large Saint Christopher medal pinned to the underside. He raised his hand to touch the image—a metal emblem of the patron saint of travelers carrying the Christ child on his shoulders—and murmured, "Now let's all say a little prayer to Saint Christopher asking him to protect us." And we did, eyes closed and hearts fervent with supplication. "Please, Saint Christopher," I thought with the uncomplicated reasoning of a five-year-old, "don't let me die on this trip." Considering what I now know about the hazards of car travel in those days—dangerous roads, no safety belts, drunk drivers at every turn—we were right to pray. After ten seconds or so the moment passed and, as we pulled away, my father announced our destination with a boyish glee that substituted the world of adventure for visions of bloody accidents on the highway: "Here we come, Rome!"

We headed out of town for the *Nationale 7*, the national highway that descended all the way from Paris to Nice and the Riviera. A network of *nationales* crisscrossed France in those days, well-maintained two-lane roads like the old system of national highways in the United States, where Route 66, say, connected Chicago and Los Angeles, or Route 1 wound its way up the Atlantic coast.

The speed limit was 90 kilometers per hour, or about 55 miles per hour, but even in those days there were speeders. Passing another car on a two-lane highway always involves some risk, but with trucks sharing the road with low-horsepower French cars, the perils increased. My dad was a good driver—steady, methodical, seemingly relaxed, but with a sixth sense for anything that departed from the ordinary. No doubt this came from his experience as a fighter pilot in World War II, where hours of routine flying at altitude would suddenly explode into frenetic minutes of combat when anything at all might happen, to be followed by another long and usually uneventful leg back to base.

Our trips weren't exactly like wartime, but occasionally the dull, predictable routine would be punctuated by real excitement and, it must be said, real danger. Early on in that drive to Italy, on the second day, we were cruising on the *Nationale 7* when suddenly my father braked rapidly as he thrust his right arm out across my mother's waist, and with his left hand steered the car off the road onto a narrow gravel shoulder. The abrupt lurch of the car and my mother's cry of fear told those of us in the back that something was seriously wrong, but before we had registered the danger, it had passed. What had passed was a truck, bearing down on us head-on in our lane. He had misjudged the time it would take for him to pass and, unable to pull back into his own lane, he drove us off the road. The truck barreled past, honking wildly, as we rolled to a stop on the graveled edge. My brother and I looked out the right side of the car and saw that Dad had judged the distance perfectly. The wheels sat only inches from a steep drop-off to a drainage ditch; had we gone any farther, a serious accident—perhaps a rollover—would have been the certain result. Things were eerily quiet in the car for five or ten seconds as we all took in the near miss. Then, pulling back his outstretched arm and sitting up straight again, my father announced in a voice that mixed lightheartedness and relief, "Well, they didn't get us that time!" I cannot say why exactly, but that line instantly became a family slogan: "Didn't get me that time!" In that mysterious way that big families sometimes have of clarifying the terms of a situation, it distilled for us the brush with fate that could change everything in an instant.

One of France's great advantages, among many, is that its geography is extremely varied. For a country whose surface area is slightly smaller than the state of Texas, it has a phenomenal variety of landscapes, from the rocky coves of Brittany, so like their geological siblings in New England, through the volcanic gorges of the Ardèche, to the mountain redoubts of the Pyrenees and the Alps, right down to the Mediterranean beaches of the Riviera. For parents on a long trip with children, this can spell salvation: a different panorama reveals itself every hour or so in France, and kids are attuned to that. There is nothing in the French landscape akin to driving across Iowa, say, and then Nebraska, where corn becomes an enemy, where the eye seizes upon anything that breaks the horizontal—a water tower, a windmill, a large tree—and then returns, sullen and disappointed, to watchful waiting as the same scenery passes endlessly by.

If there was ever any question about what particular *Nationale* you were on, it didn't last long. Not for more than a kilometer, in fact, because there was a *borne routière* every thousand meters, a stone roadside marker painted white with a red top and the letters of the road—"RN7," say—painted in black against the red. Their shape was exactly that of tombstones—that's in fact what we called them at first—with rounded tops and the distance to the next town painted where the name of the dear departed would have appeared. These are still common on the rural stretches of the remaining *nationales*, but in those days they were everywhere. Imagined after the revolution, at the same time that the French came up with the metric system, they dotted the roads of France with that peculiarly Gallic impulse to measure, to number, and to unify.

We children counted the *bornes* episodically, but there was a lot more to see at the side of the road on the *Nationale 7*. Principally the French. There were roadside restaurants, but they weren't all that numerous, nor were they frequented by most travelers. None of today's "rest areas" waited alongside the road with acres of parking lots, multiple gas pumps, and clean toilets. Instead, you bought supplies—that's what they were called, *des provisions*—in one of the towns, being sure to do so before everyone shut down for lunch from 12:00 to 2:00 p.m. Then if the weather was nice enough (and my mother used to joke that anything other than snow or driving rain was "nice enough" for the French), you pulled off the road onto the grassy margin, threw a blanket on the ground, and had a picnic. Everyone did it. On a sunny day at 1:00 in the afternoon, the sides of a French highway in the fifties looked as if some sort of disaster had struck the area, with many more cars stopped at the edge than moving along the road.

As at any French lunch, a bottle of wine generally made an appearance for the adults in the group. This seems shocking today—drinking on the road!—but these weren't quick stops where everyone wolfed down a sandwich in ten minutes and then got right back on the road. In those days, lunch, *le déjeuner*, was said to *couper la journée*, to cut the day in two, and it really did. Less than an hour was considered hurried, even on a trip, and a nap was often worked in to the break for the driver. Some people sat in their cars, eating and dozing. Others deployed elaborate trays with porcelain and cutlery, as if they were in a restaurant that just happened to be on wheels. There was always a contingent of "campers," who fired up small butane stoves and heated soups and sauces, their blue flames shielded against breezes with a hubcap or a jacket draped across a folding chair. All of this was like another planet to us, and we ogled shamelessly, until my mother told us not to stare.

By the same token, we must have looked strange to the French parked nearby. The Chevy's doors were left wide open, as was the tailgate, and we piled out along with the dog, always on a tight leash to keep him from running into the road. By this time we had been in France for a year, and the American formula of white-bread sandwiches with either bologna or peanut butter and jelly for a filling had long since fallen away. My parents did as the French did: you stopped at a delicatessen, a *charcuterie,* and stocked up on sliced sausage, *saucisson,* and pâtés of various sorts; then a stop at a cheese store, the *fromagerie,* for a large slice of our favorite Emmenthal, the French version of what Americans call Swiss cheese, holes and all; and finally the stop by a bakery, the *boulangerie,* for baguettes. These were often baked just before the lunch hour in larger towns, so you waited in line until they were handed over, warm and smelling like heaven. These were the essential ingredients, along with a few items from a greengrocer, the *épicier*: tomatoes, a head of lettuce, fresh fruit, mayonnaise and mustard in what looked to us like toothpaste tubes, and two liters of bottled water.

After eating, we sometimes played on the grass, though we were strictly forbidden to cross the road. Usually we just walked Kepi, straining at his leash, and dawdled around the other parked cars as we stole glances at their passengers. We kept an eye out for anything new or unusual by the side of the road, and soon we discovered the small markers—usually crosses, sometimes plain slabs of stone—that were placed where there had been a fatal car accident. The names of the victims were invariably inscribed, as was the date of the dreadful event. Occasionally a photo of the person who had died was affixed to the marker, usually a head shot in black and white or sepia somehow printed on a small porcelain oval. Once you knew to look for them, they seemed numerous.

Once, on this same trip to Italy, as we were walking the dog parallel to the road, we came across a stone marker with three little ovals attached to its front—a woman and two girls, their smiling faces like little pansies rising above the surrounding grass. Beneath their portraits were inscribed their names and a date and, beneath that line, four words: *Perdues dans les flammes*—"Lost in the flames." I looked at the words and tried to figure out their meaning, but it didn't make any sense. When we returned to the car, I asked my mother if it meant the three of them had gone to hell. My sense of perdition was still fairly basic, and flames figured prominently in what happened to those who strayed. I remember that she winced at my question, then said, "I'm sure that that mother and her daughters are in heaven now." Then she changed the subject in that way adults had of pretending they had answered when no words could be found to explain the horror of something like a fiery crash.

Aside from collisions, the great fear in those days was that tires would explode. A flat tire was essentially what it is today—a gradual loss of air pressure until the tire goes flat—but a "blowout" at high speed was something else altogether: loud, sudden, and potentially lethal. Tires had inner tubes that sat inside the thick rubber casing and held the compressed air fed into the tube from a mechanical pump through a high-pressure valve. If a car ran over a jagged piece of metal debris, or even a deep pothole, the inner tube could be pierced so quickly that it exploded, "blowing out" the whole tire so that in a split second you were running on a lopsided metal rim rather than inflated rubber.

I remember only two blowouts in all our family trips, but they were terrifying, the kind of shock that kids take in and then endlessly recount with the fervor of those who sense they have been near death. In both cases, my father's reactions were by the book: at the sound of the explosion, which sounds and feels as if you've run over a small land mine, you grab the wheel firmly, countersteer against the loss of pressure and stability, take your foot off the gas, and resist mightily the instinct to slam on the brakes. Strong braking with one entire wheel running on the debris of a ruined tire can precipitate a complete loss of control, a sudden catastrophe that can send the car into the path of oncoming traffic. Instead, you steer the car well off the road and let it roll noisily to a stop.

It took us three days to get to Rome, most of the time spent in the car, of course, but other long hours given over to the elaborate process of pitching the unwieldy surplus tent my dad had wheedled from the quartermaster, then striking, packing, and loading it back onto the car's roof rack the following morning. The first night we stayed in a farmer's field in the foothills outside of Nice. Dad had stopped on a side road of the *Nationale 7* to inquire about campgrounds, and struck up a conversation with two men who were refueling a tractor. Ten minutes later we were unloading the Chevy in a field that alternated deep ruts and long rows of stubble. Now we discovered why the U.S. Army was happy to lend out surplus tents. What came off the roof of the Chevy, once we had unrolled and disentangled it, was a dark brown canvas behemoth known as a squad tent: a square measuring sixteen feet on each side, with four-foot walls and a steep-pitched pyramidal roof that gave it a purposeful air. A huge tangle of lines and fasteners dangled from this dank wad of cloth, and my brothers and I had trouble making any sense of it as we opened it flat over the uneven clumps of stubble. It was murderously bulky and complicated: my dad had great trouble steadying the twelve-foot jointed wooden center pole while the rest of us did our best to pull the canvas taut on all four sides. When at last we managed an approximation of symmetry, each line pulled to the wooden peg that had been pounded into ground about as forgiving as cement, our efforts were rewarded with the sight of a huge "U.S." stenciled in black on two of the four upward-sloping faces of the pyramid roof. This was a tent meant for an invading army, one whose air force would have no trouble identifying it from on high. What those farmers in the uplands of Nice thought about it I can only imagine.

That night we challenged the odds for the south of France in early September, and lost: it rained. We had managed to wrestle seven air mattresses and sleeping bags into the big brown tent, mom had produced pan-fried steak and potatoes, and the frenzy of pitching camp for the first time had at last subsided into a peaceful calm. Everyone was exhausted and soon fell into the deepest of restful sleeps; all was quiet well into the night. At some point I crawled out of my sleeping bag to pee. ("Away from the tent, in the ditch by the road": Dad had laid down the rule after dinner.) I recall with vivid precision two things, and two things only, from my brief foray outside with the shaky flashlight. The first was visual: the night sky was awash with stars, or, rather, half of it was. The other half was hidden by something—what?—that divided the sky into a twinkling riot of light on one side, and a starless void on the other. It felt wrong, but I had no idea why. The second impression was a change in the atmosphere that flooded every corporeal sensation. As I headed back to the tent after doing my business, a sudden wind, cold and piercing, hit the field with a force as sure and frightening as the palm of a giant's hand being swatted across the exposed terrain. The trees at the field's edge rustled loudly, the summer air on my face was instantly an icy draft, bits of leaves and hay whipped through the air. I scurried back to the tent and sensed more than saw its canvas expanse ballooning outward, then quickly deflating, like some enormous bellows fed by a mysterious power. Kepi, whose leash was tied to a stake at the tent's flap, started to howl in a way I had never heard. That should have been a sign.

As I jumped back into the tent, flashlight jiggling and heart fluttering, the air was suddenly charged with a crackling illumination of light, followed instantly by a shot of thunder that shook my bones to the core. Everybody was up: alarmed, fumbling, groaning.

In one of those peculiar misapprehensions familiar to children, I felt as if my stepping back into the tent had somehow *caused* the simultaneous arrival of the storm; I needed to explain. "I just went to pee . . . ," I began feebly, but the inside of the tent had become a place where explanations weren't wanted, or needed. All the flashlights were lit, but their tiny cones of light became ludicrous as lightning turned night into brightest day with increasing frequency. Raised on a farm, my mother respected the power of lightning and sensed danger, not just discomfort. "We can't stay here!" she announced in a clear voice, and my dad added a clipped "You're right about that" and said we'd all "sit it out" in the car.

As we grabbed a few pillows and untied the dog, an eerie moment of calm was followed immediately by a new kind of pandemonium. A downpour opened above our heads—the classic cloudburst—and in an instant the air was suffused with moisture. Being inside the tent was like standing inside a huge drum, its canvas a flapping membrane pelted with furious rain. We hadn't trenched the perimeter of the tent; there had been no need and, in any event, we'd have required a jackhammer to make a dent in the rock-hard ground. Now water began to flow into the tent from one side, the ground softening to a viscous mud as if a plasma shift had just occurred.

The smaller stakes holding down the tent's four walls had by now mostly ripped out, so we cowered below the pulsing pyramid roof as rain whipped in from the sides. In circumstances like these, even children understand the need for quick and lucid action. As one, we poised for flight, my mother carrying my toddler sister, the rest of us grasping whatever was readily at hand. Then together we ran to the car. It can't have been more than twenty-five yards, but by the time we reached it we might as well have plunged headlong into a swimming pool. We scrambled into the car—frightened, excited, and relieved, all at once—and I considered how new and strange it was to discover that the impact of rain on your skin could actually hurt. The noise in the car was deafening, its metal roof far louder than the windswept tent, but we didn't care. Each of us found some dry clothing or bedding in the car, and within a quarter of an hour we had settled in as comfortably as possible, drifting off to occasional lightning flashes that revealed the sorry remains of our tent rising above a small lake.

The next sound we heard was Dad standing outside the car talking to the farmer, the rising sun reflecting off the yellow stone farmhouse in the middle distance. The center pole of our tent still stood, swathed in wet brown canvas like a bedraggled maypole. The sky was a deep, cloudless blue. Slowly we stirred, put down a window, opened a door.

"Ah, Monsieur," the farmer was saying, his two arms raised on either side to shoulder height as he shrugged, *"c'est inhabituel, ce temps-là!"* "This weather is unusual!" He and his wife insisted that we come into their home, warm ourselves, have something to eat. My father knew when to accept a sincere invitation, and soon we were all gathered in the mammoth kitchen of the house, one whole corner given over to an open hearth where a fire crackled. Coffee and cocoa were passed around, fresh bread, butter, and jam were provided by Madame; we took turns using the single bathroom. We looked more like the survivors of a shipwreck than a rainstorm.

Gradually we regained a bit of energy and a bit of humor, too; the storm seemed like another world entirely. As we sat by the fire, munching and sipping, a distant commotion was heard, then died down. Madame cocked her head at an angle, like a bird listening acutely for a worm, and after a second or two she rose to her feet and said with some alarm in her voice, *"Les poules!"* "The chickens!" Just then the commotion approached the house and its constituent elements swiftly became discernible: squawking chickens in panicky flight, and the excited barking of a dog. Now it was my dad's turn: "Where's Kepi?" All eyes swiveled around the room, and the sounds from outside suddenly took on a personal resonance.

Everyone scrambled out the door onto the gravel-covered expanse at the side of the house. Kepi flew by, in active pursuit of a half-dozen chickens, their wings flapping frantically, feet clawing the gravel for purchase as they dashed forward. My dad yelled with imperious anger, but it had no effect whatsoever on the scene. Then, in the fresh morning air, we watched as Kepi lunged with the feral agility of a hunting wolf and caught one of the chickens in his jaws. Everyone froze: the sight of our sweet family dog with a living chicken in his mouth was beyond belief. In fact, it was one of my secret fantasies that Kepi was obliquely related to a pack of wild wolves in northern Europe, part of the great poodle-wolf continuum, a kind of canine sleeper agent using a big American family to cover his true ferocious nature. And here, before me, was the dramatic proof: Kepi cavorting with a squawking chicken at the end of his soft and gentle snout.

He may not have been a wolf, but there was certainly some bird dog in him. Reverting to some atavistic instinct, he now pranced, showing off his prize with high-stepping élan just out of my father's grasp, the wolf/poodle in full display mode. My dad turned away, frustration and disgust playing across his features, but the farmer went down on one knee and spoke to Kepi in a voice you'd have thought was intended for a young child. "*Viens ici, mon chien. Oui, viens ici. Donne-moi ce joli cadeau,*" he cooed. "Come here, boy. Yes, come here. Give me that pretty prize." And it worked. Kepi slowly approached the farmer, surrendering the fluttering bird to his hand. My dad grabbed the dog's collar and gave him a swat, but the farmer protested with a shrug: "*Non, Monsieur. Il n'a fait que ce qu'il sait faire. C'est tout.*" "No, sir. He only did what he knows how to do. That's all." Madame then scooped up the injured bird and went back into the house, cradling it in her arms.

It is impossible to exaggerate the sense of acute embarrassment—shame, really—that now hung in the air. It was, my parents explained for years afterward, one of those situations from which no recovery seems possible: we use your field, accept your hospitality in the face of a storm, and . . . our dog kills your chickens! My father apologized, offered with awkward sincerity to pay for the chickens, and said that we should not trouble our hosts any longer, but Monsieur scoffed good-naturedly at these words and guided us back into the house. "*Ce n'est qu'une poule, après tout!*" "It's only a chicken, after all!" My parents exchanged a doubtful glance, but clearly a rapid flight would have been its own form of insult, and so we filed back into the huge kitchen with its welcoming fire. There we found Madame seated in a straight-back chair, the wounded chicken balanced on her lap, as she drew a line of thread through a large needle.

For the next quarter of an hour, as we finished our breakfast and warmed ourselves, she pulled together two flaps of feathery skin across a large gash in the chicken's breast. While we downed more bread, butter, and jam, Madame concentrated on her work, the chicken emitting occasional clucks. I watched, mesmerized, as the glistening white patch of muscle fascia disappeared beneath feathers. Miraculously, the chicken seemed not too badly injured, and the atmosphere lightened considerably.

After feeding us, the couple insisted that we pull out our wet sleeping bags, spread out the tent, and let everything dry in the now blazing-hot sun. As we worked together, Monsieur told my father that he was delighted to be able to help some Americans. It was, he said, like being able to make a gesture of thanks that was long overdue. It happened that his family was from the farmland outside Draguignan, a town about twenty miles from the coast. In mid-August of 1944, he explained, the invasion of this part of France by the Allies saved him, his parents, and his sisters from the effects of the German occupation that had gone on for years. He himself had been hiding out in the barn to avoid the forced-labor roundups that were common. "And then one fine summer day," he explained, "we got word that the Allies had landed near Fréjus. Within days, a column of American troops made its way up the road past my parents' farm, and the war was as good as over for us."

The invasion of southern France is a lesser-known chapter of World War II in Europe, eclipsed by the momentous D-Day landings in Normandy two months earlier. But its consequences were significant, since within a month the 200,000 troops who landed on the vacation beaches of the Riviera had liberated the entire south of France and driven the Germans up the Rhone Valley and into defensive positions near the Swiss border. In liberating the deepwater ports of Toulon and Marseilles, the American and French armies freed up precious supply facilities to sustain the vast army that had landed in Normandy. Before D-Day the Germans had destroyed the major ports on the English Channel, and the Allied advance against retreating Wehrmacht troops was seriously threatened by critical shortages of fuel, ammunition, weapons, and food. Now supplies flooded into France from the Mediterranean, ensuring that pressure could be maintained in the ensuing battles. French units played an integral part in the invasion of the south under General Jean de Lattre de Tassigny; the French resistance disrupted German communications and supply lines before and during the invasion, which was code-named "Operation Dragoon" by the Allies. Churchill bitterly opposed the whole idea—he favored a move from Italy to the Balkans—and it is said he himself baptized the invasion since he had been "dragooned" into acquiescence. On balance, though, it was an overwhelming success and hastened the push of all German forces out of France.

The farmer's account was direct, intense, and emotional. From the devastating defeat of France in 1940, through the contradictions of the Vichy regime and the direct occupation of the so-called "Free Zone" by the Germans when the Allies invaded North Africa in late 1942, he told us, his family and friends had all been made to drink a bitter cup. *"Et puis, un beau jour, voilà les américains!"* "And then, one fine day, there are the Americans!" His enthusiasm was apparent, as was his gratitude to my father, to our family, to any Americans at all. Dad acknowledged the effusive thanks and mentioned that he had himself flown combat missions from southern Italy, and the farmer stopped and shook his hand for that alone. Mostly, though, as we hauled wet gear from the car and spread it to dry, we listened to this highly personal account of what it had felt like to get your country back. I began to understand that Americans were in a special category when talk turned to *"la guerre,"* and the rules that applied weren't necessarily simple to understand.

Our first few days in Italy were a pure adventure. Before the competition started, we did the tourist circuit of Rome: the Colosseum, the Forum, the Piazza Navona, the Vatican. One morning my dad even drove the Chevy on the Appian Way so we could visit the catacombs. Who takes young children to the Roman catacombs? Everyone, it seems, both then and now. I wasn't traumatized by the experience, but neither did I think of it as fun. There we were, out in the Roman hinterland, the millennial stone slabs of the Via Appia stretching to the horizon flanked by lines of junipers and pines. At various points along the road little booths were set up with flashy signs: *CATACOMBE QUI!* CATACOMBS HERE! Each one was flanked by a guy who looked as if he had sat out in the sun for too long. For a small extra fee our host would "protect" the Chevy, a consideration that hadn't entered my dad's mind until that moment. He paid, and then we walked in out of the sun, and down flight after flight of stone stairs.

The description beforehand of where we were headed—"Open tombs where the early Christians buried their dead outside the walls of Rome"—interested me a lot more than what we in fact found. Once you've seen a skull or two, or an entire skeleton (a rare apparition in the catacombs of the fifties), the effect is neutral, at best. Even a child tires of piles of bones, no matter how old or supposedly imbued with the tragic fate of early martyrs. After half an hour of traipsing by numberless niches, many of them empty, some of them filled with ribs and feet and hands, we children had had it. For that matter, so had my parents.

As we climbed out of the ground and back into the Roman sun, we were all struck by the same sensation, almost physical in its impact: how great to be alive, and in what beautiful surroundings! So the catacombs, for all their inflated buildup, had indeed had an effect, but it was far from poetic. Life against death isn't a tough call, especially in the Italian countryside.

As it happens, Paris has its own catacombs, or so they advertise themselves, but they are far different from their Roman cousins.

Right in the heart of the city at Denfert-Rochereau, they are in fact vast ossuaries to which the remains of several large cemeteries in Paris were removed in the late eighteenth century when the city needed the land for expansion. Most of the bones are relatively recent, then, and they are arranged with a strange, almost theatrical precision: walls of femurs are punctuated with skulls placed at intervals; hundreds of tibias and pelvic bones make up a free-standing mass, as if at the center of a traffic intersection, where the paths of the labyrinthian itinerary converge. And yet this is an attraction that is hugely popular with the tourists. I see them in long, self-policed lines in the late morning, waiting for hours to descend into the relatively modern depths of Paris to look at skeleton parts.

I like to think that, whether in Rome or in Paris, the hordes who climb back out of the catacombs after their tourist "must-see" take the time to look at the sky—any sky, cloudy or clear—and consider how lucky they are that their intact skeleton can carry them to a nearby bar for a stiff drink and a fleeting laugh in the face of the swallowing earth.

Close to the site of the fencing competition, in the new part of Rome developed by Mussolini (called EUR, for *Esposizione Universale Roma*), my father had found a campground with plenty of room. We were given a large plot at the very edge of the property and spent the better part of a day pitching the tent. Now more than ever, the huge "U.S." emblazoned on two faces of the tent's slanting roof was a source of dismay to me and my siblings. We wanted to be like the other campers with their colorful tents of lightweight nylon secured with aluminum stakes.

That first afternoon some sort of large festival was held in the field immediately adjacent to where we had pitched camp with hundreds of revelers, loud music, carnival attractions, and speeches amplified over a public address system. My brothers and I investigated by letting ourselves through one of the many holes in the fence. We discovered that it was a major meeting of the Italian Communist Party, the same ones (we were later told) responsible for the occasional YANKEE GO HOME! that we saw painted on walls. They seemed very friendly to us, though, and invited us back for the party later that night. My mother was always one to take people at face value, but she drew the line since we were staying in a US Army tent. Her logic was impenetrable, and no amount of pleading could change her mind. The next day, though, we collected stickers and flags from our newfound friends, hammer-and-sickle insignia that we squirreled away like so much war booty. These many years later it occurs to me that by those guileless boyhood acts, we had almost certainly qualified ourselves as traitors and subversives in an America where McCarthy's sway was reaching its peak.

CHAPTER 24

PAINTING

My mother was an amateur artist who painted watercolors for as long as I can remember. She had intended to continue art studies after high school, but her parents blocked the way. Not long after she completed nursing school, America entered World War II, and she married my dad nine days after Pearl Harbor. Within a year he was stationed in Hawai'i, and she was raising a newborn in her parents' home. Child rearing and continual moves were the constants in her life for several decades afterward, but she always painted. Along with sewing, it was the only domain that was clearly her own, and it was an essential way for her to express creativity and play a part in a tradition that she deeply respected.

Fontainebleau in the fifties was a good place to be if you had a painter's eye. The masterpieces of Paris—Old Masters, Impressionists, medieval art, Cubists—were an hour away. Closer to home, the village of Barbizon lay on the edge of the forest, just a few miles from Fontainebleau, and it was the center of a long tradition of painting in the nineteenth century. When the railroad provided easy access in the 1850s, painters made their way from Paris to the *Forêt de Fontainebleau*. It began with the fairly bucolic Barbizon School painters: Millet, Corot, Daubigny. They were followed by some of the most illustrious Impressionists—Monet, Renoir, Sisley—who painted in and around the forest. Small museums and artists' ateliers were still part of the landscape when we arrived, though tourists had also invaded in the early twentieth century. My mom took us to Barbizon a few times, but she found the attitude overly precious, she later explained, and the town full of well-off people pretending to be artists.

The other great advantage for an artist was ready access to the countryside itself. Outside the forest, the landscape of the region known as *Seine-et-Marne* was one of rolling hills given over to agriculture. Secondary and tertiary roads threaded between the fields, connecting towns and villages, often flanked on both sides for a mile or two with lines of poplars or plane trees whose trunks bore wide bands of white paint. For much of the year these stretches would be like long tunnels of green, the overarching branches forming a broken cover through which sunlight filtered in dappled abandon. It was the same countryside of northern France that nineteenth- and twentieth-century artists made familiar to the world: an affair of gentle contours, stands of trees punctuating the plowed fields like islands, and always the villages on the near horizon with a gray stone steeple rising in a squared mass above the church.

When she had a free hour or two—not a frequent occurrence, and often at an unexpected moment—my mom would take one or two of us with her in the car and head out of town for a few miles. There she would pull onto the grassy edge of a two-lane country road with very little traffic and set up her stool and a lapboard. Often she sat in the middle of poppies or Queen Anne's lace or mustard shoots—whatever was flowering and growing. Her paint box open at her side, a jar of water at her feet, she then attended to the magic of reproducing what she saw with brushes, paint, and water. I sometimes watched closely but I never cracked the code, forever astounded that what started as a few smudges on the paper would soon reveal clouds or a stone bridge or a line of deep furrows in the fragrant turned earth that surrounded us.

Those stops were usually brief—twenty minutes to half an hour—so we kids sometimes played in the nearby fields, or along a stream if one ran nearby. Often, though, we waited in the car and played there. The Chevy's interior was like a big playroom when it was parked. A favorite game consisted of lying flat on the front or back seat with our legs propped up and feet sticking out the open windows. Then, in the quiet of the countryside, we'd listen for an approaching vehicle, a fairly infrequent event. Aside from birdsong and the thrum of insects, along with the distant echo of an occasional tractor, the air was calm, so another car was easy to hear.

When we heard one coming, we vibrated with excitement, our feet risking being ripped off, as we saw it, when the car passed. In truth, we couldn't manage to stick our feet more than a few inches out the window; the door handles and rearview mirror extended much farther than our limbs from the side of the car. My mother always pulled well off the road, so the exercise was pure childhood fantasy.

But it was our thrill and our delight to imagine that we were in imminent danger of being dismembered, as if a supersonic jet were about to buzz our car. As the sound grew and a car at last passed with a whoosh, we cried out with glee, "Didn't get me that time!" The imagined danger, the miraculous survival, the promise of more to come: all fueled our notion of drama as mom painted quietly on the other side of the car.

Knowing of my mother's passion for watercolors, Mademoiselle de Chêneville introduced her to an older gentleman who had spent a lifetime as a professional artist—both as a painter and a teacher—and whose specialty was *aquarelles,* watercolors. Monsieur Villeneuve was an aged widower, courtly without being stiff, and my mother liked him right away. He spoke in a slow, clear cadence, and my mom found that she understood most of what he had to say about painting and other matters, too. A neatly trimmed white beard gave him an air of distinction, and he always wore a dark gray suit, a tie, and a felt hat with a slouching brim.

My mom soon decided to hire him for occasional private lessons. He came to the house and they would assemble their materials, side by side, and set about painting the same scene or group of objects. About those pairs of paintings my mother used to joke, "Even when mine was passable, his was a masterpiece!" It was clear he had real talent, and she learned a lot from him about the craft of watercolors since he still embodied the rich tradition that had developed in and around Fontainebleau.

Over time my mother discovered that Monsieur Villeneuve was not only living on his own but getting by on very little. He was glad to have the fees my mom paid for her lessons, but it was hardly enough to make a difference. She knew, also, that a gift of money or things would be an assault on his dignity and had to be ruled out. It was Mademoiselle de Chêneville who proposed a way for my mom to help: commission a series of paintings of Fontainebleau that she would want to take back to America when we left. It turned out to be a good arrangement all around. Monsieur Villeneuve had another supplement to his meager income, and my mom would have images of France painted by an artist she knew and respected.

He was good at painting all sorts of things, but he was particularly good at buildings. This is far from obvious for a watercolorist. If the architecture's lines and facets are too vague, the edges blurry, then it reads as an impression of a building, and nothing more. On the other hand, if the brushwork is too fussy, the lines too precise, then it undermines the true appeal of watercolor as a medium: its very fluidity should suggest the particulars without detailing them. It's a very tough balance to strike, and Monsieur Villeneuve did it superbly well.

Two of the paintings have a special resonance. One shows the monumental doorway to the Henri IV wing of the Château, where my dad had his office. It's an impressive work of architecture, surely—instantly recognizable. But there is also a mood to its stonework and the play of light that are perfectly captured with an economy of means. The other painting is our house as seen from across the garden. Better than any photograph, it reveals the *grand bourgeois* pretentions of the court official who built it, using the conceit of a small château as a model. But it also shows the seductive, and very French, attractiveness of the garden, its meandering gravel-covered paths and sun-splashed expanses of grass, surrounded by informal but well-maintained trees and shrubs along the perimeter.

Of all the un-busy details in that painting, my mother always marveled at the way he treated the trees and bushes on one side. A line of mature chestnut and fir trees extend along the stone wall, with a clipped privet hedge below. A full range of greens and blues and yellows are arrayed to depict the foliage, pine needles, fresh growth, branches, sunlight, and yet when you hold it close and inspect it, the forms don't seem to be there. Only when you hold it at arm's length do the layered colors magically resolve into all the structure involved in trees and bushes. And yet there are very few brushstrokes, each one deftly placed in sequence. "Any artist would have been proud to paint those trees as he did," my mom always said, and I'm sure she was right.

I remember when Monsieur Villeneuve spent an afternoon in our garden working on that painting. He had substituted a broad-brimmed straw hat for the felt, but he kept his suit coat on though the sun was blazing. I was playing in the yard, riding my bike along the paths, curious to see what he was doing, but each time I rode by there was nothing on the paper. For a long while—it must have been the better part of an hour—he looked at the house, and then he looked some more. Then, as I rode by again, he picked up his brush and set to work.

Within twenty minutes he had filled the paper with paint and captured our house in a moment that is both familiar and unique. When I look at it now, it occurs to me that he must have concentrated all his attention for that hour or so of seeming inaction. Whether or not he was conscious of it, he had planned the sequence of his brush strokes. Then he entered the zone of imagination and some urgency where he could bring to bear the full force of his experience, his instinct, and his talent. The result was an image not just of our house, but of the home we made during those three years.

CHAPTER 25

NAPOLEON I

No French ruler is more closely identified with Fontainebleau than Napoleon. There is a paradox here: those who keep track of such things tell us that in his ten years as emperor of the French, he spent a total of 150 days at his favorite château, whereas Marie Antoinette stayed there for 444 days. But then, Napoleon was nothing if not original. Very often he was away on yet another military campaign, thrashing the armies of Europe's kings and teaching them a lesson in military genius.

When he decided to proclaim himself emperor in 1804, Fontainebleau became an essential part of his dynastic pretensions. He gave Versailles a wide berth; it was too closely associated with the *Ancien Régime* of the Bourbons, too freighted with the excesses that led to the revolution, too big and unwieldy and relentlessly formal. When First Consul Bonaparte became Emperor Napoleon, he needed a palace other than Versailles or the Louvre that would closely associate him with the long line of Valois and Bourbon kings. The Château of Fontainebleau nicely filled the bill.

During the revolution, the Château, like all royal residences, was sacked, its furnishings sold, stolen, or simply destroyed. Napoleon ordered new furniture and had several wings fitted out with apartments worthy of an imperial court. The new style, character-

monarchists but to the French themselves. Born and raised on the island of Corsica into a clan of local gentry, only the happenstance of an appointment to the Royal Military School in Paris steered him toward a France he had loathed in his boyhood. For a decade and more he prevailed against all odds as the most prodigious leader in Europe; then his luck ran out, and with it, apparently, his sense of political strategy. The end came at Fontainebleau.

After the disastrous campaign in Russia in 1812 and the defeat at Leipzig in 1813, Napoleon's marshals refused to follow him. On April 6, 1814, he abdicated in a small office at Fontainebleau. Two weeks later he bade farewell to his troops at the foot of the monumental staircase in the *Cour d'Honneur,* ever since known as the *Cour des Adieux,* the Courtyard of Farewells. He was ridiculed by his enemies as the emperor of Elba, his place of exile, a speck of an island off the coast of Italy not far from his native Corsica.

Once again they misjudged the man. A year later he was back, landing on the Mediterranean coast of France, raising an army as he marched north. He spent one day at Fontainebleau. History does not record what he did there, but—as with so much else around him—it would be the last time he laid eyes on what had been a home. These were the famous *Cent Jours,* the One Hundred Days, three months that ended at Waterloo. There followed a second abdication—this one at the Louvre—and a second, definitive, exile on St. Helena.

From that faraway prison island he dictated his memoirs, including his now-famous description of Fontainebleau: "*Voilà la vraie demeure des rois, la maison des siècles.*" "There stands the true abode of kings, a house for the ages." There's some hyperbole in that assessment, surely, but there is poetry, too. Napoleon was that strange and suspect creature in France, *un ambitieux,* an ambitious climber. Even today the French reserve a special place for *ambition.*

If not exactly a dirty word, it is nonetheless frowned upon as the refuge of those without real substance. But Napoleon crowned his overriding ambition with success after success, breaking the mold of an ancient line of kings whose only claim to rule was the accident of birth.

He certainly recognized a dramatic setting when he saw it, and Fontainebleau perfectly suited his search for legitimacy as the new French sovereign, more powerful by far than all his predecessors. Among the many pithy pronouncements that are ascribed to him is this one: "I found the crown of France in the gutter, and I picked it up. . . ." His imperious, and imperial, rule paradoxically furthered some of the ideals of the revolution, and changed Europe forever. A nostalgia for glory as the agent of change permeates Fontainebleau to this day, and it is the creation of Napoleon Bonaparte.

CHAPTER 26

THE STAIRCASE OF FAREWELLS

The project of restoring the Château's nineteenth-century Second Empire theater is elaborate, and will require years of work. Patrick Ponsot determined that he needed his own workshop in the Château so that his crew could construct and refine the major architectural details outside the theater itself, leaving that space clear for major structural work. He invited me to visit the area that was being adapted as a workshop for the theater's restoration; in effect, a staging area. Together with half a dozen of his colleagues, I donned a hard hat and climbed the tubular steel ladder built into the external scaffolding of one of the Château's principal Renaissance wings, *L'Aile de la Belle Cheminée*, the Wing of the Beautiful Hearth, designed in 1565 by Primaticcio. A winter wind spat rain in our faces as we slowly made our way up to the third and final floor, then stepped through one of the towering windows to the vast attic, over three thousand square feet of open space beneath the steeply pitched roof.

Coming in out of the weather was welcome, and the amount of light that flooded the space through huge skylights and windows, even on a rainy day, was truly magical. A dozen workers—masons, carpenters, plumbers, electricians—were transforming the expanse so that period architectural details could be fashioned at work stations throughout the floor. This was but the latest of several transformations. In 1856 a fire had gutted the floor below as well as the attic, and the damaged wing was closed up and not used for decades. Then in 1924 John D. Rockefeller gave money to rebuild it; the top floor was subsequently used by the newly founded American School of Music and Fine Arts. Now it was being refashioned for yet another temporary purpose.

On one side, the windows looked down on the *Cour de la Fontaine,* the Courtyard of the Fountain. The other view was across Andre Le Nôtre's extensive formal gardens to the long, canal-shaped basin and the edge of the forest. As I marveled at the patterns below, both in stone and in flowers and shrubs, it occurred to me that this was one of the highest points in the Château.

After Ponsot had made the rounds with each of the work crews and explained his choices and priorities for the week's work, we descended a narrow but graceful service staircase. "It dates from the 1750s," Ponsot told me. "It's the only part of the wing that wasn't consumed by the fire." Even here a certain elegance prevailed: the treads and landings were paved in wine-red hexagonal tiles; the banister was fashioned from a continuous rail of oak, worked in sinuous curves down the three flights and set firmly on perfectly proportioned forged iron vertical supports. This, too, is France, where a secondary staircase can still command fine work.

Our group took its time descending the narrow passage, and I realized that the large architectural elements to be built in the atelier we had just visited could never be taken down to ground level via this route. I asked Ponsot how he would bring them down. "*Comme les déménageurs, par la fenêtre,*" he said, as if it were self-evident. "Like furniture movers, we'll take them out by the window."

Inwardly I winced, but I knew it was my own exaggeration in

the face of a standard French practice that triggered the reaction. When you move apartments in Paris—and in other old city centers—the stairways are typically too narrow to take furniture down. The solution, for getting things both in and out again, is to come through the apartment's largest window. In Haussmannian Paris, the height limit is seven stories. (Baron Haussmann was the prefect of Paris under Napoleon III who rebuilt the entire center city in a late-nineteenth-century style that still bears his name.) For anything from the second to the seventh story, the moving company sets up a kind of inclined elevator that rises from the sidewalk. It looks like a ladder, but the two side rails are fitted with a motorized four-by-eight-foot platform that lies in the same plane as the sidewalk and rises or lowers as a unit. Onto this precarious perch are placed a family's belongings, and the up-and-down of the furnishings goes on for hours as the moving van is filled or emptied.

There are many ways in which my earliest instincts and reactions are those of the French, but this is not one of them. The whole operation appears to me impossibly dangerous, and every time I see them at work on the streets of Paris—a frequent occurrence—I steer clear. No history of disaster or reputation for recklessness conditions my attitude; I just see falling tables and squashed people and cars where Parisians see nothing more remarkable than house movers at work. The one time we moved house in Paris, from a Haussmannian apartment on the fourth floor on a blustery day, I had to leave the neighborhood for the duration rather than imagine the mayhem that our bedstead could cause as it was blown from its tiny perch. All went as planned, without incident. Now, to hear that the entire output of the theater's workshop would be lowered to the Château courtyard in like manner struck me as strangely appropriate. And singularly French. All will be well, but I won't be there to watch.

At the bottom of the staircase, and again along the hallways below, our group kept telescoping against locked doors, then waited for Ponsot to come forward with his weighty bunch of keys, of all shapes and sizes, to let us through. He rarely chooses the wrong key, though each lock requires that its own body language be brought to bear before opening with a satisfying "click!"

The hidden delights of a château the size of Fontainebleau are manifold, and frequently surprising. One of the locked hallways we passed through, well away from the tourist circuit, was lined with exquisite carved walnut paneling with coats of arms worked in bas relief. Those of Henri II (three crescents, fashioned as a symmetrical triskele akin to the purity of an Art Deco design) alternate with those of his wife, Catherine de Medici (the familiar six balls of Florence). Seeing me looking closely at the artistry, Ponsot said, "It's beautiful work, but we're not entirely sure of their provenance, or even when they were carved." My surprise showed, and he added, "There are a lot of things like that in a big house full of objects that have been handed down." He smiled and moved on, and I began to see the proportions of his task in a new light.

Confronted with a discrete restoration project like Napoleon III's office, say, the choices are limited to the era under question and seem relatively straightforward. But then one considers the history of the Château as a royal residence and, subsequently, as a public museum that also serves as a repository of national art, architecture, and even a certain idea of France. Looked at in that way, the scale and the complication of all the collections can quickly become crippling when a clear and lucid presentation of things is the goal. I realized that one of Ponsot's chief attributes, in addition to being highly organized and widely knowledgeable, is to keep projects moving forward by refusing distractions. The carved panels with their coats of arms may be of real importance, or they may not, but such a consideration is irrelevant to Ponsot's current projects. For now they are safe, and that is enough until the question arises out of necessity.

As I considered all these precious objects, whether hidden or on display, I understood that the entire process of restoration appealed to me because it sprang from a basic impulse that one sees every day in France. The French don't like throwing things away. Not, that is, if it can be repaired, restored, or otherwise saved. Whether it's a good coat, an old table, or an ancient château, the tradition of refurbishing valued possessions is deep seated. Paris is still full of *retouches,* or small tailor shops where clothes can be taken in, the lining replaced, the material itself rewoven to make small holes disappear. Similarly, an *ébéniste,* a specialty carpenter, can repair and strengthen almost any piece of furniture using cuts of exotic wood to match the original elements. Handing down tables, chairs, and *armoires* within the family is quite common.

So it is no surprise that the French have been restoring their principal public buildings for a long time. The most famous of the nineteenth-century architect-restorers, Eugène Viollet-le-Duc, has since been criticized for his aggressive "interpretations" of medieval architecture (the Cathedral of Notre-Dame of Paris was his most famous project), but the impulse to save masterworks from further degradation was always at the core of his work. This philosophy survives and flourishes in France, and Fontainebleau has been one of its chief beneficiaries, though today there exists a greater concern about the competing claims of a long and varied past. Seen this way, the entire apparatus of Ponsot's team strikes me as a kind of traditional recycling, a notion I find fundamentally reassuring.

We emerged from the locked back corridors into the public area, and total silence reigned: Fontainebleau is closed to the public on Tuesdays and we had the place to ourselves. We made our way up the King's Staircase, suitably regal in its cavernous proportions and luxurious materials, principally marble and frescoes. The staircase was built for Louis XV in 1749 in the space that had originally been the bedchamber of François I's mistress, the Duchess of Etampes, and so the ceiling dates from the 1540s. As we mounted the stairs, we passed underneath the unimaginably rich sculptures fashioned by the Italian Renaissance artist Primaticcio, a baroque dream of carnal delights that originally graced this most private of spaces.

The walls and ceiling are alive with white plaster statuary, larger than life, mostly of female nudes and cherubs in hedonistic profusion. Fat bunches of fruit and swags of laurel garlands festoon the languid poses of these beauties, at once sensual and inviting. This was the first great expression of late Renaissance décor in northern France, and the mix of Italian artistry and French abandon draws you in with the power of seduction. The elaborate celebration of the pleasures of the flesh recall the smiling figures that cover certain Hindu temples where the crowd of bodies is both erotic and serene.

I caught up with Ponsot in the *Galerie François I*, the exceptional art-filled corridor that lies at the heart of the Château one flight above ground level. Measuring two hundred feet long by twenty wide, this gallery was the work of both Rosso and Primaticcio in the 1530s. Many consider it the sublime expression of the Renaissance in northern Europe. The same voluptuous sculptures stretch on both sides to the far end, now flanking a series of exquisite frescoes that tell the allegorical tale of a king's duties. It is said that François I kept the key to this gallery around his neck, and admitted only a select few to this closely guarded repository of Italian art. You can understand why when you stroll its length.

These spaces are ordinarily open to visitors, who enter on the ground floor, then ascend an interior staircase to walk through the *Galerie François I*; then they can visit all the state apartments used by the endless succession of kings named Louis, the Bonapartes (both of them), and even a pope (Pius VII) when he was Napoleon's prisoner. Tuesdays are the only days when major work can be done in areas that the public usually visits. An advantage of accompanying the chief architect and his clutch of keys on the one day the public is excluded, however, is that one can pass through any door Ponsot chooses, even one that is ordinarily closed on the guided tour.

We entered the vestibule that lies just inside the Château's main door, Ponsot produced a key, *et voilà*! We walked out onto the landing that lies at the top of the double-horseshoe staircase. Tourists can mount the staircases and stand outside on the broad stone porch, and they also pass through the interior vestibule on their visit of the Château. But it must be said that walking through that door itself is something special. In all my many years of visiting Fontainebleau, I had never once seen it open, and here we were walking through, just like that. From a somber inner space, you exit to light, space, and height. It occurred to me that this was the path Napoleon took when he bade farewell to his troops. On the *piano nobile*, you're one story up with two broad staircases rising from the courtyard in sinuous curves worked in carved stone, with you at the center. It is a transition a ruler would appreciate, quite literally like walking on stage: a door opens and you pass from the personal interior to the theater of the court, the focal point of an entire architectural scheme.

It was a perk I never expected, and no one else in our small group seemed surprised or even all that interested in our route.

They do this all the time, I realized; it's necessary for their work. In the nature of these things, it was over almost before I was aware of our exit onto the balcony, but it was a lovely moment for one who had always seen that double-horseshoe staircase as leading to a locked door.

CHAPTER 27

SPAIN

After the trip to Italy, camping became part of the landscape for our weekend excursions and longer vacations. We made short trips to the beaches in Brittany (rain, sun, more rain, and sand in absolutely everything), and forays to see the châteaux of the Loire and of Burgundy. I can tell you that the picturesque fog that forms along the Loire at dawn is a bone-chilling plunge into pure humidity when you're stumbling your way to the campground's communal toilets.

We weren't as impressively equipped as some of the families, but we were getting there. Gone were the unwieldy surplus tents stenciled with "U.S." and the massive wooden posts, replaced by a state-of-the-art Dutch model that was light, easy to put up and take down, and truly weatherproof. The sectional poles and stakes were all of lightweight aluminum, and the longer outer rain shell sheltered two separate inner tents—like two bedrooms—that were separated by a covered space. The drudgery of pitching the field tent was a thing of the past; instead of soldiers on bivouac, we felt like we had luxurious accommodations.

The French had a pared-down attitude to camping that we never mastered, or even tried to adopt. Perhaps there were just too many of us, or maybe the Chevy just had too much room for "extras." Four or five people would emerge from their tiny cars and proceed to put up a neat nylon tent with one of each essential, and nothing more, arrayed for each person: one cup, one metal plate, one set of folding cutlery, one sleeping bag, and on and on. They had a no-nonsense, almost abstemious approach to the undertaking, part of the legacy of the Gallic version of Boy Scouts (pronounced "scoots" in French) that is far more associated with Catholic religiosity and a certain do-gooder mentality than in the United States. Somehow they would always manage to fashion a table, and they'd sit together and eat cold cuts, soup, cheese, and bread as if it were a feast, the blue glow of their butane camp stove lighting their features from one side. In the evening the young people sang songs together, softly but earnestly, and occasionally we'd hear one or another group murmuring prayers. This shocked me as I recognized a cadence and a susurration that I had always associated with church.

We sometimes met other kids along the paths and, as our French got better, we'd talk with them. Invariably they wanted to know about us—where we were from, what we were doing here, what we ate—as if we were so insanely exotic that we must subsist on other food entirely. In fact, we had the great good fortune to be able to mix with the French and do as they did on vacation, and yet still remain ourselves: Americans in a big, strange-looking American car. At times we didn't see it as an advantage; we kids would at first have been happy to be cocooned in comfortable hotels and do our version of the grand tour. But the savings of campgrounds, and the autonomy of having our own car to visit the different regions, meant we fashioned this hybrid form of camping. Not only did it not hinder us, it allowed us to know Europe in a way that was entirely different from the conventional tourist experience.

Our next big trip after Rome was a two-week visit to Spain the following summer. Our path over the Pyrenees took us through Lourdes. This cannot have been a coincidence. We were headed to the Mediterranean coast and Lourdes lies inland, but my father pretended this was a happy turn of fate and we would simply "stop by" Lourdes. Bad call, Dad! Lourdes is not a place you visit lightly. There are so many others visiting it at the same time that subsistence, if not survival itself, becomes an essential piece of the undertaking. It's a pilgrimage site, and who knew there were so many pilgrims in this world? Renowned for the apparitions in 1858 of the Virgin Mary to Bernadette Soubirous, a fourteen-year-old local girl, the town is all but overrun by visitors. In all of France, only Paris has more hotels, and more than five million faithful make the pilgrimage each year.

We stayed one day and one night, and the images for a child were not those of religious transcendence. I had never seen so many people on crutches or in wheelchairs, or just generally old and unhealthy in a visible way. In one of the shrines we visited, people had abandoned their crutches after a "miraculous" response to their prayers, and they were hung from the ceiling of the church in their dusty thousands. I can't be sure why, but it was a very menacing sight, deeply spooky in its strangeness.

The grotto itself was a colossal disappointment. After hearing how Mary had showed up eighteen times for a girl the age of my older sister, I expected a glow, at least, from the place that was regarded as holy. We shuffled forward endlessly with others, and finally got close to see this: a shallow cave of gray rock that resembled dirty cake frosting, with a simple niche about twenty feet above the ground into which was set a statue of Mary holding a rosary. I recall very clearly thinking, when we stood below the dank wall, "That's *IT*?!?" Faith is a mystery, and in those days I still believed, but nothing about this place seemed holy or particularly special.

Another surprise was the puny river, *Le Gave de Pau*, that ran alongside the grotto and was the source of the miraculous water that was piped into spigots throughout the grounds. It sometimes turns into a roaring torrent during heavy rains, but in the ordinary course of things it's a placid stream. The creek that ran across my grandparents' farm was far bigger than this watercourse, and a lot more inviting for a summer swim. Pilgrims filled numberless bottles from the faucets, then swigged down the contents for relief if not salvation, as if they craved a new kind of drunkenness from plain water.

The one thing I loved was the candles. Indoors and out, there were thousands of tiny flames flickering, even in daytime. I had never imagined so many candles! Inside the churches, between the clouds of incense and the candle smoke, the atmosphere was intoxicating. Thinking this was surely an instance of youthful exaggeration, amplified as I tried to remember, I checked the current statistics, and the numbers are in fact astounding. Over three million candles are sold to pilgrims each year; that's seven hundred tons. The Church has a monopoly on their manufacture and sale.

Before heading back to the campground, we participated in a nighttime "rosary procession" with many thousands of others. Each pilgrim carried a long white candle with a four-sided wind baffle made of thick paper to protect the flame. On its four faces were printed the lyrics of the hymn to Mary: *"Ave, ave, ave Maria!"* This we chanted together, over ten thousand strong, full-throated and fervid in our unison.

Groups from throughout the Catholic world carried multicolored banners which swayed overhead, lighted by the sea of candles as we made our way across the broad plaza to the basilica that was designed for crowds. My dad liked it; my mom did not. The spectacle enchanted me—all those candles in the dark!—and I was captivated by the powerful spell of singing with thousands of others, over and over the same melody praising Mary, praising the very idea of her. It was glorious in the full sense of that word, but I have long since decided to give a wide berth to any such mammoth displays: sports cheering, political slogans, religious ardor of this sort. Something about the grouped mass of others, all united in their passion, is both seductive and disturbing.

The road we took over the Pyrenees was anything but the main route. There were no divided highways to Spain in those days, but good two-lane roads led over the mountains at several points. Not for us, though; my dad was intent on taking "local roads," which meant roads that grew increasingly narrow as one climbed into the mountains. My mother had a lifelong fear of heights, and she protested when two lanes shrank gradually to one. Worst of all, no guardrails separated the macadam from sheer drops of five hundred to a thousand feet. If there was any question of the dangers involved (and there certainly was not for my reasonable mom), small crosses had been erected at intervals—intervals that shortened as you climbed higher. They bore the Spanish version of Catholic imagery that honored those lost, just like the crosses along the French roadsides marking the place of accidents.

It's true that there was very little traffic on this tiny road, carved into the bare flank of the mountain. But then it didn't take much traffic to block passage altogether; one vehicle sufficed. The standard procedure was for the vehicle traveling uphill to back down to a slight widening of the road, where one could squeeze past the other. Under pressure, you were confronted with the phenomenal difficulty of backing down a narrow mountain road, a maneuver that demanded a sure hand on the wheel, a delicate foot on the brakes, and nerves of steel.

The worst moment came when we were blocked by a descending truck; the two drivers of the truck determined that it would be far more dangerous for us to back our car down than to turn it around in the width of the road. They were locals and knew every twist of the mountain, and they carefully eyeballed the Chevy's overall length as well as its wheelbase (the distance between its two axles). There was just enough room, they assured my dad. My mother objected, in vain; she had us all pile out and hug the rock cliff on the inner side of the road, a short way down the grade.

Paralyzed with both excitement and fear, we watched as my dad turned our station wagon inches at a time under the whispered supervision of the two Spanish truck drivers. When he had gotten the Chevy fully perpendicular to the road, its nose was touching the rock face and its tail actually stuck out over the void. There can't have been more than a couple of feet between the back tires and oblivion. Gently, he continued the operation by tiny degrees—back and forth, back and forth, turning the wheel by minuscule increments (no power steering!). My mom gave a little whimper of fear and, no doubt, rage. We were all scared for Dad in what seemed an endlessly extended point of danger, but my mother's anxiety must also have given way to a more practical thought, on the order of this: "He's going over the edge with that car, leaving me with five children to raise on my own!"

Once over the mountains, we headed for the beach, a small fishing town called Palamos on the Mediterranean *Costa Brava*. All the other vacationers we ran into were Spanish, and the area was not crowded; only a few other families were using the campground. In the evenings we'd go to informal restaurants that were really houses with a room or two added on and the women of the family cooking in a big kitchen. They were always glad to see us and made a fuss over the kids, with lots of older girls ready to dote on my younger sister and me.

"Do you have only the five?" One exuberant lady greeted us with this apparently sincere question as she watched us filling up a large round table. It wasn't quite disappointment that colored her voice, but there was a form of concern there. My mother later repeated this line at times with a wild smile on her face, as if to remind herself that things might, in fact, have been even more complicated. Only the five.

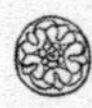

After a week at the beach, we spent the rest of our vacation in Barcelona. This consisted of two things: numberless churches and endless bullfights. I'm not sure what led my parents to think of bullfights as suitable family entertainment. In the fifties it was inseparable from the very idea of Spain; Hemingway, Picasso, and Hollywood stars were regularly photographed in the stands. Like many of their generation, my parents had read *Death in the Afternoon,* Hemingway's paean of praise for what was regarded as a mythic confrontation, unique in the modern world. Whatever the reason, we went to the *corrida* as a family.

First false step: my dad had no way of knowing that the cheaper seats were cheaper because they were on the sunny side of the arena, and the July sun in Barcelona can be brutal. We baked in the sun, taking it all in. At first it seemed like a different kind of circus: entrance parade, band with trumpets, guys in shiny clothes with strange hats and shoes, horses prancing. Then things got serious in a hurry, and stayed that way. The bull entered, full of pride and energy, running around at first, then confronting the matador and his assistants as he rushed their capes. This was exciting the first time: nothing bad happened, the men moved like special kinds of dancers as they dodged the bull's horns, the crowd roared.

Soon, though, the atmosphere changed. Every time a man entered the arena he did something hurtful to the bull: the guy on horseback thrusting his lance in his shoulder muscle, the runners with colorful spiked sticks who stuck him in the same place, and ultimately the matador himself with his sword hidden in folds of silk. The *picador*'s horse was clearly terrified, no matter that he was encased in a mattress-like covering and his eyes hooded. The *banderilleros* ran like deer, and always seemed about to be caught when they scooted behind the panels of wood that protected them. I wanted them to get away, but I wanted them to stop hurting the bull, too. Every time, the bull ended up with more hooks stuck in his back and more blood streaming down his shoulder muscle, neck, and back. Soon I was on the side of the animals. Let the horse get out safely! Let the bull escape! But everyone seemed to accept that that wasn't part of the deal.

A single *corrida* featured six bulls with three different bullfighters; we went to several. Inevitably we saw a lot of blood, and a lot of death, too. Mistakes happened. A *picador*'s horse was rammed against the wall, then the bull got his horns under the protective covering and the horse was disemboweled as the bull went wild, trapping horse and rider from below. A *banderillero* slipped as he stuck his barbs in the bull, and the wounded animal gored him badly as we watched. His pant leg of green silk and silver embroidery darkened rapidly, soaked with his blood, before his comrades could carry him off. At the moment of truth, a matador misjudged the thrust of his sword and the blade entered the bull's torso without wounding him mortally. The animal stood, dazed and paralyzed as blood poured from his mouth. I understood that the men could be injured, too—even killed. Death on all sides.

After the bull had been killed—and if it was a "good" kill—the matador walked around the circumference of the arena accepting the crowd's acclaim and bestowing the symbols of his prowess. An ear sliced from the bull's head, perhaps two; a tail if it was special. And then, most exceptionally, an entire hoof; this we actually saw once. At our first bullfight the matador had been awarded two ears, and I didn't understand what was then to happen. He circled, waving, smiling, then suddenly tossed an ear into the crowd at a smiling *señorita*. I had seen the way American baseball crowds went after balls hit as home runs or even foul balls, but this was a whole different order of business. She caught it and waved to him, brandishing the ear as a token of respect. One ear remaining in his hand, the matador continued his progress, his suit a dazzle of lights as he approached our part of the stands. Then he spied my blond sister, smiled at her, and flung the ear at our row.

Nothing approaches the effect of a thrown bull's ear headed toward you: furry and large, strands of streaming blood trailing along with it, a strange and terrifying projectile (unless, it seems, you happen to be Spanish). We all recoiled, and a man next to us caught it with panache. With unaffected chivalry, he offered it to my sister, but she declined the honor. Murmurs came from among those in nearby rows, and the matador moved on to continued applause.

I left the bullfights confused. I knew that this was a bloody sport, "cruel" even, by usual standards. But these weren't usual standards. I didn't understand the reason for it, but I sensed that something was very different from any other "sport" I had seen, something that captured the crowd's attention as if together they formed a single person. The bullfighter usually walked away unharmed as a pair of horses dragged the bull's carcass from the arena and the trumpets blared. But occasionally the matador died, too, or was badly injured. This possibility was surely the very thing that made the whole undertaking so stirring, and even attractive, in a way that was troubling.

Years later when I returned to Spain, I declined to attend a *corrida*. I had seen enough to know that something powerful and compelling was being played out, a blood feud that was real and yet that didn't feel like it was my fight. Watching as an outsider now seemed like a puny intrusion on a matter I couldn't pretend to understand. It occurred to me that those hours I spent in the Barcelona *corrida* as a boy were as close as I was ever likely to get to the world of antiquity: brutal, direct, captivating, and fundamentally different from what we call our worldview.

As we made our way out of the arena with thousands of other spectators, we happened to be in a side street that sheltered the bullfighters' entrance, a kind of stage door for the principals—*matadors, banderilleros, picadors*—and their extended retinues who maintained them on the circuit of *corridas*. Inevitably there was interest from an adoring public, anxious to catch a glimpse of a favorite. People lingered near the guarded door, hoping for an autograph or a hurried word with their idol.

My eye was drawn to the matadors' cars, a half-dozen old limousines from the thirties that looked like something that Al Capone might have ridden in. Big squared-off cars with massive front fenders that swooped back from shiny chrome grilles, their passenger compartment was like a small room with comfortable bench seats facing both forward and back on a few. Highly polished black or brown, they were like an apparition to me, who loved seeing new and unusual automobiles. I counted a massive Hispano-Suiza, and several other impressive cars, a grouping of old-fashioned vehicles like something out of a time machine. Several had roof racks, and on these were strapped, upright, large clay pitchers of wine, corked and wrapped in rope.

Now handlers started to load the cars, and a matador's "suit of lights" was carried with a reverent air in a transparent bag. It shocked me to see it so soon after it had adorned the body of a young god, but here it was like a spectacular article from the dry cleaner, being laid carefully in one of the deep car trunks. A couple of the *matadors* themselves soon made an appearance, and a cry went up from the small crowd on the sidewalk as flowers were offered, kisses blown. Close up they were smaller and more wiry than what I had seen in the *corrida,* but their aura filled the air for every onlooker, adult or child. Then five or six people piled into each car, and they were gone. The men who challenged death for all of us disappeared into traffic.

The bullfights were new and peculiar, no doubt about it, but then so was walking around Barcelona. If violence, excitement, and death were what you encountered in the *corrida,* there was a different kind of death—equally dramatic, in its way—everywhere in the city. I was fascinated by the number of wounded and disabled people: walking by, in restaurants, all around us. Crutches, wheelchairs, prosthetic limbs, facial disfigurement, terrible mutilation: for a child it was like a freak show on the sidewalks of a major city, strangely disturbing and impossible not to notice. I knew about war—there were still many reminders of World War II in France—but it wasn't until I was an adult that I understood what civil war had meant for Spain.

In France in the fifties every bus and train and subway car had places reserved for *mutilés de guerre*, mutilated war victims, a program started after World War I. The combination of trench warfare and long-range artillery made for a deadly combination in that conflict. Ordnance does terrible things to human tissue, and yet the rapid advances in the early twentieth century against sepsis and other deadly infection meant that survival was often possible, even when shrapnel had done its bloody work. You did still see terribly injured people—soldiers and civilians alike—on Paris public transportation, but it was a relative rarity. How brutal and widespread must have been the carnage in Spain to leave so many "mutilated" in its wake?

We went into a lot of churches in Spain, both in Barcelona and in towns and villages. We weren't particularly religious—Sunday Mass was our weekly limit—but it was one of the things that tourists did. Being Catholic, we had no hesitation about walking in, blessing ourselves with holy water, genuflecting to the altar, then taking a look. But before long each church started to resemble every other one, no matter how important historically or architecturally. It's not a place kids want to spend a lot of free time. In French museums and châteaux, my mom always set a limit of an hour for a family visit before, as she claimed, *mal de musée*, museum sickness, would set in. This was her way of keeping the pot from boiling over with five children in tow.

The same might have been necessary on this trip if my eldest brother, Tom, hadn't discovered something peculiar to Spanish churches: relics! We were familiar with the concept and even the various rankings, and French churches sometimes had a small relic on display. But this was entirely different: Spain was awash in relics. Every side altar in every church seemed to have another saint's body part—a foot, a thumb, an entire skull—brown and misshapen and presented in a glass case with elaborate gold decorations. It was a bit like the House of Horrors ride at a carnival, except that the spooky bones and skulls were . . . real! Once we discovered this, churches were, for a brief while at least, no longer boring.

Death in the arena, death on the sidewalk, death in the churches! And, come to think of it, near death crossing the Pyrenees, too. These all merged in my mind without any real system: that seemed to be a lot of what Spain was about. Perhaps it was and, for that matter, still is. It sure didn't feel like France. Before long we started, all of us, to feel that gravitational pull that only a trip that takes you somewhere truly different can exert. Gray stone buildings punctuated with pink brick, green lawns, and occasional rain: these seemed attractive, like something we missed and even needed. It was time to get back home, and home was Fontainebleau.

CHAPTER 28

GUIGNOL

When the merry-go-round stopped turning, we sometimes saw white-haired couples lifting their grandchildren onto a particular animal they themselves had favored as children. My own kids were not enthusiastic about the Luxembourg Gardens carousel. They were happy to ride one of the banged-up camels or elephants when they were very young, but the wild delight of the ring snag wasn't the same for either Sara or Nicolas. By the time I took them to the Luxembourg Gardens, giddy with anticipation to initiate them to my boyhood delight, they had ridden numerous other carousels in Paris, all of them more modern and more elaborate than the homely version I cherished. Near the Eiffel Tower there's even a version with an entire second floor, reached by staircase, that revolves with the lower level, gleaming with lacquered paint, polished brass, and twinkling lights. Luxembourg's doesn't even have a floor: the animals hang suspended from a rudimentary structure of steel struts, and you walk on the tamped-down earth and climb on.

Soon enough I saw that I was projecting my enthusiasm for a long-ago adventure on my own children. As every parent must, I realized my mistake—this was a different age, a different world—and I gave it up. Then my pokey brass-ring fantasy started to look like a tired merry-go-round, the sort of thing adults would maintain in the name of nostalgia and tradition: a sweet endorsement of the past, their *own* past. But kids pick up on such well-meaning subterfuge pretty quickly, and will play along for just so long. They need to find their own adventures, and they rarely coincide with the claims of others. "How you gonna keep 'em down on the farm / After they've seen Pareeeee?" Or that double-decker carousel wonder across the Seine from the Eiffel Tower.

And yet some things do translate whole for multiple generations, and work their magic over and over. One such is the French puppet theater tradition known as *Guignol* (pronounced "gheenyole"), presented regularly in the larger parks of Paris. Luxembourg is equipped with one of the more elaborate setups, a minitheater scaled for kids, with a ticket window, rows of well-anchored benches, and theatrical lighting focused on the large rectangular aperture where the puppets appear when the curtain opens.

The repertoire is based on standard folk and fairy tales—"Little Red Riding Hood," "Puss in Boots," "The Three Little Pigs"—with some French variations. The action is frenzied and melodramatic, often spilling over into slapstick. The central character is always Guignol, a kind of everyman dupe, who gets himself into impossible situations with various bad guys, then gets himself out again. The key element in the dynamic is that the kids identify with Guignol, and loudly warn him when something bad is about to happen, usually in the form of an unexpected bonk on the head with a wooden bat.

My mother took us to *Guignol* once on one of those lazy Sunday afternoons, a performance of "The Three Little Pigs." I'd been to movies before, but never to live theater, so the whole thing seemed exciting. As soon as the lights went down, it was clear that this was participatory theater of the first order as all the kids started to chant rhythmically *"Guignol! Guignol! Guignol!"* When at last he appeared: pandemonium! Wild shouts of glee, of approval, and of derision, too. We joined in, of course, understanding only that shouting was expected, even encouraged.

At some point not too far along in the action, the wolf made his appearance, and the screams doubled, tripled in volume and intensity. This continued periodically for the duration, a kind of audible roller-coaster ride that gained velocity without warning, then sustained a thrilling momentum until Guignol was again threatened and another shrill peak was scaled. I remember only that I left that theater half dazed with a ringing in my ears that I considered cool, an invisible badge of honor that I shared with all the other kids. We never went back. Somehow the hours were always inconvenient, my siblings didn't want to go, or it was always sold out.

Fast-forward forty years when my own children were youngsters and *le Jardin du Luxembourg* was not far from where we lived. They both liked the pony rides. For a few francs they'd be plonked on a saddled mount, then led with eight or ten others, tethered together, down one of the dusty *allées* and back again. Early on, Sara favored the little carriage pulled by a donkey, more refined and princess-like in her mind than the shuffling clump of ponies. For a while Nicolas enjoyed the rented sailboats, too—small craft that you rented for a half hour and put in the large central basin. But there were limited possibilities since the boat was unsteerable once you set it in the water, and there lurked the peculiar hazard of the fountain in the middle. If your sailboat happened to tack in that direction, it could be caught in the toppling column of water from the fountain, a child-scaled Scylla and Charybdis. Once the sails became drenched the hull would bob hopelessly against the fountain's stone pediment, unable to make way, visible in its distress but lost to its captain across the basin's wide sea.

Then one day I proposed *Guignol*. We walked to a tree-shaded area in the park, bought tickets, and contemplated the large sign on the front: *Les Marionnettes font plaisir aux enfants et aux gens d'esprit*, "The puppets bring joy to children and to clever people." No longer a child, I wondered if I was a clever person. As if by coincidence, the performance was "*Les Trois Petits Cochons*"—"The Three Little Pigs."

When the doors opened we burst inside with the gaggle of kids, parents, and grandparents. The rows of miniature benches filled quickly, adults sitting on the ends or standing at the back. The room came alive with the electric charge of children's anticipation, followed by total silence as the house lights went down. Shouts for Guignol were followed by a few murmurs and laughs as the action began, and then rapt attention as the pigs made their appearance.

All of the figures display the classic configuration of handheld puppets: head held straight with the index finger, thumb stuck into a tiny sleeve and hand on one side, the other three fingers jammed together as an arm on the other. The peculiarity about *Guignol* figures is that the heads are disproportionately large, as if a bunch of cartoon characters had gathered. Each head is made of wood and is hand painted to show the distinctive features of the familiar cast of characters in each play. They are both sturdy and easily recognizable to young children. The wooden heads, not coincidentally, are strong enough to withstand a blow with a small wooden bat, a key driver of the action in each *Guignol* show. Sooner or later, many of the characters wield bats in their hands with that peculiar kind of hugging grip necessitated by the puppeteer's handhold. Repeatedly, one character sneaks up behind another with a bat almost as big as his body, then suddenly pops up, inclines his entire body, and whaps the wooden head of the unsuspecting victim.

Very little had changed over the years. The urgent whispers, the nervous giggles and laughs, the rhythmic calls for Guignol. When he does finally show up, the whole place erupts with shouts that never really subside. A wall of sound builds from some bottomless well of energy that only the very young can draw upon. The three pigs elicit a rolling swell of cries, then Guignol himself draws a crashing wave of delighted screeches. Finally, when the character of the *Gendarme*—the Policeman—is the first to wield a bat, the room explodes with noise, as if a chemical reaction had loosened the vocal cords of anyone younger than eight years. My reaction was instantaneous, a mix of shock and extreme discomfort. I waited for perhaps ten seconds for it to subside, but it continued to build, against all reason. Together with many of the other parents, I bolted for the doors at the back, driven from the tiny theater by intolerable noise: it was less a choice than a biological imperative.

A group of us assembled outside, many lighting cigarettes and visibly willing themselves to be calm as they drew smoke deep into their lungs. This, too, is part of a *Guignol* set piece: parents sitting with their kids in good-natured tolerance, then engaging in wild flight when a limit is breeched. We cast sidelong glances at one another, united by a bond of adversity both intense and ludicrous in its contours. A few of the women offered ironic remarks; they seemed more knowing in the ways of *Guignol* than the few dads who stood in a stupor worthy of shell shock.

"C'est les bâtons qui les rendent dingues!" a mom with a practiced air declared as she waved her cigarette. "It's those wooden bats that make them crazy!" Nods all around. The door opened and a young man staggered out into the light, like a wild animal straining to escape his cage; the screams swelled around him until the door latched shut. He looked at us with a puzzled half smile.

"I thought I could take it, but I was wrong," as if discovering for the first time that he was no longer seven years old. "I hope they'll be okay in there."

One of the women laughed, blowing smoke derisively. "What could happen to them? They're in heaven!" she said—*"Ils sont aux anges!"*—and she meant it, then added, *"A leur âge, j'étais pareille."* "At their age, I was the same."

There was about our little colloquy a strange and enticing air of camaraderie among strangers, as if we had just been through combat together, or had great sex—or a combination of the two. Perhaps the childhood experience of *Guignol* is what, in fact, initiates the French to the pleasures of the senses, taken to an extreme. Perhaps not. But the intensity of it alone argues for significance. Those were our children in there, submerged in shrieks and yells that were clearly audible through the walls. Real fear, sudden delight, abject terror, warnings and commands: a broad spectrum of human emotions hurled upon the stage, upon each of the characters, in the full-throated charge to WATCH OUT! that only the young can sustain with sincere fervor. The experience is understood to have been enjoyed by parents and even grandparents in their own youth, and this is one of its chief pleasures for kids: knowing that it's now pure hell for adults, and sheer bliss for them. What could be better?

My kids liked it well enough, though Sara pointed out that she could hardly ever hear the words. There is, indeed, a script to each play, and extensive lines of dialogue among the characters. But after that first bat makes its appearance, you might as well be on a deep-sea dive as in a theater for all the intelligible words that will reach your ear. *Guignol* can be seen as a thin pretext for allowing kids to scream their heads off, together, in a closed space. It surely satisfies some deep-seated, atavistic need to yell. You just need to make sure you're not in the room when it starts. Unless, of course, you happen to be one of those *gens d'esprit.*

We went back a few times, but I have to confess that I always waited out front from the beginning. Eventually, as happens with all childhood activities, *Guignol* became for my kids a "kiddie" thing—the kiss of death—and all interest vanished. Me, I'm waiting for the day to encourage them to take their own children, and to sit with them on those little benches when the fun begins. I'll be the first out the door.

Years later I asked my own mother if she recalled *Les Trois Petits Cochons* in the *Guignol* theater at the Luxembourg Gardens. She stifled a smile and merely replied, "Yes, I remember." Well knowing it was a provocation, I asked why we had only gone to one performance when we were so often in Paris on Sundays. Now my mom's eyes assumed a steely aspect, and she answered slowly, as if by choosing her words carefully she wanted to be sure that I grasped an essential truth about life on this earth. "That screaming was the loudest noise I've ever heard human beings produce in a closed space," she declared with clipped precision. "No one needs to experience that more than once."

CHAPTER 29

NAPOLEON III

P*arce que nous avons eu Napoléon le Grand, il faut que nous payons Napoléon le Petit.*" "Because we had Napoleon the Great, we must now have Napoleon the Small." Uttered in 1851 at the beginning of what many French claimed would be a return to greatness, Victor Hugo's withering judgment has come down as a prescient truth. Less than forty years after Waterloo, Napoleon I's nephew, Louis-Napoleon, declared himself emperor of the French in 1852. The path that led to that moment could hardly have been more different from that followed by his uncle.

When Napoleon I was shipped off to St. Helena, the victorious Allied powers—England, Prussia, Austria, Russia, all ruled by kings—imposed on France a return to the Bourbon monarchy. The two younger brothers of the guillotined Louis XVI ruled successively for fifteen years. Then the French rose again, there was a minor version of the revolution in the streets of Paris, and the Bourbons escaped to exile in England. A cousin, Louis-Philippe, took over the reins of power, calling himself the Citizen King and declaring France a constitutional monarchy with a representative assembly. That arrangement lasted until 1848, when France again revolted and overthrew its king. He, too, took refuge in England.

All this while the Bonaparte clan bided its time, every family member having been expelled from France when the Bourbons were restored. Napoleon's nephew began life as the ultimate insider. Born in Paris, he was baptized at Fontainebleau in 1810 with the emperor and empress as godparents. He grew to adulthood in exile in Italy and Switzerland, agitating constantly for a return to France. Captured in an unsuccessful attempt to overthrow the king, he spent six years in captivity. Then came the convulsion of 1848, and he saw his chance.

The remarkable thing is that he managed to get himself elected president of the Second Republic (the First Republic was during the Revolution of 1789); the Bonaparte name still had considerable resonance. Within three years he dissolved the Assembly, suppressed all opposition, and declared himself emperor, a step that was ratified by a national plebiscite. Once again the tension between those who proclaimed liberty in the name of a constitutional Republic and the conservative monarchists who insisted on the need for a strong leader, a sovereign, erupted in the theater of French political life. The initial compromise—the current Bonaparte as an elected president—tipped to repression, and suddenly Napoleon III was sitting on a throne. (The first Napoleon's son, who died at the age of twenty at the Austrian court of his Hapsburg mother, Marie Louise, was considered Napoleon II, even though he never ruled.)

The man who came to power in 1848, Napoleon III, had been raised in awe of his uncle, a cult figure to exiles and disillusioned French citizens alike. The new emperor, unmarried at forty-four, left a long string of mistresses behind him from his various ports of call in exile. He married a young Spanish aristocrat, Eugenie, in 1853; within three years she bore him a son, their only child. They visited Fontainebleau regularly, strengthening in the public eye their association with the habits of the first Napoleon.

The railroad had come to Fontainebleau in 1849; Paris was less than an hour away. The technological advances of the industrial age reached the Château, and life changed. Central heating was installed, heavily upholstered furniture favored comfort over style, gas lighting replaced candlelight. Instead of courtiers, guests from the arts, industry, and the professions—the flourishing bourgeoisie of an affluent France—were invited for the weekend. An elaborate theater was built in a wing of the Château. Concerts and balls and outings in the forest punctuated these visits.

And yet. And yet the siren call of empire seduced Napoleon III, and his adventures called for a military genius and a political sagacity that were beyond him. The Crimean War of the mid-1850s was a transparent bid for prestige by Napoleon III, and its cost and savagery affected the balance of power in Europe for decades to come. He dispatched an expeditionary force to Mexico in a misguided effort to install a Hapsburg as a New World emperor. The entire undertaking was a fiasco; when the French withdrew, the archduke Maximilian was shot by Mexican partisans. Finally, in 1870, this Napoleon declared war on Prussia over a relatively minor matter, and the end came swiftly.

Within three weeks the Prussians had invaded French soil and prevailed at several battles. Thinking to reverse matters with a stroke worthy of his uncle, Napoleon III assumed command of the army, took to the field, and was dealt setback after setback. When defeat was apparent within six weeks of the beginning of hostilities, he sought the salvation of "death on the field of battle," but even that was not granted him. He was captured, like François I three centuries earlier, and held prisoner in Prussia. The empire was dissolved, France descended into yet another revolution, and the emperor went into an ignominious exile in England, where he died two years later.

More than for any of his considerable accomplishments domestically—the rebuilding of central Paris; the elaboration of a modern infrastructure of bridges, roads, railways, and dams throughout France; the development of a flourishing economy with an extensive and sophisticated banking system—Napoleon III is remembered for this defeat and the ensuing loss of Alsace and much of Lorraine, two important regions on the border with Germany. The shame of a diminishment of national territory hung over France like a pall for decades, and was a significant factor in French entry into World War I. The region was returned to France in 1918; Hitler appropriated the same territory for Germany in 1940. The initial loss was always laid at the feet of Victor Hugo's "Napoleon the Small."

The fate of his only son marks a strange footnote to this last of French monarchs. The *prince impérial,* as Louis-Napoleon was styled, survived his father in exile by six years. In 1879, at the age of twenty-three, he insisted on joining the British unit with which he had trained when it was posted to South Africa to fight in the colonial war there. On a patrol in the bush, the soldiers were ambushed by Zulu warriors. The French prince was trapped away from his horse and speared seventeen times by the attackers. So died the last Bonaparte pretender, sometimes called Napoleon IV, trying to win glory in battle in order to live up to his name.

France would never again have a king or an emperor, though factions of Bourbons and Bonapartes still squabble among themselves about legitimacy and reclaiming "the throne of France." They are in no sense a serious part of the political landscape, providing instead endless fodder for gossip magazines and society parties that have become a small and silly industry.

The monarchy is a thing of the past; its trappings remain. After the end of what is known in France as the *Second Empire,* Fontainebleau was used by elected presidents of the Third Republic, its grounds and gradually its rooms opened to the public as a museum. So it continues to this day, the Château cared for by the architects, curators, and artisans who work in the name of the French Republic. Surely their work, too, is one of the glories of France.

CHAPTER 30

A SHIP WEATHERS THE STORM

Four months after first visiting the crowded work site where Napoleon III's office was being refurbished, I wanted to see it as the finishing touches were being applied before it was opened to the public. It was the first restoration site Patrick Ponsot had invited me to visit; I wondered what the transformation would be. Vincent Cochet, a curator I had met on my previous visit, agreed to show me the suite of three rooms that I had last seen stripped to the underlying timbers. He, too, had a huge set of keys; he found the right one immediately and ushered me into a quiet anteroom, entirely transformed.

As we entered the emperor's office, the impression was different from that created by any of the Château's other rooms. Comfort rather than ostentation seemed the main consideration, though the space was certainly richly appointed. The herringbone-pattern oak floor I had watched carpenters repairing was now entirely covered with a thick carpeting, laid wall to wall, specially woven in a strong Persian pattern of reds, blues, and yellows. A light brown cloth with a nubby horizontal grain covered the walls—this was the color called *havane* about which there had been so much speculation until a tiny sample of the original was found beneath the window surround, and the right tint to suggest Cuban tobacco could be agreed upon. Electric-blue silk bell cords hung from the wall at several points, an arresting contrast against the brown, and the same cords were worked vertically in each of the room's corners as well as along the cornice line. The substantial brown marble mantel dominated one side of the room, its simple lines a striking departure from the curved tracery of mantelpieces in other parts of the Château. This was clearly a late-nineteenth-century aesthetic. The mirror that I had watched being repositioned so perilously those months before now gleamed above the hearth. Forced-air heating, a great innovation of the late nineteenth century, would again be circulated through polished brass vents that had been set in the carpet.

These rooms must have felt remarkably modern in their day, worlds away from the pull of the *Ancien Régime*'s furnishings. The aesthetic was one we commonly associate with a plush, mid-Victorian order, with ponderous desks and tables of precious woods placed at right angles, interspersed with comfortable armchairs upholstered in a rich blue. After all, the office was first decorated in 1864, the curator reminded me, at a time when the American Civil War was still being fought. The industrialized world was coming to the fore, and even French palaces reflected that tendency.

A slender man with a watchful, curious air, Cochet was responsible for the historical accuracy of the transformation that had been effected in these rooms, and he talked about the process with enthusiasm. "On one hand you want to display the original use with utmost accuracy, in a way that can be understood by a visitor. At the same time, you need to protect the original pieces, often fragile, from the very public whom you want to educate. It's a constant balancing act."

I peered out the open door where a half-dozen stairs led down to greenswards and a view of the forest in the distance. Now that the piles of equipment and materials had all been cleared away on the garden side, the windows in the office afforded extraordinary views to the English Garden and the lovely lake pavilion. However, curtains and shades blocked the views; I asked Cochet if that would change when the public was admitted.

"No, that is a compromise we have had to make throughout the Château. Otherwise, the sun will destroy everything."

Visiting the long succession of rooms and periods in the Château's many wings, all richly furnished, can now seem like walking through a faintly lit tunnel. The magnificent vistas—to the gardens, the courtyards, the forest—are almost all cut off from view by shades tightly affixed to the windows. It is a necessary concession to the power of the sun's rays to diminish and destroy original materials, but the visitor has to work at imagining the rooms with light and air streaming through open windows.

When the sovereign was in residence, curtains were opened or closed as a function of his personal comfort, but never because of concern about sun damage to rugs, furniture, paintings, murals, or tapestries. The prevailing mentality was that these could always be replaced, as they indeed were with some regularity. What seems to us like bottomless profligacy was in fact the right exercised by the monarch to have what he wanted in his immediate surrounds. With the state's entire apparatus of artists and artisans at his command, silk could be allowed to fade, paint to chip: a newer version would be imagined and created as the fancy struck.

After my discussion with Cochet in the completed office of Napoleon III, I headed toward the Château's shop—*La Boutique*—to consider what was available that suggested this rich and largely hidden process of restoration. As I ambled around the tables piled high with books, my eye settled on a thin book—a booklet, really—with an arresting cover photo in black and white. In the Château's *Cour d'Honneur,* the main courtyard that leads to the famous double-horseshoe staircase, lines of helmeted German soldiers were arrayed around the greenswards with military precision. Then I read the title: *Le Château de Fontainebleau sous l'Occupation, 1940–1944.* Its author was Albert Bray, one of Ponsot's predecessors as chief architect at Fontainebleau. To him fell the thankless but essential task of seeing to the Château's welfare during the war years.

Intrigued both by the cover image and the title, I bought a copy of the slender volume and read it in the Château's gardens. It is a journal kept by the chief architect from the arrival of the Germans just after their victory in mid-June 1940 to their eventual departure in late August 1944. During these four long years, the Germans requisitioned the Château for use as a major military headquarters. Most of the artworks had been removed to another château in France's unoccupied zone, but the Fontainebleau buildings remained fragile shells, poorly suited for use by an occupying army. The daily entries are generally short, and they tell the melancholy tale of a concerned and vigilant official trying to protect the domain for which he is principally responsible.

Much of the work involved the formal confrontation of two redoubtable bureaucracies, the French museum expert challenging, delicately, the initiatives of the victorious German army. Bray's requests seem reasonable and necessary, but one gets the sense of a man who fears the worst for his storied buildings. Will the officer commanding kindly insure that the officers do not persist in smoking in state rooms, where the fire danger is extreme? Will the officer commanding please see that the German garrison does not continue to fish and eat the carp in the decorative pond? For the concert to be given by the Berlin Philharmonic in the Ballroom, can the army's technical corps please take care to install the electricity needed for lighting and radio so as to avoid damage to the irreplaceable Renaissance frescoes that grace the room? Mostly Bray's mix of arm's-length formality and dogged persistence seems to have prevailed, and one wonders that the premises did not suffer more physical damage.

Another, more personal dimension to the situation seeps through, however, particularly as one comes upon the snapshots that Bray himself took and that illustrate some of the entries with an air of resignation. The cover photo that first grabbed my attention was shocking to consider. As it happened, in the euphoric flush of victory the Germans organized a series of celebratory events at Fontainebleau. The photo on the cover was taken on July 20, 1940, just after the invasion, during a rehearsal for a nighttime ceremony in the courtyard. It was organized after a banquet held in Henri II's magnificent Renaissance ballroom attended by eighty high-ranking German officers and presided over by the overall army commander, Field Marshal von Brauchitsch.

After their dinner under Primaticcio's matchless frescoes, the generals and the colonels came out in the dark onto the landing at the top of the double-horseshoe staircase, there to be greeted by hundreds of soldiers bearing lighted torches. One photo from inside the booklet shows them lining the perimeter of the vast courtyard, another has them massed in front of the staircase in perfect rows, flaming torches held high. Bray's text describes as dispassionately as possible the martial band music and the hymns sung by the massed troops. He notes that German army film crews recorded the scene in order to display the splendor of victory to the people at home. Even in grainy black and white the power of the images comes through. The impression of desecration—and of defeat—is absolute.

The rest of Bray's account continues with desultory entries about the constant but courtly battle between the two bureaucracies. The chief architect emerges through these pages as a devoted civil servant who cannot bear to see the Château damaged. Even in this flat chronological catalog, though, some darker aspects of the German presence come briefly into focus.

Toward the end of their invasion in 1940, on June 16, the Germans bombarded the Château's gardens, but only minor damage to the roof resulted. When Bray returned to Fontainebleau on the 18th, however, he found that the town's synagogue, adjacent to the Château's inner garden, had been pillaged. On the floor he found the Torah, torn and trampled, but underneath, miraculously intact, he found a gold-embroidered tallit, or prayer shawl, which he kept in his apartment at the Château for safekeeping. From the very first days of the occupation, then, a Jewish place of worship had been targeted, even in a provincial town like Fontainebleau. Worse was to come. The following spring, on two nights in April 1941, just after the curfew, forty German soldiers broke into the synagogue and set it aflame. By the time he arrived a half hour later, Bray could only watch, helpless, as a German patrol allowed the building to burn; the firemen saved little but the walls.

The last photo in this little book shows the first tank from Patton's army to enter Fontainebleau on August 28, 1944. The tank's American crew members are posed in front of the Château, striking mock heroic poses around the tank's turret as a few townspeople look on. Less than three months after the Normandy landings, the euphoria of the evolving victory is all but visible in the air. The intact Château in the background seems a miracle, an apparition that floated across the four long years like a fragile ship that has found a safe port.

CHAPTER 31

FOLIES D'ADOLESCENCE

In all the time we lived in France, my parents left us children only three or four times so that they could have some time to themselves. Usually it was for their wedding anniversary, and they were never gone for more than a few days. Annick took care of me and my younger sister, spending the weekend at our house. An adult had to be there, too, for Sally, Tom, and Judd, and that meant arranging things well ahead of time.

The first time my parents did this, they merely went to Paris on a Saturday and stayed overnight in a hotel. An aunt was visiting from the United Sates at the time, so she took over responsibility for, as she put it, "holding down the fort." Her choice of words was eerily prescient, but that became clear only much later. All went well with my parents' "adventure" in Paris, and it was fun to see them come home as if they had actually been on a trip.

Their next venture came about a year later, after our first family camping trips. My mom flew to London to join my dad who was there on business, and they spent a weekend together. The arrangement that time involved having a childless couple, American friends of my parents who lived in Paris, come and stay with us, occupying the big bedroom *in loco parentis*. They insisted it would be "a lark" for them, a veritable "idyll in Fontainebleau" to move into the big old house with the huge garden for a few days. It's fair to say they had no clue about kids—*any* kids, much less our crew of five. So they indulged us without reason, and we, being clever enough to recognize a good thing while it lasted, acted shamelessly, as if it were our due.

Every kind of caprice was played out. Sally was already a teenager, and lipstick and eye shadow that my mother would never have abided were applied with abandon in the morning. Tom suggested it was his weekend duty to take Kepi for a long walk, and he disappeared for hours. Kepi returned first, dragging the leash, and Tom showed up much later, smiling and self-satisfied, with no explanation. The rest of us must have picked up the unspoken message—we could get away with murder!—and I recall that weekend as if it were one long birthday party/sleepover, when we were spoiled, and then spoiled some more.

We slept late, then stayed in our pajamas past noon. We told our minders that we often ate in the garden, a pure fabrication, but they responded as if this were received wisdom and required action. Nothing could have been more inimical to an indoor/outdoor flow than that great ark of stone, bricks, and mortar, but somehow they fashioned a "picnic style" setup on the lawn, then bought every delicacy and delight that we named. The local *pâtisserie* did good business that weekend. After twenty-four hours of this the adult couple seemed astonished at how much five hungry children could wolf down among them. They described us as "perfect angels" when my parents returned. That should have made Mom and Dad wonder, but they were so relieved to hear that all had gone well that they were deaf to nuance.

The last time my parents escaped from us for a few days, things took a different turn. They were off to Venice for a weekend, a romantic getaway when they stayed in a fancy hotel and indulged themselves in ways that were usually unimaginable. I still have the photo of them bobbing in a gondola on the waters of the Grand Canal, oblivious to what was happening at home. More than most, that snapshot illustrates for me that ignorance truly is bliss. Their ignorance, and their bliss, continued until their return.

Meanwhile, our home life in Fontainebleau during their absence headed into a tailspin. Sally was fourteen, Tom already twelve. Judging that they could manage a bit of responsibility, my parents arranged for friends to "check in" with us on each day at dinner time (my mom had left food prepared in the refrigerator) and ensure that all was well. Big mistake! Everything was calm on that first night, and the adults must have been reassured at what a model family we seemed, responsible and caring. On Saturday afternoon, all hell broke loose.

Who knows where an adolescent boy comes up with ideas for what we would now call "acting out"? Tom had a particularly fertile imagination, and he was an excellent student whose composure erupted every now and again with a baffling streak of wild behavior. With my parents gone for more than forty-eight hours, all restraint vanished and his fantasies could become real. What he imagined was that he and Judd, his necessary sidekick talked into an uneasy complicity, would fashion themselves as "Beats" (who wouldn't be termed "beatniks" until 1958) and pass unrecognized along Fontainebleau's main street, causing a sensation in town.

We subscribed to *Time* and *Life*, and there were plenty of images in both to give an idea of the "cool cats" from our mother country and how they dressed, never to be seen in provincial France. Tom got the basics of what was already a stereotype: dark turtleneck sweaters, jeans, sandals, berets. For a Vandyck beard and mustache, he held a match to a wine cork, then used the blackened tip to draw facial hair on his smooth, preadolescent face.

The last detail was the killer: Tom decided they should carry empty wine bottles and act drunk, as if this would strengthen their disguise and make the whole thing appear plausible. I was bitterly disappointed that I couldn't go along in disguise, too, but I was the true "little brother," three years on the wrong side of a divide that may as well have been an ocean. Little did I suspect my good luck in this event.

They set off late on Saturday afternoon. Sally tried to stop them, and even Judd emitted a few Sancho Panza–like misgivings on the order of "I'm not sure this is a good idea. . . ." But for Tom, the Beats were marching on Fontainebleau and would not be stopped. The reaction of the shopkeepers can be imagined, though my dad learned soon enough, and in painful detail, what had transpired. The lady at the wine shop thought at first they had come to return empties, but when she saw their dress and their erratic behavior, she threw them out. At the bakery the owner recognized them, of course—they regularly stopped by to pick up baguettes—and thought they must be headed to a costume party (*un bal masqué*). *"Mais ce n'est pas encore Hallowe'en, non?"* "It's not Hallowe'en yet, is it?" There was in France no dress-up tradition for Hallowe'en, but they had a vague idea of what Americans did when that holiday rolled around. . . .

This failure to convince only egged Tom on. By the time they got to the local café, he was stumbling and mumbling like a true drunkard, and the owner played along for a while. He poked gentle fun: "You look like Basques with your berets and beards." And then he kicked them out, too, with a sobering admonition: *"Votre père ne sera pas content!"* "Your dad won't be pleased!" They must have known how right he was, and the jig was up. They slouched home in a blue gloom, all trace of the initial high jinks gone as they slipped in the door. By the time the adult friends checked on us at dinnertime, they were out of costume and out of character; unless you'd wandered into one of the shops on the main street earlier, you'd never have suspected what had happened.

The final act was swift, inevitable, and grim. My parents returned Sunday evening and Tom, no fool when it came to damage control, knew a voluntary confession would be better than being found out. Taking a cue from the bakery lady, he told my father that he and Judd had "played Hallowe'en" on the main street the day before. My dad knew enough to be alarmed, and questioned the two of them relentlessly until a version of the truth spilled out. We could hear the yelling from behind the closed door of his office. Then he gave them each several straps with his belt on their rear ends and sent them to bed without dinner. The dimensions of our family's shame (for so my father saw it) emerged in the next few days.

He made the rounds and heard from the merchants that it was "nothing" or just "*des folies d'adolescence*," "teenage craziness." My dad later told how the café owner tried to make light of it: "*Alors, mon colonel, ils étaient bien exubérants pour deux adolescents!*" "Well, Colonel, they were quite exuberant for two adolescents!" Now, *exubérant* is one of those French words that can mean a lot of things. Like its English counterpart, it can describe one full of enthusiasm and unrestrained joy. It can also be the polite way of signaling behavior that is licentious, unbridled, wild. Not a good thing to hear about your sons.

Tom and Judd were made to apologize in person to each of the shopkeepers, who must have felt as uncomfortable as my two brothers. For a while there the two of them ranked even lower in my father's esteem than Kepi. My dad was incensed by the insult to the French, "our hosts," and the aping of the ways of homeless alcoholics when we had so many advantages. The "Beat" theme never resonated with him.

My mom took the long view, being herself the middle child of a large "exuberant" family. While she didn't blame herself, she knew Tom would never have dared this kind of venture if one or both parents had been present. So there were no more weekend getaways for Mom and Dad.

One can only imagine what the French must have thought. The *bourgeois,* if it reached their ears, would be scandalized that two sons of an officer at the Château had made a spectacle of themselves in public. But then they'd have chalked it up to the Americans and their inscrutable behavior, a mix of arrogance, insouciance, and unpredictability. The Communist Party occasionally tagged walls with the familiar slogan, YANKEE GO HOME! (usually rendered phonetically as "Yanqui"), and this would add a drop of fuel to that self-righteous fire.

The shopkeepers, actually, seemed to take it in stride, laughing at both the audacity and the foolishness ("Did they think we wouldn't recognize them when they are here daily for *charcuterie?*"). But they had seen a lot—barroom brawls, political demonstrations, family feuds, the bitterness of the war years—and this must have seemed both funny and trivial in comparison. *Folies d'adolescence,* indeed.

CHAPTER 32

SOUVENIRS

In the fifties France was a country in transition, both domestically and internationally. The peace accords ending the conflict in Vietnam were signed in the summer of 1954, and France withdrew from Southeast Asia. Closer to home, the rebellion in Algeria was growing, and increasing numbers of troops were being sent to North Africa. I knew nothing of such political upheavals, but I occasionally caught sight of some of the consequences of turmoil in the adult world.

In the fall of 1956 my dad was making plans to travel to Australia in November. He had been selected as a member of the U.S. fencing team for the Olympic Games in Melbourne. Two major events kept him from going: the worsening of the Hungarian uprising against Soviet-imposed policies, and the eruption of the Suez Crisis in the Middle East. NATO forces were on high alert, and sports took a backseat to military duty, so he traveled a lot, but not to Melbourne. Before long, my parents were welcoming Hungarian fencers for dinners and social gatherings. Hungarians were widely acknowledged as superb fencers, and we had often seen them beat my father—and everyone else—at international matches in Paris. Now they were refugees, and France was a favored destination for those who could escape. In our house they were fun and funny, always joking around with us children, but I realized only much later that things were grim for all of them.

The Suez Crisis, which put the United States at odds with both Britain and France, meant my dad went to Egypt. My dad was no shopper, but he must have had time enough in Cairo to visit the bazaar. That, and an empty airplane, meant that we ended up with two fancy versions of camel saddles—polished wooden frames and soft leather cushions—that we used as stools around the coffee table. They were perfect for long board games.

My father also came back with several official photos from his discussions in Cairo. He was the liaison officer for a group of NATO officers, uniformed and standing in a row. Next to him was his opposite number from the Egyptian military, another lieutenant colonel who played the smiling host. It was Anwar Sadat. Years later, when I discovered that photo and asked my dad if he had had important meetings with the future president of Egypt, he said, "Sadat was already somebody. He was a great guy." That was it. But then my dad never—neither then nor later—talked about his duties as an Air Force officer. "A great guy" in fighter-pilot speak can mean anything from "He had serious responsibilities and acquitted himself well" to "He showed us all a wild time in Cairo." I'll never know; the spirit of the Sphinx was long since part of my dad's *modus operandi*.

In addition to the camel saddles, there accumulated at our house in Fontainebleau a store of souvenirs from various trips—either Dad's travels or our family camping jaunts—that spoke of the four corners of Europe. We had Venetian glassware (soon broken, or at least chipped); Florentine leather goods; Spanish wine flasks made of soft leather; a pair of lethal Spanish *banderillas* from bullfighting (the colorful sticks with harpoon-like points jabbed into the bull's shoulder muscle); boxes and ice coolers and even life preservers made from pieces of Portuguese cork; wooden clogs from Holland; Alpine skirts and blouses from Switzerland; silver (soon dented) from Ireland and England. With a family of seven, it didn't take long to build up a store of mementos—some useful, others not—from our multiple destinations.

The only true dud in the list was an outfit from Germany that my parents bought for me: lederhosen, shirt, sweater, and green felt Bavarian hat with a feather stuck into its band. I shunned the lederhosen like poison. Who wears thick leather shorts with horn buttons? I wondered—but I wore the hat to school. Once was all it took. What seemed to me like a plain green hat with a bit of the hunter's flair was immediately seen by my classmates for what it was: *allemand,* German! Or "*Boche!*" as the mocking taunts had it, the French insult whose nearest English equivalent might be "Kraut!" Reconciliation between France and Germany was under way, but some things run deeper—including Bavarian headgear in France.

On a more practical level, my mom set about filling out the house's furnishings with French pieces. In this she was helped mightily by the discovery of a venerable Fontainebleau institution, the weekly *vente aux enchères,* or auction. Held on a weekday evening, the proceedings were presided over by the town mayor, an apparent conflict of interest that bothered no one. Once a week he would lock up the Town Hall at the end of the day and make his way to the nearby auction hall, where he picked up his gavel and delivered a lively performance for a couple of hours.

Fontainebleau was a strange amalgam of a provincial town in a prosperous agricultural district with a heritage of affluence and a certain pretention from the families associated with court life at the Château. The things that went on the block were a wild mix of agricultural implements, rustic country furniture, elaborate tables and chairs, porcelain and crystal *bibelots*, fancy mirrors, all manner of paintings—in short, an assemblage that was generally mediocre, but that occasionally held surprises.

"Even French junk looks good!" my mother enthused at first, but she knew enough to wait and watch. My dad wasn't so reticent. On the few occasions he accompanied my mom, we came away with purchases that tended to be ungainly (a ponderous throne-like oak chair that had to be reupholstered—expensively—and that was never comfortable), impractical (a pair of huge pewter goblets that looked as if they had been used in a production of *Parsifal*), or plain broken (an old nineteenth-century upright piano with attached candelabra that looked nice but was irreparable as an instrument). Over time we acquired some household essentials, including sets of dishes, glassware, and extra chairs. We also gained an insight into the priorities in France at the time.

Both my parents were shocked to learn that big pieces of furniture fashioned from solid hardwood were hard to sell. In particular, *armoires*, the big freestanding closets that are an essential part of French life (built-in closets were until recently a novelty in France), were going for centimes when they were made of solid oak, chestnut, walnut, even mahogany. They were considered old-fashioned and—the kiss of death—"*bourgeois*." What did the French want instead? Anything relentlessly modern with showy veneer, plain lines, and stainless steel handles. Modern was good, old was bad—it was that simple.

But before we dwell on the apparent folly of it all, we should remember that this was ten years after the war, and as things started to pick up economically, many people wanted a complete break with the past. That solid walnut chest, delicately carved with a motif of scrolls and palm fronds, might as well have been a horse and buggy to a population that craved automobiles. The pendulum has by now swung back, and old, heavy *armoires* and sideboards are again desirable, and quite expensive. But the richer irony is that trendy shops have lately been springing up in Paris doing a flourishing business in selling the stripped-down, veneer-covered furniture that brought full price in the fifties. French boomers are experiencing their own wave of nostalgia, and "retro" is as pricey as "bourgeois" these days.

My mother kept our household together with help. With five children and an enormous house, there was a colossal amount of work. Monsieur Jérôme continued to polish the parquet floors with his foot brushes, the gardener clipped the hedges and planted flowers and raked leaves. There was no question of closeness since my father was an officer and, moreover, an American: the rift, both social and cultural, was wide. There was, however, a respect that ran both ways. My parents weren't hard to work for, and they understood that life sometimes took quirky turns.

Each morning our maid arrived late on her Mobylette, the French motorbike that was the precursor of cars for young working people in the fifties. "*Quel brouillard!*" "What fog!" she would exclaim, stamping her feet on the kitchen tiles as she warmed up. She lived in a village on the far side of the forest, and ground fog was endemic and brutally chilling; this was no fabrication! She spent an inordinate amount of time in the kitchen, either near the Mary Hotcakes clothes washer, around the stove, or ironing sheets. My mother never wanted the sheets ironed, but she never said so. "All of those activities in the kitchen were reliable sources of heat," she pointed out to me years later. "And being cold in your bones is a terrible thing."

Another young woman who worked for us got into the habit of taking Kepi for a walk on a leash, but only in the weeks following his occasional clipping, when he looked like a show dog. Then Yvette would disappear for an hour or more, dog in tow, saying he needed "*une bonne promenade,*" "a nice walk." Kepi ran free in our garden, an enclosed acre of land, so exercise wasn't lacking.

By happenstance, on one of those days my dad took another route home on his bicycle from his office at the Château. There on a street adjacent to ours he passed by the entrance to the French army barracks, where he noticed a beautiful poodle. Then recognition dawned and he saw it was Kepi, uncharacteristically leashed and standing patiently while Yvette chatted with two soldiers. "All dolled up," he said later, "with perfume, makeup, red chiffon scarf, heels." He pedaled on. It seemed harmless enough in its way: Kepi as unwitting shill. But my parents were hardly surprised when she gave notice soon after Kepi's next haircut. The gardener told them that she intended to marry a soldier. "I hope she got what she wanted," was my dad's only comment.

At times, as I revisit that period and consider the challenges my mom faced, it's easy to imagine the house staff and all the locals in cahoots, ready to take the rich Americans for a ride. But that's an American view of things, an "Anglo-Saxon" regard based on irony that fails to take into account the supreme individuality of the French. That, and the extreme respect for order, tradition, and hierarchy that still prevailed. These were people who were going on as before, and we were the ones who had upset the order of things, failing to comprehend how matters proceed in France, in Fontainebleau, in this house.

Had they wanted, individually or collectively, to take advantage, the opportunities were not lacking. The French expression for duping innocent newcomers, *rouler dans la farine*—literally, "to roll in flour" (implicitly, before frying to a crisp)—combines the fascination with food and the enthusiasm for expressive language in one colorful metaphor. But the plain fact is that we weren't rolled in flour. There was no pilfering in the house, no petty theft. One of my mother's rare blanket statements about France and the French captured the attitude: "They are proud and they are honest, period."

But there was one instance in which this code was broken, an eventuality so shocking that it passed from the domain of professional relations to what is called *faits divers,* literally "different things," a category that includes petty crime, scandal, and bizarre events. One morning in December my dad left the equivalent of $600 in French francs sitting on his dresser. Adjusting for inflation, it was worth about $5,000 in today's currency. It was highly unusual for him to have that kind of cash in the house; he intended to use it to pay for school tuitions, and for Christmas presents when he drove up to Paris the next afternoon. When he returned for lunch the following day, the money had disappeared. It soon developed that a young maid who had worked for us for only a few months was also gone; she had stolen the money. In addition to feeling suddenly poor—that was a colossal amount of money for us—my dad felt both stupid and foolhardy. "You don't tempt someone who has so little with a pile of cash," he said many times, blaming himself.

He reported the theft to the French police. In a week, word came back that the maid had been found in Nice, and they pieced together the story. She went on a spending spree in Paris, buying a number of luxury goods followed by a first-class train ticket to the *Côte d'Azur,* the Riviera on the Mediterranean coast. In Nice, she checked into a suite at the Negresco, the city's legendary luxury hotel, and after a few days the money ran out. Then things got complicated.

Apprehended by the police, our former maid threatened to commit suicide out of shame, and was held under guard in a hospital. Discussions ensued. My parents declined to press criminal charges, but the French insisted on restitution of what she had acquired. After the travel, the fancy hotel, elaborate meals, and plenty of expensive champagne, little remained. When matters were finally resolved, my parents received two objects: an exquisite Catholic missal, bound in dark green pebble-grain Moroccan leather, its pages gold-limned; and a large leather purse from Hermès the color of honey with a purposeful look, almost like a doctor's bag, whose brass clasp clicked importantly when closed. "This bag will last longer than any of us," my mom used to say, and so far her words have proved to be prescient. My dad used the missal for the rest of his churchgoing days. Every once in a while, when he returned it to its shelf after Mass, he'd wink and say, "This was one pricey prayer book."

CHAPTER 33

A CRIME OF PASSION

That February morning in our final year in France had started like any other at the *Ecole Internationale*. At the sound of the first bell we hurried to our classrooms from the courtyard. Those just arriving came in the front door, racing along the fast-emptying hallway in order to be in the classroom and seated before the second bell rang, five minutes after the first. The classrooms for the *section française* were on the *deuxième étage* (third floor in American usage) with the hallway running the length of the room on the street side. On the opposite side of the building, inside the classroom, a large bank of windows looked out to the gravel-covered playground. Two doors opened from our classroom into the hall, one at the front of the room, the other at the rear. A third door was placed behind our teacher's raised desk and to the right of the blackboard, away from the windows; it connected our classroom to the one immediately adjacent, though I never saw it open and, in any event, we were all too short to take advantage of the glass pane at eye level that our teacher, whom I'll call Madame Langlois, sometimes glanced through.

We had started the morning with reading, each of us reciting aloud three sentences from a thin book, *Là-haut sur la montagne*, that told the story of a family of chamois (small goat-like animals) high in the Alps. François, two rows in front of me, was laboring through the dramatic passage where Flack, the young chamois, is swept away from his family in the talons of an enormous eagle.

With no warning, an explosion of cries erupted from next door. This had never happened before. We sometimes heard a single loud laugh or cry, usually followed by the teacher's sharp reproof and then silence, but never a commotion like this. François stopped in midsentence and looked nervously at the teacher; she nodded for him to continue as the screams seemed to subside. Just as he began again, however, the cries from next door became louder and changed from a tone of surprise to desperation. Madame Langlois now strode to the door separating the two classrooms, looked through the small window, and took a sudden step backward, as if she had been struck hard in the chest. She held on firmly to the doorknob, however, as the screams became a wall of sound, young voices making a noise unlike any I have ever heard, before or since.

She turned her head quickly from one side to the other, as if she were trying to see something in the corners of the next room, then she opened the door halfway and children just a year older than us—seven or eight—came tumbling through, screaming, crying, and falling over one another in their panic. Madame Langlois half dragged a few children through the door, then lunged in to grab a final little girl as if she were retrieving something precious from a blazing fire, her face a mask of concentration and feral energy. As soon as the sobbing girl was through the door, Madame Langlois closed and locked it. Immediately she went to the door at the front of the classroom that opened to the hall and retrieved children who had fled in that direction. Both doors to the hallway were then locked, and we began to hear from the desperate children who were now closed in with us, without at first understanding the words that were being shrieked between sobs and shouts: *"Il l'a tuée!" "Avec un poignard, il l'a tuée!" "Elle est morte!"* "He killed her!" "With a dagger, he killed her!" "She's dead!"

I remember what followed as a long period of anxious waiting, though I don't suppose it lasted more than ten or fifteen minutes. Most of the children from the class next door continued to cry, some of them hysterically, and a few of my classmates started to whimper with fear and incomprehension. In the middle of this chaos I kept my eyes on Madame Langlois. *"Calmez-vous, les enfants!"* "Calm down, children!" she cried from the front of the room, and the level of shouts and sobs went down appreciably. Then, as if remembering something, she walked to the windows and looked down to the courtyard. I can see her as she flinched visibly, straightened, put her hands over her ears for a moment, then turned to us. Some of the more daring boys at the back of the classroom had raced to the windows and were relating what they saw—*"Il est là, il est là!"* "He's there, he's there!"—and Madame Langlois turned on them with an unaccustomed fury and demanded that they return to their desks. She then announced that we should all move to the back of the room where we would stand in two big circles, hold hands, and sing songs together.

This is when I understood that the whole thing was real, that *Madame la Maîtresse* from next door was indeed dead, that some devilish force had made its way into our schoolrooms and was now, apparently, outside in the courtyard. *What, exactly, had happened? Who was "he"?* we all wondered, but Madame Langlois now insisted on our participation in nursery school songs we hadn't sung for a year or more. The student next to me in our circle was one of the boys who had run to the windows, and between verses he whispered his special knowledge to me with an air of triumph and certitude: *"Il a sauté, le tueur. Il est là-bas toujours, les jambes cassées."* "He jumped, the killer. He's still down there, his legs broken."

This was the first reliable information I had heard in all the commotion, at once terrifying and strangely reassuring: someone had killed the teacher next door, but he couldn't get to us because he was down on the playground with his legs broken. Madame Langlois made the rounds of both circles, comforting as best she could, taking one child or another in her arms for a moment, then moving on as the singing continued with a false sense of gaiety. Even then I think I recognized her obdurate insistence on routine—any routine—for what it was, a form of courage in the face of the abyss, though I would never have known the words to describe it that way. Only years later, when I considered the facts as I knew them, did I understand enough to admire her improvisation as an uncommon reaction to an awful event.

After what seemed like a long time, a sharp knock at the door interrupted our make-believe world of childhood songs and forced insouciance. The director of the school identified himself from the hallway and Madame Langlois unlocked the door as if air could finally be let into our closed and temporary world. Then the wall of sound built itself up again, though this time the shrill edge of panic was missing. Everyone cried now, a deep sense of release welling up from below. In a few instants we were surrounded and scooped up and protected, with the same incessant questions put to every child: "*Vous allez bien? On ne vous a pas fait de mal?*" "You're okay? No one hurt you?" There were teachers, police, firemen, parents, and ambulance crews: the front of the school was pandemonium as parents arrived, aware only that there had been a *drame* at the school, to claim their children in tearful embraces.

My parents came, too, along with all the others. They had never been inside the school before and the uproar on all sides must have been bewildering. I recall their taking me home in the late morning and patiently, earnestly explaining that a "bad man" had killed a teacher, but he was in the hands of the police now and couldn't harm anybody else.

The facts were dreadful enough, even in our present era of random shootings in schools, banks, and offices. It happened that the teacher next door was Dutch, a young woman described in newspaper accounts as "*de bonne famille,*" "from a good family," as if this made her death more shocking still. Her killer was another teacher at the school, a young black man from Africa: "*bien habillé, bien élévé,*" "well dressed, courteous."

Not until I returned to France as an adult did I research and find the particulars of their story. Both were twenty-nine years old, both had arrived at the school only months before, both were realizing a dream of teaching in France. Reading the local newspaper articles from that era that describe this drama is like visiting another world. Both the style and the substance are suffused with the moral code of the times, and the facts are shaped to a narrative that suggests the hand of fate. The reporting is admirably thorough: friends, colleagues, even the concierge and landlord are interviewed, quotes assembled, personal details scrutinized.

And yet the descriptions of the two principals are embroidered in a way we no longer accept as reasonable in crime reporting. She had "*un visage angélique,*" "an angel's face"; he described himself to her as "*le pauvre Noir,*" "the poor Black." His teenage students dubbed him "*Boule de neige,*" "snowball," and the reporter assures us he laughed when he heard about his nickname. What alternative did he have? Though the vast gulf between the races is always implied, the story line adopted by all was one familiar to the French: *le crime passionnel,* a crime of passion. Their backgrounds and interests and life choices until the day they met are cited as proof of a shared destiny that was fatally flawed.

Until the previous year the young Dutch teacher had always

lived with her family in Amsterdam, taking a university degree there, but chronic asthma had kept her at home. Then her health improved and she took the job in Fontainebleau. She lived alone in a small apartment at the center of town that the paper described as *"sobre et impeccablement entretenu,"* "sober and perfectly maintained."

The African teacher was born in rural Togo, a West African country that was still part of the French empire in the fifties. He won a scholarship to study in Paris and spent the next eight years tutoring private students and working odd jobs while he acquired a teaching certificate. The job at the school was a godsend, giving him hands-on teaching experience and a modest but steady salary. He was described by his colleagues as *"excessivement timide,"* "terribly shy."

When they first met, months earlier, they hit it off. Perhaps fascinated by each other's different paths in life, they were seen over lunch engaged in long discussions of the books they both cared about. Both of them lived solitary lives, and a new friendship surely enlivened things. Each evening he took the train back to Paris, where he lived in a *chambre de bonne,* a maid's room, on the northern edge of the city. Generally no bigger than a closet, with a common toilet down the hall, a *chambre de bonne* has just enough room for a single bed and a small table and chair. The rent is cheap because these rooms are found under the eaves, an eight-floor walk up to a tiny space. Maids used them in the nineteenth century.

It is impossible to know what misunderstanding arose between these two young people, what series of crossed signals led to distance, and then disaster. It seems clear that they both were seeking companionship, but the form it might take was different in the mind of each. Did her initial sympathy and fascination send a message she never intended? Was he so cut off from the code of behavior among new colleagues that he projected his feelings in a way that could only end badly? Whatever the specific misapprehensions, by the late fall she realized that what she considered a friendship was for him becoming a towering passion, and she refused to see him. When she opened the door of her classroom that morning, he thrust a letter into her hands, a declaration of love and devotion that she glanced at, then handed back. It was then he produced the knife and plunged it into her chest before running from the room when she fell to the floor.

I knew the Dutch teacher by sight because her classroom was next to mine, and she greeted her students at the adjacent door. The African teacher I recognized, too, but only because he was the single black person in the school. He may well have been the only black person in Fontainebleau at the time.

In Washington I had seen plenty of blacks; they were still called Negroes in the early fifties. They worked at grocery stores and gas stations in the otherwise all-white Virginia suburb where we lived. In Paris, despite France's West African empire, they were all but invisible, with two exceptions: diplomats from African countries, and the street sweepers, who swept the sidewalks and gutters with brooms fashioned from the supple switches of briar bushes. A few impeccably tailored representatives of their country on one hand, and the lowest rung of manual laborers on the other, pushing with their brooms down the water-filled gutters the leavings of city dwellers. There were other blacks living in the Paris region at the time—workers from Senegal, Cameroon, Mauritania—but they were concentrated in outlying neighborhoods and rarely appeared on the human landscape of a white person.

For the young Dutch woman, France was doubtless filled with strange and new experiences. Simply being white didn't open all doors, or dissolve the loneliness of a small apartment in a provincial town. But the sense of excitement, of adventure, must have been great, especially as a victory over chronic illness. Was her initial openness to a fellow teacher a step that a young French woman would never have taken? Or was she just in the wrong place at the wrong time?

CHAPTER 34
RETURN

My deep attachment to France began with the lucky circumstance of living there as a child. Children don't have a voice in such matters—it just happened—and I didn't suspect how deeply it would affect the direction of my path in life. When we returned to the United States, there was no one with whom to speak French; my facility with the language didn't end, but its practice did. It would be an exaggeration to say I missed French consciously, and yet, for years to come, I felt something akin to nostalgia and regret whenever I encountered a French speaker or saw a French movie.

Before returning to live in France over twenty years ago, I had visited Paris several times, and I had often returned to Fontainebleau for an afternoon. Like so many French downtown areas, the center of town had been modernized, the shop façades gussied up and, in many cases, covered with the colored glass panels of chain stores and their ubiquitous logos. A new Town Hall now stood adjacent to the old one, its lines simple and contemporary, sharing only the classic mix of Fontainebleau materials: red brick, gray stone, and blue slate. But the layout of the streets was basically the same, and the slightly sleepy air of a provincial center still prevailed.

I drove by the two schools I had attended, both of them still functioning. The International School was now flanked by several new buildings, forming a complex of schools that ran from kindergarten through *lycée*, or high school. De Gaulle had expelled all NATO troops from France in 1966, and the school now served those associated with a new international business school, INSEAD.

Our house still sat on its quiet corner, between the dead end on the front side and the little street onto which the big iron gate opened. I knew from peering in from the sidewalk that there had been at least two major changes: the house was no longer lived in, but had been transformed into offices. More surprising was the presence of two modern houses, with severely raked roofs like ski chalets, in the far side of the garden. They were identical and ungainly looking; access to them was via an opening in the stone wall farther down the street. The house itself looked the same, though some cosmetic repairs had clearly been made. I can't say the transformations shocked me; I had feared the house might be gone altogether. The near side of the garden was intact, leaving the structure of the house still floating on its sea of light yellow gravel.

Sometime after I moved to Paris with my own family, I decided to visit both the house and the school in Fontainebleau. They were the two poles of my private world there, different entirely from the public Château, and I wanted to see how each had weathered the years. The house was now the French office of an international partnership of professionals. I wrote to the on-site managing director, explaining my interest, and asked if it would be possible to see the interior briefly, and we set an appointment.

It happened to be a splendid April day when I drove down from Paris. A small parking lot had been fashioned on the side of the house nearest the Château's outer gardens, and I parked the car there. Approaching the front door felt unsettling; we almost never used it since we came in the side gate and up the stairs at the back entrance. As I hesitated before ringing the bell, I realized I had no idea what to expect, and I hadn't given the matter much thought. I had a vague notion of all those rooms as we had left them, with desks and computers somehow worked in among our things.

When I was shown in to what had been one end of the main hall—the same hall where we had found the boar's head and deer trophies when we first arrived as kids—I felt as if I had entered the wrong building. Nothing whatsoever was familiar: the interior had been entirely gutted and then reconfigured and remodeled with uncomplicated lines and tasteful materials. Gone were the endless expanses of polished wooden floors that creaked and shined in their nineteenth-century splendor. Gone, too, were many of the walls and all the heavy dark paneling that had made the dining room and the big reception rooms so weighty and formal. As I waited for the director, I took in the new décor. I felt a surge of excitement, and a kind of relief, too. Somehow it was better that way.

Nowadays the practice of keeping the shell of an old building while stripping its interior is increasingly frowned upon. It's the sort of cosmetic restoration that would never be tolerated, say, in a national monument like the Château, since the interior is deemed at least as important as the façade, and the two go together as examples of a particular moment in history. Here, the exterior of our house was still convincingly Second Empire, but the inside captured the sleekness and purity of the most modern rooms.

My reaction to this change was more personal and, I suppose, more selfish, too. Seeing our house with different rooms and none of the dark, ponderous elements—somber wood, thick rugs, heavy draperies, weighty furniture, wooly animal heads, brass light fixtures—was like walking in an agreeable dream. It looked like all the bourgeois elements the landlady had so prized had vanished, as if those countless pieces of Louis XV gilt furniture hidden on the top floor had dissolved in thin air and floated through the open windows as dust. In their place was a stylish, efficient, and light-filled space that suffused good taste without being heartlessly corporate.

When the director appeared, a lively Spanish man with animated eyes, he described how he had made the choice to renovate the house for his firm. Colleagues in other offices around the world poked gentle fun at the unlikely premises, so different from their modern corporate buildings. "They call it my little French château," he confided with a smile. "But in fact they are jealous." The light on all sides, the fresh air and trees in the garden, the proximity of the Château's outer gardens for a lunchtime stroll made it a delightful place to work, he assured me.

I showed him a few snapshots of our time in the house in the fifties, and he seemed as surprised as I was at the contrast. He then showed me around the different floors. It was not a sense of nostalgia I felt, but one of discovery and surprise. The lighting fixtures were sculptural, the colors light and airy, the feeling throughout one of openness. And since the house still stood by itself, bathed in light from all four sides, the interior glowed with the sun's rays. It had been reduced to its skeleton and a few load-bearing walls, and the proportions were pleasing at every turn. It had good bones.

When we lived there it had been a wonderful, quirky, improbable place to call home, as French as French could be. All the claptrap that had kept that apparatus going—coal-fired furnaces, half-broken stoves, heavy curtains against drafts—was gone now, and it had become something else altogether. That seemed right to me.

As he showed me out, the director asked me with a note of concern in his voice, "You are not disappointed to see it this way?" I assured him that I was enchanted with the transformation; he accepted that pronouncement and told me I was always welcome to return. I lingered in the garden, considering all that was different. The little I know of the house's life before our stay seemed to recede further: built by a wealthy court official, then transformed into an inn, requisitioned during the war by the Germans as an officers' residence, life again as a house for a big family. The French call this *la mémoire des lieux*, "the memory of a place," and they are keen to preserve it when they can.

As I started back to the car, I passed the side of the house that had sheltered the two kitchens, and a concrete dilemma presented itself. How on earth, I wondered, did they ever remove the colossal Rosières stoves that seemed as essential to the house's structure as any beam or wall? They must have had an ironworker come in and break them up for scrap, and it cannot have been inexpensive. I wished then that my mother had been there to see the result, and to wonder at the change in the place. She was no iconoclast, but she was forward looking; "modern" was not for her a dirty word. This would most certainly have tickled her fancy as an exercise in how to leave behind absolutely the weight of the past.

When I contacted the current director of the International School, I didn't know what to expect. I figured that to be named the head of an elementary school with an international component in Fontainebleau would be a sought-after assignment. I imagined a seasoned veteran with decades of experience behind her.

One of the questions I faced was whether to bring up the matter of the teacher's murder during my last year at the school. Would a school administrator necessarily know about such a thing? Or would the passage of time—more than fifty years, half a century—have done its work and obscured the tragic story? When I asked French friends, they all suggested mentioning it only after I had met the school principal and assessed what kind of person she was. "*C'est au feeling*," one of them told me, using a French parallel to "Play it by ear."

It felt funny to park my own car across the street from where my parents had dropped me off so many times in the past. I discovered that the big doors of the main entrance I had used, while still there, were no longer open; a new gate had been built at one end of the building with an elaborate system of cameras and remote buzzers. I said my name into the squawk box and was buzzed in, recognizing my surroundings but unsure of where the director's office was located. I passed the closed-in schoolyard I had known, much smaller than I remembered, where the high drama of our marbles competitions was played out. The tamped-down earth had been paved over, though, and colorful swings and gym sets placed around the perimeter. No bullies lurked in the shadows.

On the far side of the building I found some older students from the adjacent middle school who directed me to the top floor of my old school, where my classroom had also been located. Each level had an identical configuration: an exterior hallway running the length of the building alongside two classrooms, then a set of offices, followed by another two classrooms before the stairway.

I wandered along the hallway, passing my *salle de classe*, my classroom, but unable to peek in. The inner wall was lined with white plastic coat hooks; in my day they had been forged iron. The door handles had also been changed to plastic, but otherwise all was virtually indistinguishable from my time there as a student. Differently from the fifties, the central offices now had glass walls separating them from the hallway so that the view extended all the way to the windows on the other side of the building. In the first office I saw two women working at desks and I knocked, asking the nearest one where I could find the school director.

"*Je suis là!*" the woman sitting near the far window sang out. "I'm here!" She rose and extended her hand as I made my way to her desk. "And you are doubtless Mr. Carhart," she said, referring to our exchange of letters. She was tall—perhaps five foot ten—with an attractive, finely drawn face and shoulder-length auburn hair. Where I had expected the ages-old French uniform of gray skirt, white blouse, and navy cardigan, she wore well-tailored jeans, a full-cut flower-print cotton blouse, and low heels. The impression was one of energy and a sort of no-nonsense intelligence. I guessed her to be no older than thirty-two.

She invited me to sit, told me that she was glad to make the acquaintance of an *ancien élève*, an alumnus, from the school's early years, and then she was interrupted by a phone call. Within two minutes she had negotiated with a plumber whose work was unsatisfactory, polite but inflexible when it came to the main point. ("*Monsieur,* in my experience, faucets with pressure fittings stop flowing when the hand is taken away. Ours continue to dribble.") She looked forward to seeing him at the school the following day so that he could remedy this "small problem," and ended with the French pronouncement that engages the other morally, and to which there is no possible response: "*Je compte sur vous.*" "I'm counting on you." Click.

She turned her attention back to me and I pulled out my *Carnet Mensuel,* the monthly grade book that contained grades and comments for all subjects, as well as a few of my notebooks, *cahiers.* I had brought them as quaint artifacts from another era that I assumed she would glance at and rapidly set aside. Instead, she examined several of them closely with a teacher's appraising eye, starting with the grade book to get an overall sense. I had consistently made the *Tableau d'Honneur,* Honor Roll, but she wouldn't have missed that my grades in *conduite,* conduct, were beyond bad (1, 3.5, 2 over 10), and the teacher's comments got worse ("*attention à la conduite*" became "*conduite exécrable!*"). She murmured that my grades were excellent, then picked up the *cahiers.*

Another series of interruptions intervened: a teacher who

needed her signature urgently; a student who had fallen on the playground and needed to be sent to the local hospital; a couple of phone calls. She was the director of a good-sized elementary school, I reminded myself, and this came with the territory. I thought that she would forget about my notebooks, and that we could talk a bit more before I'd be overstaying my welcome. As I sat there waiting, I realized we were directly next to the classroom where the Dutch teacher had been killed.

When she hung up the phone, she dived right into the notebooks, savoring the period details and commenting on the endless complication caused by pens that needed to be dipped in inkwells. The *cahier du soir,* take-home notebook, contained the punishments meted out in class; they took the form of copying ten or twenty or even forty times a rule that had been broken. It didn't take her long to find mine, and she exploded with laughter as she paged through from one to the other.

Je ne dois pas bavarder pendant la classe. × 20
I must not chat during class.

Je ne dois pas crier dans les rangs. × 20
I must not shout in line.

Je ne dois pas courir dans le couloir. × 10
I must not run in the hallway.

Je dois être sage pendant la classe. × 10
I must be well-behaved during class.

Si j'étais poli, je ne parlerais pas en même temps que les grandes personnes. × 20
If I were polite, I would not speak at the same time as grown-ups.

On it went, each one signed by one of my parents. They must have thought this was a typical French notebook, but the principal in front of me knew differently. "*Vous étiez un élève bien exubérant,*" she said with a mild note of reproach. "You were a lively student." We left it at that and she handed back my *cahiers.*

The effect of her easygoing banter about my *mauvaise conduite,* bad conduct, was to lighten the mood considerably. I was the elder in the room, but I had also shown myself to be a bad schoolboy, or at least a lively one. It gave us a common ground. Another interruption, and I realized I couldn't reasonably take much more of her time. I decided to mention the murder.

I began hesitantly, explaining that my classroom all those years ago had been just two doors down the hall. "And as I sit here today, I cannot help thinking of a drama that took place in the adjacent classroom when I was here." She looked puzzled—I had said *un drame,* which is strong language in French, something like "a sensational event." I had begun, and I knew I had to continue. "A teacher was murdered by one of her colleagues in the next room," I said quietly.

The principal flinched almost imperceptibly at my words, and I had the feeling that I had misjudged, that she must think me a fantasist, or worse. A long pause ensued, both of us motionless, and then she said, "So it's true then." Now it was my turn to be confused. I had imagined the possibilities as binary—she'll know, or she won't know—but now I seemed to be confirming what was only a rumor.

Briefly, I explained the facts as I had lived them, with the children tumbling into our class in terror. The image of our *maîtresse* at the door, looking through the window, then grabbing kids and hauling them in, particularly moved the director. "*Quel courage!*" she murmured. I mentioned that our teacher had carefully locked the door between the classes, and the principal now looked puzzled, then almost relieved as she said, "But we have no locks on our classroom doors." My account was false, it hadn't really happened after all; this one flawed fact would save us all from the weight of the past. We were sitting only a few feet from a door that opened from her office to the adjacent classroom. We both turned and saw that where a keyhole would have been, a plain white plastic roundel had been fitted over it. Clearly there had been keys when the hardware was forged iron; teachers were the only ones who used them.

A silence descended as we turned back, the principal now holding a hand to her face. She told her assistant to hold her calls, and she shared with me her version of things. She had begun as director just two years previously, and she insisted on teaching one class in order to remain connected with students. The classroom she was assigned was the one next to her office. A couple of comments from other teachers referred obliquely to the classroom where a teacher had ended her days as "the jinxed classroom." She didn't know what to make of their words and, being new, didn't press the matter. She figured it was their way of ragging her a bit, a fairly common practice among new colleagues in France. "It never occurred to me that a teacher had actually been killed." Both of us were shaken, knowing that it was on the other side of the nearby door where the tragedy had been played out.

When I wrote to thank her for her time, I also sent a copy of the newspaper article that contained all the relevant facts. I expressed the hope that she, like me, preferred facts to rumors, even if the facts are atrocious. Otherwise, how to justify shedding light on a somber history?

I can't say the memory of that murder haunted me in the intervening years—I had been one room away from the active horror of the situation, after all—but its aura stayed with me, coloring my notion of some strange and troubling things that lay beyond the school doors. It had been peculiar to find myself the one to confirm to the principal what she already half suspected. But I felt it had been necessary, too—part of *la mémoire des lieux,* the memory of the place, that helped to exorcise the hurt that dwelt in the past. As an adult, I saw it more clearly as a tragic story of two young people—neither demons nor angels—whose misapprehensions had led to disaster. Now I was the older person here, more than twice their age at the time, looking back and accepting the facts for what they were in a way the child never could.

CHAPTER 35
LEAVING

Toward the end of 1956 my father was informed that he would be reassigned to the United States the following summer. Three years was a standard tour of duty in an overseas posting. I had nothing to compare it to since the move to France was my first; many more were to come. We never lived anywhere longer than four years (Washington, D.C.) or less than two (Minneapolis), and we would have another foreign assignment, to Japan, when I was in high school. But that was all in the future. For now we knew only that we'd be going back "home" to America, and that our adventure in France would end.

I wondered what it would be like to live in a place where everyone spoke English, to go to an American school, to have American friends and play American sports. We'd had glimpses of how things were different when we drove onto the American base in France: the cars were immense and colorful; a version of a burger/fries/shake could be had in the snack bar; we saw recent Hollywood movies at the base theater. But I knew this was just a cookie-cutter version of the real thing, and it was hard to imagine what the real thing would actually be like. I remember studying carefully the photos in *Life* magazine, trying to picture myself as one of the kids in a Little League game, or showing livestock at a state fair, or competing in a spelling bee, but the images refused to come into focus. The people and the clothes looked familiar enough, many of them, but the situations seemed foreign.

The most prevalent aspect of American popular culture in our house was rock and roll, its explosion coinciding with the adolescence of both my older sister and brother. We had a portable record player that played both 45 and 33 rpm discs. In the evenings my dad sometimes listened to classical music from his extensive collection of "long-play" 33 rpm records. Then, by common consent, there would be "kid time" when the record player would be spirited into Sally's or Tom's room and single-play 45s took over, loudly. I didn't much know what I was listening to, but I *did* know it was different from my parents' music. It raised the energy level among us kids in a hurry, and it was American.

So we felt a kind of nostalgia for America without really knowing how the puzzle parts fit together. On one of her weekend visits from her school in Paris during that final year, Sally, by now a full-fledged teenager of fourteen, came up with one of the all-time great adolescent laments. "I want to go back to ELVIS!" she keened, as if he were waiting for her on the dock. My mother, for once, laughed out loud, but it was a generous laugh, and sincere. But that didn't matter to Sally. My mom was "mean" and "old" and "didn't even know who Elvis WAS!" This last was technically almost true, but my mom did understand what Elvis stood for in her teenage daughter's yearnings, and there was no easy remedy for that. Imagine a world with that kind of adolescent ardor, if you will, and then consider that the Beatles were nowhere on the horizon yet. The world has been changing for a long time, and the fifties were no exception.

In our last spring at Fontainebleau, a controversy arose having to do with the NATO command of the Château. Maréchal Juin had retired the previous fall, and the political decision was made by NATO member states—with the United States as first among equals—that a German general should for the first time assume major responsibilities with the unified NATO command structure. I didn't understand any of the politics at the time, but in looking back at contemporary press accounts, it's clear what the fuss was about. A dozen years after the war, many Europeans were not ready for a German military commander, and certain French combatants were particularly sensitive to the notion of a German general on French soil.

The candidate was a certain Hans Speidel, and he was about as "clean" a German senior officer as it was possible to find. A classic staff officer who had worked his way up after serving in World War I, he was not a member of the Nazi party. Moreover, he had been among the inner circle of conspirators in the July 1944 plot to assassinate Hitler. The only one not executed for lack of proof, he was held in prison by the Gestapo for seven months, then freed by the French when Germany capitulated.

But he had also served during the war as chief of staff to General von Stülpnagel, the notorious and reviled commander of German forces in France. Terrible reprisals were carried out during that time against French partisans and civilians: cousins and nephews and friends had been summarily shot. Emotions remained raw and a deep bitterness persisted. The newspapers of 1957 described a heated debate, letters of protest from veterans, and several demonstrations.

It was against this background that my mother received a request from our landlady, through Mademoiselle de Chêneville. Would she be so kind as to show the house to Madame Speidel, who had heard that it was of an appropriate size for a general officer, and suitably close to the Château? The visit was arranged. We children were kept out of the way, but I heard the story from my mother so many times that I felt as if I had been there.

The introductions were cordial enough, with Mademoiselle de Chêneville acting as an intermediary for practical questions. Madame Speidel loved the huge yard, she announced, and was anxious to see the interior. But soon enough, as they made their way through the central hall with the hunting trophies, the darkly paneled dining room, and then the gloomy double kitchens, it became clear that the inside didn't pass muster. The visitor clucked and sighed, and then turned to my mother with a declaration of candor: "No, I'm afraid I can't see us here. It would take a great deal of work to make it comfortable. Things just look too tired." (Later my mother joked, "I think she was thinking of me when she said 'tired.'")

Then, as if to mollify a sharp assessment and explain her reasons, Madame Speidel said with a regretful tone, "You know, things were so good for us before the war." If she was looking for sympathy, she used the wrong logic with my mom. An icy silence ensued; then my mother said, "Yes, the same could be said for a great number of people." Another pause, unrelieved by pleasantries. Then my mom used the mask of manners to move on. "Well then, since the house does not suit you, let me show you out." The typical effusions of thanks were expressed at the door, and that was that. The war would not be over until a new generation lived beyond the unspeakable onus of history.

In the last months before our departure we had to get ourselves organized for the return to the United States. This time we'd be traveling by ship. We could take with us a pair of suitcases each, but all the other personal effects had to be packed and sent ahead.

At the same time we were all finishing up our school year, the Chevy needed to be sold to another American stationed at the base, and we were fitting in some of the "essential visits" we'd never managed to schedule over three years.

One of the final acts in this busy landscape involved the end of our lease of the house, which required another visit from the emotional proprietor to "verify the inventory." One morning in June she arrived, accompanied by Mademoiselle de Chêneville and armed with her list of furnishings. She started in as she had three years previously, a strange combination of histrionics and precision. To hear her tell it, the house was about to fall apart because of us. Valuable cutlery had disappeared, the floors were worn almost to nothing, the heirloom stove was hardly useable, and on and on.

By now my mother knew the score, and she understood that this had to be played out. In truth, the house was in at least as good condition as when we moved in, thanks to Monsieur Jérôme for the floors, the honesty of the maids for small pieces, and my mom's own efforts at sprucing things up. But she also knew that *Madame la propriétaire* was after a piece of the considerable security deposit. So they traipsed from room to room, listening to lamentations as Mademoiselle de Chêneville disagreed on details and pointed out the notations she had entered by hand on the original inventory list three years previously.

Finally they gathered in the main hall to reconcile matters. The owner recited her list of woes and unforeseen expenses, my mom listened impassively; she had an ace up her sleeve. For all the large windows in the rooms of the main floor, my mother had sewn sheer white nylon curtains that could be drawn separately from the full, heavy drapes. She did the same for the full-length doors that led off the hall to both the grand salon and the dining room, covering their glass panes on both sides with gathered nylon curtains stretched vertically between two horizontal rods. Nylon was still hard to come by in France, and prohibitively expensive, but my dad had brought back yardage from the United States on one of his trips. These were clearly part of *le mobilier*, private furnishings, and did not belong to the house.

When the owner mentioned a sum "for damages" that was both exorbitant and unsupported by the facts, my mother told her she would be willing to leave all the curtains in place "as compensation." At first the woman didn't grasp what was being proposed, and her reproachful tone did not vary. Then something clicked, and she interrupted herself, as if startled. "*Quoi? Offrez? Vous me les offrez?*" "What? Give? You will give them to me?" Her features changed in an instant as if there had been a chemical reaction, mendacity transformed to avarice, and the deal was done in a flash.

After the proprietor was shown down the stairs from the exterior landing, Mademoiselle de Chêneville raced back in saying she had an extra key to leave with my mother. Whether or not this had been agreed upon beforehand, I'll never know. But as soon as she entered the hall, my mom knelt down beside the glass-paneled doors to the dining room, pulled the nylon back on both sides, and stuck her hand through the empty lower panes in full view of Mademoiselle de Chêneville. The two of them erupted in laughter, and the real estate agent, still in her ragged fur coat, protested with mock surprise: "*Je n'ai rien vu!*" "I have seen nothing!" The bottom row of panes in those doors were mostly broken—five kids in a house will do that over three years—but my mom considered that the experience of being called to task with such unwarranted pettiness justified this failure to disclose the missing glass. Something tells me Mademoiselle de Chêneville felt as she did.

CHAPTER 36

THE MOST BEAUTIFUL ROOM IN FRANCE

Over the years, I have returned to the Château many times. I took my own children there; they learned to ride bicycles in the Château's outer gardens, not far from where I lived as a boy. People who visit us in Paris get an expedition to Fontainebleau, and none has come away disappointed. And I discovered entirely new aspects of the Château's history and ongoing restoration when I met Patrick Ponsot. But Fontainebleau is so vast and so varied that even a lifetime of visits would not exhaust its riches and delights.

What continually intrigues me is how its profusion of styles coheres, even though few elements are rigidly balanced, much less symmetrical. Over the course of seven hundred years, each king left his mark with a new wing, a chapel, a ballroom, a theater, so that the accumulation of styles is itself a history of French architecture. Somehow—and this is Fontainebleau's great allure—they add up to a poetic and deeply satisfying whole.

Fontainebleau says something very profound about the French approach to history, and to life itself; Versailles says something else entirely. To my way of thinking, you can learn more from a day well spent in Fontainebleau than from a month of Sundays at Versailles, but I am most certainly biased in the matter. The Louvre is the only other place in France that has this same richness of successive periods, but given its vocation as a world-class museum, it is impossible to experience it as a palace that was lived in. Its rooms are almost all galleries for the display of art, one of the world's very greatest collections. This is no fault of the Louvre; the shell is essentially intact and has in most instances been beautifully restored, but its function is entirely different. Add to this the numbing crowd of visitors, and you may as well be walking through an endless, crowded train station. Fontainebleau is also a museum, but one whose aim is to preserve the setting of the Château's original function.

From his exile in St. Helena, Napoleon wrote of his favorite château as the true home of the kings of France, including himself in that long line of monarchs. Despite the shadow of Bonaparte, I have my own favorites on the tour of the Château, and they are not related to his era. One place in particular is entirely enchanting to me, and I make a point of visiting it whenever I am there.

The most beautiful room in France is not the Hall of Mirrors at Versailles: while certainly very grand and famous, it is essentially a long narrow room with a dazzling décor that softens, but does not hide, its inflated proportions. Nor is it the lovely gallery at the *Château de Chenonceau* that spans the River Cher and looks on both sides to the waters below: though it is deeply poetic, it is inescapably a gallery, a corridor of remarkable beauty, but a corridor nonetheless. The list of candidates would be very long; France abounds in architectural delights, of course, and taste is always highly personal. But for me the most beautiful room in France is in the *Château de Fontainebleau*, and, like so much else in this effusion of royal exuberance, you come upon it almost unawares. It's *La Salle de Bal*, the Ballroom. Completed in 1558 under the reign of Henri II, it captures perfectly the French spirit: sensuous indulgence married to sober discipline.

Entering from a series of small antechambers, you are unprepared for the subdued glory that is revealed: a room both long and wide of majestic proportions, bathed in light from colossal window bays on both sides. Outside to the left lies the *Cour Ovale*, one of the most intimate courtyards in the Château, while to the right you look across the formal gardens to the beginning of the forest in the middle distance. Richly decorated above with frescoes painted by Niccolò dell'Abbate after the drawings of Francesco Primaticcio, the wood-paneled walls are delicately limned in gold. Together with the patterned marquetry of the vast oak floor, the expanses of honey-hued wood suffuse the room with a warm luster. You feel immediately this was a wonderful room for a party, and the massive hearth at one end confirms the feeling of pleasure and comfort that is everywhere apparent.

If one wants to understand the genius of the French in making Renaissance themes their own, no site in France tells the story better than Fontainebleau. It's not a coincidence that the *Mona Lisa* was displayed in the king's rooms at Fontainebleau, as was a statue of Hercules (since lost) by Michelangelo. There exists a perpetual dialogue with the out-of-doors; beyond the formal gardens, persistent and breathtaking vistas of ancient trees speak of this place's origins as a hunting lodge in the depths of a forest.

A small lake stocked with fat carp recalls the tradition whereby a single one—"the emperor's carp"—bore a ring of solid gold through its snout, to be admired as the fish were fed from the overhanging terrace. A small and perfectly proportioned seventeenth-century pavilion at the lake's center, accessible only by boat, reminds the visitor of a Japanese teahouse in the exquisite simplicity of its lines. In the summer you can rent a rowboat and taste something of the voluptuary's delight as you glide among swans, floating leaves, and breezes redolent of boxwood and roses. Just as it has for centuries, the perfect inverted image of the Château shimmers slightly, then disintegrates as you paddle around its flanks.

Perhaps the most fun is to do what we did in the fifties, and what the locals have always done: set yourself up in the outer grounds with a picnic lunch. Outside the gates and the manicured gardens, you spread your blanket along the banks of the long canal, lie in the sun, and relish the goods you have gathered at the town center: *saucisson* and *rosbif* from the butcher, a warm baguette from the *boulanger,* fresh tomatoes and salad greens from the morning's street market, a selection of tiny fruit tarts from the *pâtissier,* and a good bottle of wine. Others are doing the same, or fishing lazily for perch, or riding their bikes between the double rows of linden trees that run the length of the canal on both sides for more than a kilometer.

As you look back to the Château in the middle distance, it occurs to you that the outline of its roofs, irregular and massive, is akin to a small village that has been built up, piece by careful piece, over an interval of many centuries. "Someone made this all fit together," you think to yourself for a moment, and then you realize that that someone is France.

ACKNOWLEDGMENTS

Writing about one's past is a tricky business, so I was lucky to have a close friend to jog my memory, press for details, and encourage me to tell the story of how France became so important in my scheme of things. Marion Abbott reviewed drafts and edited passages that didn't cohere, always assuring me that this was a tale worth telling. To her I owe an immense debt for her pithy suggestions, her sharp wit, and—not least—her unfailingly Irish sense of humor.

I am grateful to those who read all or part of the manuscript and offered ideas and comments, including Simo Neri, Nicolas Carhart, Sara Carhart, Judd Carhart, Bonnie Carhart, Lorna Lyons, Helen Britt, Rachel Hooper, Grazia Peduzzi, Norman Packard, Claire Miquel, Ronnie Scharfman, Richard Dolan, Jan Benzel, Judith Hooper, Joni Beemsterboer, Lisiane Droal, C.J. Maupin, Robert Wallace, and Rosalind Brackenbury.

My agent, Eric Simonoff, encouraged me in this project from the outset, and offered ideas for shaping the narrative so that the Château assumed its proper place. He is that rare find, an attentive and deeply literate advocate for the writer who knows just how to advance a book's main points. I am lucky, too, that my editor, Melanie Tortoroli, was always clear about what worked and dubious about what did not, constantly proposing solutions that made the story tighter. To her and to the entire team of professionals at Viking Penguin goes my deep gratitude.

I could not have undertaken this book without the continuing cooperation of the staff of the Château of Fontainebleau. The Château's chief architect, Patrick Ponsot, gave freely of his time and included me graciously in meetings and site visits. To him and to Vincent Cochet, the chief curator, I am most grateful. The organization of volunteers who support the work of the Château, *Les Amis du Château de Fontainebleau,* graciously allowed me to paraphrase in chapter 30 their published account of Albert Bray's *Le Journal de l'Occupation,* his fascinating account of the Château's survival under the German occupation of World War II. My thanks in particular to Hélène Verlet for her agreement to my proposed use of this document.

François Brosse granted his permission to use his remarkable illustration of the Château's buildings and near gardens. I am very pleased that his splendid hand-drawn work should give the reader a look at the Château's layout.

I used several passages from chapter 36, "The Most Beautiful Room in France," in an article that appeared in the October 2009 issue of *Departures* magazine.

As ever, some of my most fruitful hours—and most pleasant ones, as well—were spent in various libraries whose specialists were unfailingly helpful in making sure I could find just one more key source or document. Among them are the *Bibliothèque Municipale de Fontainebleau* and the *Bibliothèque Nationale de France* in Paris. I'd particularly like to thank the entire staff of The American Library in Paris for their unflagging help over the years.

My wife Simo was beside me every step of the way. No thanks can ever be adequate, but I thank her just the same. This book would never have seen the light of day without her ideas, her encouragement, and her support.

In no sense is this account meant to be a guide book to the Château. However, the reader will not be surprised to find that I am still fascinated with this singular place, and I trust that some of that deep bond comes through in the story of my relationship to Fontainebleau over the years. If that spirit presses the reader to visit, then I would count it a very good thing. It's no secret that France is full of delights, whether they be châteaux, museums, landscapes, or architectural wonders. But I can assure you that there is no place in all the land quite like the Château of Fontainebleau.

A PENGUIN READERS GUIDE TO

FINDING FONTAINEBLEAU

An American Boy in France

Thad Carhart

A CONVERSATION WITH THAD CARHART

Q. You've lived in Paris for more than twenty-five years and could have chosen any number of subjects that are better known. Why write about Fontainebleau?

A. The short answer is that I lived there as a child, and so there has always been a gravitational pull to a place that had such a strong effect on my early life. The longer response is that I came to understand the extraordinary importance of Fontainebleau as a site only as an adult. In that sense my arc has been from the happenstance of childhood to the appreciation that an adult can bring to bear only after learning much more about France.

I've visited most of the great châteaux of France over the years—Versailles, of course, but also Chambord, Chenonceaux, Vaux-le-Vicomte, Chantilly, and many others. I have my favorites, naturally enough, but I am not the only one to observe that there is no site quite so rich, storied, or delightful as Fontainebleau. It is one of the oldest places continually occupied by the kings of France, a direct connection to medieval times. For example, Thomas Becket, the exiled Archbishop of Canterbury, consecrated the original chapel at Fontainebleau in 1169. A line of rulers favored Fontainebleau from the late Middle Ages through the Renaissance, the French Baroque, the Enlightenment, and past the Revolution to the two Napoleons of the nineteenth century, and each left his mark. Now the French Republic attends to its treasures on behalf of the people of France.

My story is twofold: the account of living in this remarkable town as a boy—going to French schools, visiting Paris on weekends—and my return to the Château as a grown-up when I was able to witness significant parts of the ongoing restoration of its rooms by French experts. I think there's an inherent allure about the site that will capture the imagination of readers once they know the contours of the story.

Q. Why is it that Fontainebleau isn't better known?

A. The simplest reason, I think, is that Versailles occupies the field as the "go to" château for visitors to Paris. Fontainebleau, by contrast, is a kind of Sleeping Beauty that has yet to come into its own. But the reasons are in fact more complex than that. No single personality is associated with Fontainebleau, unlike Louis XIV and Versailles. One of Fontainebleau's most attractive features is the fact that an unbroken continuum of French art, style, and architecture can be seen intact. A particularly French notion of restraint infuses the rooms: grand, certainly, but seldom showy. Fontainebleau's subtleties are multiple, and they cohere over time, creating an atmosphere that is both captivating and unique. It takes some time, and some imagination, to drink in its splendors.

Q. Many parts of *Finding Fontainebleau* are written in the same vein as *The Piano Shop on the Left Bank*. What do you feel are the similarities and the differences?

A. I've been very lucky with *The Piano Shop on the Left Bank*. A writer is never entirely sure why a book captures the public's imagination, but I think a big part of *Piano Shop*'s appeal has been the look at French life away from the familiar tourist circuit. It's not that easy to get below the surface of things in France, and readers seem to have been hungry for stories about a French approach to things in Paris. In this respect, *Finding Fontainebleau* has a similar voice and scope, though the setting of the little Parisian shop is replaced by our family's big old rented house in Fontainebleau and the adjacent Château.

What separates the two books is a focus in *Finding Fontainebleau* on France in the '50s, as experienced by an American family. The period covered is greater, too, moving back and forth from my childhood to more recent times, when my wife and I settled in Paris and raised our own children here.

A point both books share is the story of two Frenchmen—the shop's owner, Luc, in *Piano Shop*; the Château's chief architect, Patrick Ponsot, in *Finding Fontainebleau*—who go about their business with a seriousness of purpose coupled with an abiding sense of light humor that could only be French. While *Finding Fontainebleau* is in no way intended as a kind of "prequel" to *Piano Shop*, I like to think of them as companion volumes, drawing the reader in to aspects of French life that are otherwise inaccessible.

Q. Your family arrived in Fontainebleau less than ten years after the war, and throughout *Finding Fontainebleau* there's an almost palpable sense of the war and the occupation in France. Why is this?

A. I was born well after the war, so everything associated with it seemed to me at the time like ancient history. But of course a decade is not long at all in historical terms. It was only much later that I came to understand how World War II had shaken the entire country to its core. This was the France we arrived in; it was still recovering from the trauma of battle, privation, shortages, and the presence of the enemy on French soil for four long years.

The parts of my narrative that touch on this are the things I noticed as a child: people picking up dropped pieces of coal from the gutter; the shock when my mother found that our babysitter was illiterate because of the war's convulsions; the discovery that our house had been used to house German officers during the occupation. Only when I returned with my own children did I fully appreciate the remarkable achievement of the French in first surviving, then thriving as a nation. That, too, is part of the book's story.

Q. When you lived in France as a boy, you arrived when you were four years old and left when you were seven. How can you recall so much detail all these years later?

A. One important aspect of my time in Fontainebleau in the '50s is that it was a shared experience, one that our family went through together. Anyone from a big family knows the kind of support and solidarity that arises among siblings when a new adventure is undertaken by all. At first we were almost like colonizers of a new planet, relying on one another for help to get us through some rough patches. Our three years in Fontainebleau became a part of family lore, full of stories, anecdotes, and surprises that we shared again and again over the years. I consulted my siblings carefully about the specifics of my story, as well as about the general contours.

There's another aspect, though, suggested by several readers, that may be even more important in my ability to remember so much from an early age. The fact is that I learned French that first autumn in a kind of "full immersion" setting at school where English was not an option. In a way,

I was the luckiest of us five siblings, since I learned to read and write French before English. A reader who is a cognitive psychologist has suggested that my vivid memory from that time likely has as much to do with my learning French at that young age as with regular recall abilities. In fashioning a working knowledge of French, I had to name my surroundings twice, both in English and French. In so doing, the images imprinted on my young brain in a way that would anchor them beyond a regular experience. The "sink or swim" proposition raised the stakes but also my attention. I feel as if becoming French-speaking made the memories of those times far more vivid.

Q. In *Finding Fontainebleau,* as in your other books, you touch on the whole notion of living "in between" two languages, two countries, two cultures. Why is this important?

A. My immersion in French during the years in Fontainebleau changed everything. Children aren't given a vote in such matters; it just happened. As with anyone who grows up conversant in two languages, it altered the way I look at the world, in big ways and small. It meant that I developed a healthy skepticism for occasional French posturing, but also an abiding affection for a country that is far more beguiling than the prevalent ideas of many outsiders would suggest. I don't regard myself as a missionary for things French, but I do enjoy telling stories that allow others to appreciate the human qualities that still set France apart.

QUESTIONS FOR DISCUSSION

1. A memoir lies at the heart of *Finding Fontainebleau,* a story of the author's life in France in the '50s. Carhart begins the narrative with his boyhood account of the long prop airplane trip to France, and then the impressions this new place made on him. Are there aspects reminiscent of other stories—fiction or nonfiction—where the reader discovers a new world at the same time as the author? Is the France of sixty years ago more "exotic" than the country we know today? Discuss why that might be the case.

2. The Château of Fontainebleau figures prominently as the focus of restoration efforts in the present day. Similar work goes on in almost all countries, but the French have their own approach. How does Carhart's account set forth the French philosophy of restoration? Are there similarities to how Americans care for their own national treasures?

3. Carhart's experiences and adventures in France as a boy are always seen against the background of a large family—five children—living immersed in things French. They had no TV, one portable record player, and only French radio. How would things be different in the present day for a big American family living abroad?

4. *Finding Fontainebleau* gives us accounts of many of the kings and queens who lived at Fontainebleau and built its many parts. What traditions did they share that made their projects at Fontainebleau distinctive? Now that the monarchy is a thing of the past, how does the French Republic square its democratic ideals with the safeguarding of France's oldest royal residence?

5. Carhart tells us how the Château has been threatened with ruin several times over its long history, most recently during the German occupation of France during World War II. How would its loss diminish the cultural inheritance of France in particular, and of Western civilization in general? Why is its survival important?

6. Discuss the ways in which Carhart's account of his upbringing in Fontainebleau of the '50s differed from the ways he and his wife raised their own children in Paris in the '90s. What similarities—and differences—struck you?